D0941237

KINGDOM
for a STAGE

KINGDOM
for a STAGE

MAGICIANS & ARISTOCRATS
IN THE ELIZABETHAN THEATRE

JOY HANCOX

SUTTON PUBLISHING

First published in 2001 by
Sutton Publishing Limited · Phoenix Mill
Thrupp · Stroud · Gloucestershire · GL5 2BU

British Library Cataloguing in Publication Data
A catalogue record for this book is available from the British Library

ISBN 0 7509 2239 7

Typeset in 11.5/15pt Garamond 3.
Typesetting and origination by
Sutton Publishing Limited.
Printed and bound in England by
J.H. Haynes & Co. Ltd, Sparkford.

Contents

	List of Illustrations	vii
	Acknowledgements	xiii
	Preface	xv
1	THE DERBYS AND THEIR MEN	1
2	ASTROLOGY AND OTHER INFLUENCES	18
3	JOHN DEE	30
4	THE THIRD GLOBE	56
5	THE MISSING DIMENSION	87
6	CONTRIBUTING FACTORS	112
7	THE CAST WIDENS	133
8	ELIZABETHAN ENTERPRISE	157
9	A SCRAPBOOK AND ITS PICTURES	178
10	OUT OF THE SHADOWS	210
	POSTSCRIPT	229
	Appendix 1 Additional Illustrations	231
	Appendix 2 The Geometry of Human Life: An Analysis and Commentary	237
	Appendix 3 Genealogies	242
	Glossary	248
	Notes	253
	Bibliography	258
	Index	262

List of Illustrations

		Page
1.	Elizabeth I (From the Collection at Parham Park, West Sussex, UK)	xviii
2.	John Dee (Ashmolean Museum, Oxford)	3
3.	*Monas Hieroglyphica* (The Governors of Chetham's Library, Manchester)	4
4.	Ferdinando Stanley (© H.W. Bateman, by kind permission of Mary A. Porter)	9
5.	Lathom House (The Governors of Chetham's Library, Manchester)	15
6.	Gorhambury (Manchester Central Library)	20
7.	Robert Dudley, Earl of Leicester (From the Collection at Parham Park, West Sussex, UK)	21
8.	William Cecil, Lord Burghley (TFE Graphics, Canada)	25
9.	The Grand Priory, Clerkenwell (The Order of St John Clerkenwell, London)	28
10.	The Theatre, parametric (The Byrom Collection)	34
11.	The Monad (The Byrom Collection)	38
12.	The College, Manchester (The Governors of Chetham's Library, Manchester)	53
13.	The Globe and Fortune combined (The Byrom Collection)	55
14.	The first bays at the New Globe (Photograph by Joy Hancox)	59
15.	Hollar's *Long View* (Guildhall Library, Corporation of London)	62
16.	The Carpenters' Regalia (Manchester Central Library)	63
17.	St George's, Islington (Suzie Hardie)	68
18.	Radar scan of the Globe site (© The Museum of London, The Clark Laboratory, Dr W.A. McCann)	72
19.	The Globe composite (© The Museum of London, The Clark Laboratory, Dr W.A. McCann, Joy Hancox)	73
20.	Radar scan of the Theatre site (© The Museum of London, The Clark Laboratory, Dr W.A. McCann)	75
21.	The Theatre composite (© The Museum of London, The Clark Laboratory, Dr W.A. McCann, Joy Hancox)	76
22.	The Rose archaeology in a frame of 72 (English Heritage)	77
23.	The Rose ideal (The Byrom Collection)	78
24.	The modified Rose, parametric (The Byrom Collection)	79

25. The Globe parametric with dimensions (The Byrom Collection) 82
26. The Globe schemata (The Byrom Collection) 83
27. An hexalpha of the Globe (The Byrom Collection) 84
28. Triangle and hexalpha (The Byrom Collection) 84
29. Cross-section of solids from *The New Carpenters' Guide* (Peter Howcroft) 85
30. An elevation from a German catalogue (Studienbibliothek Dillingen, Germany) 86
31. The Chapter House, Westminster Abbey (Drawing by Joy Hancox) 94
32. The Seven Churches, Westminster Chapter House (English Heritage) 94
33. The Dome of the Rock (R. Walker) 95
34. The Temple Church, London (TFE Graphics, Canada) 98
35. Temple effigies (© Pitkin Unichrome by Peter Smith of Newbery Smith Photography) 98
36. Elizabeth of Bohemia (© National Gallery, London) 110
37. Eight-sided Globe (Front) (The Byrom Collection) 120
38. Eight-sided Globe (Reverse) (The Byrom Collection) 121
39. 3: 6: 9: a rule for itt, front and back (The Byrom Collection) 122
40. 3: 6: 9: – with additions (The Byrom Collection) 123
41. 72 square based on 3: 6: 9: (Original drawing by Joy Hancox) 124
42. 72 square with Globe added (Original drawing by Joy Hancox) 125
43. The Bear Garden. 'Bare' 18 (front and reverse) (The Byrom Collection) 130
44. Feature from *The Magical Calendar* (The British Library) 132
45. Visscher engraving of the Globe, 1616 (Guildhall Library, Corporation of London) 134
46. Ms 471 (The Trustees of The Science Museum) 136
47. The brass plates (The Trustees of the Science Museum) 139
48. Catalogue of the George III Collection (The Trustees of the Science Museum) 140
49. Catalogue of the George III Collection (The Trustees of the Science Museum) 140
50. Surveyor's plate (The Trustees of The Science Museum) 142
51. Surveyor's plate, detail (The Trustees of The Science Museum) 143
52. Tintern Abbey (Julian C. Hancox) 149
53. Philip Sidney (T.F.E. Graphics, Canada) 161
54. Mary Sidney (Herbert) (TFE Graphics, Canada) 166
55. William Herbert, third Earl of Pembroke (TFE Graphics, Canada) 167
56. Philip Herbert, fourth Earl of Pembroke (TFE Graphics, Canada) 169
57. Sir Thomas Herbert (Manchester Central Library) 174
58. 'The Game of Tennis' (Schweighardt) (The British Library) 183
59. Reverse of 'The Game of Tennis' (Schweighardt) (The British Library) 187
60. 'A Philisophical Enigma' (Schweighardt) (The British Library) 189
61. The Symbolic Hand (Schweighardt) (The British Library) 191

62. 'The Key of Alchymie' (Schweighardt) (The British Library) 193
63. A narrative in picture form (Schweighardt) (The British Library) 197
64. 'The Sun Speakes' (Schweighardt) (The British Library) 202
65. 'A purpleish ground' (Schweighardt) (The British Library) 205
66. A geometric drawing (Schweighardt) (The British Library) 206
67. 'Mercury Speakes out of the Ashes' (Schweighardt) (The British Library) 207
68. Francis Bacon (Van Somer) (T.F.E. Graphics, Canada) 208
69. *The Illustrated London News* (Manchester Central Library) 212
70. *Daily Express*, 25 February, 1911 (Manchester Central Library) 213
71. Roman amphitheatre, Caerleon (Janet & Colin Bord/The Photolibrary Wales) 220
72. Map showing St Julian's and Mount St Alban's (Elsa Wood) 221
73. House at Tintern Parva (*Tintern & Its Vicinity*, by W.H. Thomas, 1839) 222
74. House at Tintern Parva (Llandogo & St Michael's Parish Council) 222
75. House at Tintern Parva (Adrian & Elsa Wood) 222
76. Francis Bacon (Hollar) (Fisher Rare Book Library, University of Toronto) 225
77. A geometric model of the first Globe (Commissioned by Joy Hancox from Kenneth Peacock) 231
78. Tiring house drawing (The Byrom Collection) 232
79. Tree of Life (Drawing by Joy Hancox) 233
80. Palladio, Plan of Roman Theatre (The British Library) 234
80a. Palladio, Plan of Roman Theatre with additional lines showing correspondence with the geometric drawings (The British Library) 235
81. Emblem from *Atalanta Fugiens* (© Special Collections Department, Glasgow University Library) 236
82. The waterside at Tintern in the nineteenth century (Llandogo & St Michael's Parish Council) 236
83. Theatre of the World – in geometrical form (The Byrom Collection) 238

Additions to any of the illustrations are the work of the author and remain her copyright.

A Kingdom for a stage, princes to act,
And monarchs to behold the swelling scene.

Shakespeare, Henry V

Acknowledgements

First of all, I would like to thank the staff of Sutton Publishing. In particular I am grateful for the discreet support of Christopher Feeney, the Commissioning Editor for History, the felicitous pen of my editor, Sarah Moore, and the skills of Martin Latham, designer, and Nick Wright, assistant editor. Special thanks are again due to my agent Anne Dewe of Andrew Mann International Ltd for her characteristic care, which I value highly.

This book has been the culmination of many years' work. In the process I have become aware, first and foremost, of my debt to my parents in providing me with an education in which music and its allied disciplines played a major role from early childhood and which has proved invaluable to this undertaking. Secondly I am grateful to my husband, Allan, for his encouragement and assistance in so many ways. Without his support, the challenge facing me would have seemed almost insurmountable.

The book has taken me into a number of unexpected areas of enquiry where I have been fortunate in being able to draw upon the specialist knowledge of experts whose readiness to help has eased the sense of responsibility I have felt in venturing to reinterpret events surrounding the development of the Elizabethan theatre.

I would like to acknowledge the Reverend Neville Barker Cryer, Past Grand Chaplain (UGL) and Past Master and Editor of the Quatuor Coronati Lodge, for his informed assistance with the iconography in Chapter 9 and his careful scrutiny of the completed typescript. I would also like to express my great appreciation to Leon Crickmore, former HM Staff Inspector of Music, for his illuminating geometrical contribution in Appendix 2 and for the Glossary, to Kenneth Peacock and Peter Howcroft for their invaluable expertise in Chapter 5 and to Dr W.A. McCann for generously placing the results of his geophysical examination of the original Globe and Theatre sites at my disposal. I am indebted, as ever, to Michael Darlington for his constant and scrupulous legal counsel, and to Mark Ash and Elaine Ogden for their loyalty over the years. I owe them and David Almond special thanks for the indefatigable preparation of the Index. I must also acknowledge the great help of Dr Peter Northover of Oxford University for his analysis of the brass plates, and

Jane Wess and Kevin Johnson of The Science Museum, London, for their interest and unfailing support during my researches for this book.

Many others have contributed to this project in either a professional or private capacity: Ellen Barnes of English Heritage; Margaret Darlington; Tim Fitzpatrick, Director of the Centre for Performing Arts, Sydney University; Professor John Gleason, Professor Emeritus, San Francisco University; Suzie Hardie; Professor Park Hogan, Professor Emeritus, Leeds University; Miles Huntington-Whiteley; Marke Pawson; Anne Rainsbury; Mark Rylance, Artistic Director of Shakespeare's Globe, London; Ian Taylor of TFE Publishing, Canada, for a significant intervention at a crucial moment; Claire van Kampen; Ron Walker; and Elsa and Adrian Wood. I would like to honour the memory of one contributor who has died: George Murcell. It is also a matter of deep personal regret that the untimely death of my brother, Malcolm, prevented him from carrying out the art work for the geometric illustrations in the text.

I am indebted to many institutions for their cooperation and help, in particular: the university libraries at Bristol and Manchester; the British Library; the specialist collections at Chetham's Library, Manchester, and The Science Museum, London; Cardiff Civic Library; Chepstow Public Library; Guildhall Library, London; Newport Public Library; Manchester Central Library; the Chetham Society for its invaluable series of scholarly publications.

I owe a special debt to Ronald Singh of Blueprint, Colyer Thorpe, Manchester, for his infinite pains in preparing many of the illustrations and to John Downey for rescuing the typescript from an exhausted word-processor. I would like to salute all those writers included in the bibliography for their knowledge and wisdom along the way. To these and many others too numerous to mention I express my sincerest thanks. Finally, the Byrom drawings remain in private possession and I am grateful for the continued support of the Trustees.

Preface

It has long been my conviction that the Elizabethan theatre did not evolve simply by accident. While it is possible to see its origins in earlier, primitive forms of play-making, the rapid and spectacular rise of Elizabethan drama owes more than we have perhaps realised to Queen Elizabeth herself, her own political agenda and the select circle of aristocratic courtiers and servants who acted as patrons to the theatre companies as part of that agenda. Just as Elizabeth strove to establish a settled church to heal the religious divisions of her realm so, too, she sought other means to forge a sense of national unity and found one in the public playhouses. Her love of the theatre is well documented, but she realised that plays could provide something more than entertainment. They could also instruct. These public arenas could be used indirectly to demonstrate the growing stability of England. The sense of fellow-feeling produced in an audience, whether watching comedy or tragedy, was a valuable unifying factor. It became important for Elizabeth to encourage a fitting stage for her kingdom.

In part, this book continues the investigation of the unique cache of material which I first presented to the world in *The Byrom Collection* published in 1992. It is not a sequel but a necessary development of some of the ideas first broached in that book. *The Byrom Collection* was by its very nature an introduction to the geometrical drawings which had at one time been in the custody of John Byrom (1691–1763), poet, inventor of shorthand and a secret Jacobite. Only a selection of material could be examined and it was my hope then, and remains my hope now, that the importance of the drawings will be sufficiently realised for a facsimile edition of the complete collection to be printed – a formidable but, I believe, essential enterprise.

Over the years in which I have been able to study the drawings at first hand, I have become more and more convinced of the integrity of those responsible in the first place for their execution. The discovery of the accompanying brass plates has added an incalculable richness to the material and widened the context of its origins considerably. With increasing clarity, it has become evident that the largest part of the resource is concerned with the Elizabethan theatres and the ideas which led to that miraculous first flowering of English drama.

Since 1992, I have continued my search for evidence to corroborate my interpretation of the theatre drawings. In the process, a number of startling facts have emerged to vindicate my thesis. Some of those facts date from the time of the theatres themselves. Others belong to the present day, such as the latest developments in archaeological techniques which are able to throw new light on the remains of the old playhouses.

Such corroboration is very reassuring when those responsible for the rebuilding of Shakespeare's Globe in Southwark, for the most part, greeted the appearance of the Byrom theatre drawings with a long and uncomfortable silence. Perhaps, in hindsight, it was naïve of me to expect anything else. The Byrom theatre drawings were such a major discovery with far-reaching implications, not only for the design but also for the purpose of the Elizabethan theatre. In addition, the drawings came to light from a private owner who wished to remain anonymous, and their last known custodian, John Byrom, had no obvious connection with the theatre. Thus, the shock which the drawings produced among those responsible for the rebuilding of the Globe was, to a certain degree, understandable; the reluctance to examine them thoroughly, however, was less so. For myself, I could only interpret the initial reception which the drawings received as a challenge – a challenge to establish beyond doubt their provenance and purpose. Happily we have progressed to a stage where the Executive Committee of the Globe stated in 1999 its support for 'the creation and publication of a Facsimile of the Byrom Collection drawings'. However, I cannot wait for that to happen. Other discoveries have arisen concerning the Byrom drawings and other related material, which in effect make the reconstruction of the Globe secondary to bigger and wider issues.

In seeking to establish one truth, others emerged. It became clear that not only was the design of the circular playhouses revolutionary, but the role of the patrons of the theatre companies had not been properly understood. The following pages are an attempt to redress that. The road to discovery of the truth has been a long one, with a number of digressions *en route*. At the end, however, I trust a picture emerges that will enlighten and enrich our understanding of Elizabethan drama as a whole.

The fact that much of the material involved is archaic and multi-layered should not deter us from our pursuit. The Reformation accelerated the breakdown of the world-view that once united the scholars, churchmen and rulers of Europe. In the reign of Queen Elizabeth I, John Dee was perhaps the last, certainly the finest, of the polymaths who could claim to have studied and to understand the complexities of the post-Renaissance philosophical tradition, mathematics, religion and alchemical pursuits. The fragmentation of knowledge, arising with the emergence of what we now regard as science, has proceeded with ever-increasing speed. The need for specialisation makes it difficult now for many to sustain a wider view of the phenomena of creation. We also have to face head-on, in the immediate context, the problem of dealing with areas of intellectual endeavour which valued secrecy and people who enveloped their most precious thoughts and activities in ciphers or codes.

The increasing rigours and multiple pressures of academic life, where the time for research is in competition with the demands of teaching, often leaves little opportunity for reflection. It has been my good fortune that, as a free spirit, I have been able to seek out vital connections often in the most diverse and unexpected quarters. I have been fortunate, too, in having the support of a group of professionals, whose skills and expertise are of the highest order, in helping to unfold some of the enigmas surrounding the legacy of the Elizabethan theatre.

1. Elizabeth I, 1533–1603.

CHAPTER 1

The Derbys and Their Men

The Elizabethan playhouse was a major cultural influence in England during the period of its existence, second only in importance to the rituals of the established religion. The following attempt to reconstruct its genesis, however, involves an investigation of a wide range of topics and personalities. Unravelling the many strands in the story is a complex and lengthy process, while arriving at the objective truth when none of the original theatres has survived presents a particular difficulty. In the following chapters I shall present a fresh look at the leading personalities behind the Elizabethan theatre, the nature of their involvement, and the ideas that led to the design of the playhouses themselves.

The three-storeyed, polygonal, open-air Elizabethan theatres flourished for over seventy years and were the birthplace of the world's greatest drama. The first appeared in 1576, north of the Thames, with the building of the 'Theatre'. Eight more were to follow, two of them (the Curtain and the Fortune) to the north, the remaining six south of the river.[1] The Rose, built *c.* 1587, saw the production of most of Christopher Marlowe's plays, while the Globe, constructed first in 1599 and again in 1614 following a catastrophic fire, was home to Shakespeare, one of the seven sharers in its ownership and profits. Because of that association, the Globe has achieved world-wide fame. It is also the only theatre to be rebuilt – close to the original site in Southwark in 1997.

It may be surprising that, despite the work of countless scholars, for a long time we had no exact idea of the size of the Globe, nor of many of its features: the seating capacity, the size of the stage, the numbers of doors to the tiring house, the original decor. There are clues littered in many of the plays, tantalising references in diaries or letters, the famous drawing of the Swan made in 1596 by Aernout van Buchell from a sketch by a visiting Dutchman, Johannes de Witt (which raises almost as many problems as it solves), contemporary panoramas of London by several engravers, and, above all, details in the contracts for the construction of the Fortune and Hope theatres which have, miraculously, survived. However, most of the foundations of the first Globe have long been covered by a major bridge across the Thames and a terrace of buildings already listed for preservation. Consequently, when it came to rebuilding the original playhouse, academics from across the world met regularly to pool their considerable knowledge and arrive at a consensus as to exactly what Shakespeare's Globe looked like. It is not surprising also that, as they neared the end of their deliberations, they felt reasonably optimistic that they had indeed achieved an authentic re-creation, ready to open its doors in June 1997.

Nevertheless, I had long had misgivings. The belief has been rife that the theatre and the works it produced were seen as a low-status pursuit in their own day. There are a number of reasons for this. One was the generally accepted view that writing as a profession was beneath a gentleman. (It was perfectly acceptable for Sir Philip Sidney to write poems as a private diversion, but not for a living.) Others include the persistent disapproval of the Puritans, the admittedly low life of the actors and the behaviour of the apprentices from all kinds of trades, who absented themselves from work in order to watch a play. However, an emphasis on these issues ignores the ideas of the aristocratic patrons of the play-acting companies, and of the sovereign herself. There was, I believe, a totally different attitude to drama at the highest levels of Elizabethan society. Moreover, this attitude encouraged the creation of amphitheatres which demonstrate a holistic and harmonic unity of concept, resulting in acoustic brilliance and excellent sight-lines. Theatre practitioners, as opposed to scholars, have already expressed dissatisfaction with the modern reconstruction of the Globe. The claim of authenticity has now been modified. The building is the 'best guess to date'. This being so, it is important to remember that, according to one point of view, the nine London playhouses were revolutionary in design and that a unifying philosophy lay behind them: eight were circular, the ninth, the 'Fortune', was purposely built to be different – a square version of the Globe, a deliberate squaring of the circle.

I soon came to realise that it was not sufficient simply to introduce the theatre drawings from John Byrom's collection to the general public. Their draughtsmanship cannot be surpassed even today, but the ideas expressed by it are so detailed and rarefied as to suggest an exclusiveness to some sort of secret order. In recent years my aim has been to validate this conclusion.

With the drawings as a tool, I have had the opportunity to investigate untapped sources and re-evaluate familiar ones. I recognised that drawings in the collection were those of Elizabethan mathematician and philosopher John Dee's Monad. Leaving aside for the moment the philosophical content of this figure, it was necessary to re-examine the connection between Dee and Robert Dudley, Earl of Leicester. This connection was significant because Dudley was the conduit that carried many of Dee's ideas to the royal Court. I had to take account of two features in the Monad illustrations. Firstly, in the Byrom Collection the sequences of drawings for each of the playhouses were differentiated by a system of colour coding. The Monad drawings

2. John Dee,
1527–1608.

were part of the Globe colour sequence. Secondly, the texture of the card used for both Monad drawings was the same as that used in the Globe sequence.

What must be established at the outset is the central place of John Dee with regard to the theatre drawings in Byrom's collection and his influence in the creation of the Elizabethan playhouse. His role in the story begins with his position as tutor and life-long adviser to Robert Dudley and to his seminal 'Preface' to the first English translation of Euclid's *Elements of Geometry*. Leicester's high regard for him played an important part in establishing Dee in the queen's esteem, and helped him to become the close confidant and friend of the most powerful members of her Court. He played a part in the birth of the Elizabethan theatre directly through the design of playhouses, and indirectly through his encouragement of aristocratic patronage of the players' companies.

Many scholars have offered explanations of the Monad and the treatise *Monas Hieroglyphica* which Dee wrote about it in 1564. Its relevance to the concept and

3. Frontispiece *Monas Hieroglyphica*, J. Byrom's copy. The symbolism devised by Dee for this philosophical tract proved useful in the creation of secret codes for matters of state.

design of the Globe will be explained later. However, during my research into Dee and his close associates, I realised that, in addition to all his other talents and activities, he and others who feature in this account were part of a network concerned with codes and espionage. His close friend and neighbour, Sir Francis Walsingham, developed a highly effective spy network. That in itself proved nothing, but it has been said of the *Monas Hieroglyphica*: 'This book has always been regarded as a study of esoteric symbolism, but Sir William Cecil, a leading member of Elizabeth's government, stated quite clearly that it was work which had been of great value to the security of the state.'[2] Cecil's comment made me reassess Dee's relationship with Walsingham and the meaning of certain entries in his diaries, such as his meeting with Francis Bacon and Thomas Phelippes, the master code-breaker of Elizabeth's reign. Dee consciously used the symbolism of the Monad for more than one purpose. On the most profound level the Monad represents, in one hieroglyph, Dee's perception of the unity of the cosmos. In his diaries he uses either the complete figure or different parts of it as a secret sign for Tuesday or Friday. At times it stands for one of the various meanings of 'Mercury', the metallic element itself or the alchemical process. He even uses it as a code for 'messenger'. In pursuing my investigations, I was venturing into territory inhabited by secrecy and suspicion, the world of a flawed genius.

Against this uncertain background one figure stood out clearly: Robert Dudley. Elizabeth's Master of Horse and supreme favourite, had been a strong champion of the theatre since its beginning. Mention of 'Lord Dudley's Players' first occurs in 1559, and, after the passing of the Acte for the Punishment of Vagabondes in 1572, he offered the protection of his official household to James Burbage and his company of actors.[3]

Patronage was everything. The success of a venture or an individual depended less on merit than on an advocate. Dee's mathematical skills included the ability to calculate the motion of the stars. Leicester had such confidence in his former tutor that he recommended his services to Elizabeth on her accession. One winter morning found him riding out with the Earl of Pembroke to Dee's family home at Mortlake to inquire of him 'the most auspicious day foretold by the stars for the holding of' the coronation of the young queen.[4] Sunday 15 January 1559 was the date Dee named and it was subsequently approved by the queen; such was the trust Elizabeth put in both Dudley and Dee.

THE WARDENSHIP OF MANCHESTER

Thirty-six years after the coronation, in 1595, John Dee was still Elizabeth's 'beloved and faithful servant' when she awarded him 'the place, office and dignity with all rights whether present or absent' of the Warden of the Church and College of Manchester (now Manchester Cathedral).[5] Leicester's patronage had not been misplaced and over the years Dr Dee had served the queen well. Even so, he had had to wait a long time for official recognition of his worth. Not many records survive of the nine years Dee spent in Manchester. To fill in some of the gaps we must look at the role played by his predecessor.

The warden he succeeded had also been a member of Leicester's household. Dr William Chadderton, a moderate Puritan and Master of Queen's College, Cambridge, had been appointed Dudley's chaplain in 1568. He was thus chaplain when Leicester became patron of Burbage's company of actors prior to the building of the Theatre in 1576. The earl proved to be a valuable patron to Chadderton too, obtaining his appointment as Bishop of Chester in 1579. In return, Chadderton allowed Leicester to nominate the next Archdeacon of Chester. At a time when religion and politics were inextricably entwined, these alliances were important in the power struggle between rival factions at Court. Chadderton was made warden at Manchester on 5 June the following year, 1580. He was also appointed to the Commission responsible for rooting out recusants in Lancashire and Cheshire. Eager to carry out this duty efficiently, he decided to live in Manchester, close to another member of the Commission, Henry Stanley, fourth Earl of Derby.[6] It is interesting to note how Chadderton carried out his duties with Derby, and in particular his attitude to the players who were members of Derby's household or visited the great Derby houses in Lancashire to perform.

THE EARLS OF DERBY

Derby was one of the most influential men in England, with vast estates in the North-West and magnificent country houses at Lathom and Knowsley, where he lived in great style, as well as a London property in Cannon Row. After the queen herself, Henry kept the greatest household in the country, with a staff of 140. Bishop Chadderton frequently preached at Lathom and Knowsley. The following entry from the Stanley Household Accounts is typical: 'Lathom House January 6 1588 Sondaye Mr. Caldewell preched & that nyght the Plaiers plaied. Monday my Lord Bishop pretched . . .'[7]

However, from 1579, Lord Derby frequently stayed in Manchester at Alport Lodge, an estate of some 95 acres not far from the college. The task entrusted to him and Chadderton was important, and they needed to be close to each other. They were expected to bring the dissident Roman Catholics in the surrounding countryside to heel. The commission went so far as to remove the children of some of the more distinguished and wealthy Catholics from their parents and place them under the direct supervision of Chadderton at the college, where he zealously tried to indoctrinate them with devotion to the queen and her reformed church. In the process bishop and earl became close associates. When I considered all these facts, and that Chadderton was happy to exchange the mastership of a Cambridge college for the wardenship at Manchester, the received view that Dee's arrival as warden in 1595 was in some way a convenient form of banishment did not ring true. On the contrary, Manchester College was evidently an important base from which to carry out the queen's commands.

Derby had served other monarchs before Elizabeth. As a youth of sixteen he had been a gentleman of the privy chamber to the Protestant King Edward VI. When Edward died, Derby retained his post under the Catholic Mary Tudor and her husband, Philip of Spain. Derby's own marriage, although unhappy, brought with it strong royal connections: his wife, Lady Margaret Clifford, was grand-daughter of Henry VII. They had married as Catholics at Whitehall Palace in the presence of

Queen Mary and Philip, and became Lord and Lady Strange. Nevertheless, on the succession of Elizabeth, they remained prominent members of Court and Derby was entrusted with several important missions. He was one of the nine earls appointed to try Mary, Queen of Scots, for treason. In 1571 he felt obliged to move to Lathom to look after his dying father, leaving his wife at Court. Despite his earlier connections with Mary and Philip, Elizabeth looked to him to keep the North-West in order. On the whole, Henry Stanley no doubt had more sympathy with Elizabeth's church than Rome, but he was understandably reluctant to persecute friends and neighbours he trusted simply because they remained faithful to their old religion. The queen managed him with a characteristic combination of charm and threats. It was said that 'All the Keys of Lancashire do hang at the Earl of Derby's old girdle.'[8] Suspicious that three generations of Stanleys were absent together from her Court, the queen decided to hold Henry's eldest son, Ferdinando, a boy of no more than eleven or twelve, as a surety. On 6 December 1571, she wrote to Henry requesting him to:

send up youre Eldest Sone to be here some tyme that both we might see him and his Mother might have some comfort of him, and chiefly that he might here learn some nurture and be fashioned in good manners mete for one such as he is and hereafter shall be by cours of nature mete to serve the Realm . . . and with his good lyking you may send him up to be here this Christmas and which we will now assuredly look for.[9]

Ferdinando was dispatched to Court and Henry continued his work on the commission. Despite his efforts, however, in 1572 Lancashire was described by the queen's council as the 'very sink of popery'. Part of the trouble lay with the ineffectual Bishop Downham of Chester. After his death in 1577 the government looked round for a more vigorous successor. This was the opportunity Leicester needed to promote his own candidate, Chadderton, a man with the proven energy for the task. One of Chadderton's roles was to spur on Lord Derby, while orders from the Privy Council kept the bishop himself up to the mark. The queen ordered a counter-offensive against the Jesuit priests who were moving secretly about the North-West in an effort to keep the old faith alive. Unfortunately, the recusants in Lancashire and Cheshire were proving difficult to subdue, and Elizabeth encumbered Derby with other responsibilities, including in 1589 the trial of the Earl of Arundel for high treason. Dutifully, right up to his death, Derby continued to root out Roman Catholic priests and their supporters. He died in 1593 and Chadderton delivered the funeral oration. After praising Henry for the virtues which 'made him the best beloved man of his rank', the Bishop turned to Ferdinando and urged him to 'learn to keep the love of your country as your father did'.[10] Chadderton's role was still to stiffen the resolve of the Derbys in the campaign against the recusants. Leicester had chosen wisely in recommending him for bishop. Even though Chadderton now moved his household from Manchester to Chester he still retained close contact with Ferdinando.

The Stanleys were among the aristocratic families who had long been associated with playwrights and actors. Thomas Stanley, the second earl, had been patron of the Chester players, who in the early sixteenth century were responsible for the performance of the cycle of mystery plays around the festival of Corpus Christi. The Reformation suppressed these, and the Chester dramas became a festival of secular plays and masques. Earl Henry had continued the already established family tradition of patronage and, as we have seen, the household accounts record visits from companies of players to Lathom and Knowsley. The practice of a sermon on Sunday morning and a play at night is more in keeping with the relatively relaxed atmosphere of pre-Reformation England than the habits of the new Puritans. Chadderton had been a popular cleric at Cambridge, 'able to lay aside his gravity even in the pulpit'.[11] He evidently had no problem with listening to a sermon on the morning of the sabbath and watching a play in the evening. On 12 and 13 July 1587, the Earl of Leicester's Men performed at Lathom as part of a month-long festival of plays. The following January, Sir Thomas Hesketh's players visited. In October 1588, the queen's company arrived. In September 1589, both the Queen's Players and the Earl of Essex's Men performed at Knowsley on the same day. It being a Sunday, the earl and his guests were subjected to a particularly vehement sermon in the morning, only to have their consciences soothed by the Queen's Players in the afternoon and Essex's Men at night. This private behaviour was in striking contrast to Henry Stanley's more public stand about the proper observance of the sabbath. In 1576, he was summoned to parliament and took his seat on 8 February. With the queen's high commissioners, he assembled in Manchester and issued stringent orders forbidding pipers, minstrels and bull baitings on sabbath days, wakes and feasts.

The records of the Stanleys' players are somewhat complicated by the fact that one company might be performing under the patronage of the earl as 'Lord Derby's Men', while another was touring under the patronage of the heir as 'Lord Strange's Men'. This overlap only serves to show the intensity of the family's love of plays. Before succeeding to the earldom, Henry supported one company of Lord Strange's Men which toured the provinces between 1563 and 1570. Later, as Earl of Derby, he had a company which we know performed in Coventry (1573–4), and then in Dover and Coventry again in 1577–8. It travelled as far afield as Ipswich, Nottingham, Bristol and Bath. Then in 1580 it had the distinction of performing at Court.

Henry's son, Ferdinando, who succeeded as fifth earl, was thoroughly groomed by his enforced stay at Court. He inherited his father's love of theatre and at the age of

4. *Left:* Ferdinando Stanley, 1560–94, fifth Earl of Derby, patron of a company of players, 'Lord Strange's Men', later called 'Lord Derby's Men'. *Right:* Detail showing Ferdinando's hand resting on a helmet.

twenty-one had his own company of tumblers who performed before the queen at Christmas for four years running: 'sundry feates of Tumbling and activity were showed before her Majestie on New Yeare's day at night by Lord Strange his servants.'[12] Later, this company extended its repertoire to plays, for, when Leicester died, actors were recruited from his company and the Lord Admiral's Men to form a new acting troupe. This included leading performers of the stature of Richard Burbage and Edward Alleyn. In 1592 they were resident for part of the year at the Rose theatre.

In addition to being 'fashioned in good manners' at Court, Ferdinando appears to have acquired stronger Protestant convictions than his father. In 1582, at the age of twenty-three, he wrote secretly to Chadderton: 'I ame throughe with my father.'[13] Describing Lancashire as 'so unbridled and bade an handfull of England', he complained that his father was not firm in his prosecution of recusancy, adding with a touch of deviousness, 'But we must be patient perforce, & make a vertew of necessitie and folow his humour. This secret letter I sent your lordship.'

Ferdinando was highly regarded by the queen. In 1575, still only a youth of fifteen, he presented her with a new year's gift of 'an eare picke of gold enamuled, garnished with sparckes of rubyes, blue sapphires and seeded pearle'.[14] That year he was included in the large retinue of nobles Elizabeth took on her royal progress to Woodstock. In 1576, Ferdinando gave her another gem in gold, this time a squirrel 'sett with iii sparckes of dyamondes, iii sparckes of emeralds and iv sparckes of rubyes with iii mene perles'.

In 1579, the year Chadderton became warden in Manchester, Ferdinando married Alice, daughter of Sir John Spencer of Althorp, Northamptonshire, a wool magnate and one of the richest men in England. Alice was a great favourite with her father-in-law and, with her children, was a frequent guest at Lathom and Knowsley. Like her husband, Alice found favour with the queen. In fact they named their youngest daughter Elizabeth after her. It was Bishop Chadderton who visited Knowsley to perform the ceremony of 'churching' Alice after the christening. Ferdinando and Alice were evidently a charismatic couple, for they were popular with all the old families in Lancashire, forever visiting and being visited when they were in the North. Among these families were the Heskeths of Rufford. Robert Hesketh and Ferdinando had known each other for years, and Ferdinando and Alice saw much of him in London, too. Robert's father, Sir Thomas, kept a company of players and musicians at Rufford Hall, and the Heskeths are associated with the mystery of Shakespeare's 'lost years' – an old folk tradition claims that Shakespeare had been at Rufford as a young man.[15]

This same Sir Thomas is mentioned in the will of Alexander de Hoghton of Hoghton Tower, a member of another important Lancashire family. Hoghton's will of 1581 mentions 'all maner of playe clothes' and musical instruments in association with two servants: Fulke Gillom and William Shakeshafte.[16] Hoghton wanted to leave the clothes and instruments to his half-brother, but, if he did not choose to keep a company of players, then Hoghton wanted his friend Sir Thomas Hesketh of Rufford to: 'have the same Instrumentes & playe clothes: And I most hertelye requyre the said Sir Thomas to be ffrendlye unto ffolk Gyllome and William Shakeshafte nowe dwellynge with me & eyther to take theym unto his Servyce or els to helpe theym to some good master as my tryste is he wyll.' Was Shakeshafte a careless slip in transcribing Shakespeare's name? Could it be that Shakeshafte, alias Shakespeare, had indeed worked for Hoghton and now stood in need of a new patron? Certainly when Alleyn and Burbage joined Lord Strange's Men they helped to turn them into one of the best companies of the day. Did Shakespeare/Shakeshafte join them? Their repertory included Marlowe's *Jew of Malta* and Shakespeare's *Henry VI* (marked in the diary of Philip Henslowe, the London theatre owner, as a new piece), and *Titus Vespasian*, thought to be the play on which Shakespeare based *Titus Andronicus*. Plague drove them from the Rose in the summer of 1592 and forced them to close again the following year. But the patronage of 'our verie good the Lord Strange' obtained a special licence from the Privy Council in May 1593 for them to: 'exercise their quallitie of playing comodies, tragedies, and such like in anie other cities, townes corporacions where the infection is not, so it be not within seaven miles of London or the Coort, that they maie be in the better readiness for her Majestie's service whensoever they shall be thereunto called.'[17]

In September the same year, 1593, Ferdinando inherited his father's title and the company became Lord Derby's Men. On Ferdinando's death they were taken under the protection of Lord Hunsdon, the Lord Chamberlain, and, as the Lord Chamberlain's Men, they performed regularly at the Theatre and later across the river at the Globe.

Ferdinando enjoyed many of the fashionable recreations of the day: hawking, coursing and stag hunting in Lancashire and the more chivalric sport of tilting in London. From contemporary accounts he emerges as a polished courtier who was also a man of energy and religious conviction, a generous patron of revels and plays, and a conscientious servant of the crown, in fact a worthy successor to his father. Much could have been expected of a man with his talents, wealth and position. Yet he survived his father for little more than six months, his name tainted with rumours of treachery and poisoning.

Ferdinando's troubles began the day his father died. Richard Hesketh, a member of another branch of the Hesketh family, arrived in Lancashire from the continent on a mission from a group of leading Catholic exiles hoping to find a successor to Elizabeth, now sixty years old, who would be more tolerant towards recusants in the practice of their religion. Ferdinando was considered a possible candidate because he was a descendant of Henry VIII's sister, Mary. However, Hesketh was mistaken. Ferdinando's Protestantism was stronger than his father's. Hesketh approached the young earl who promptly arrested him; eventually, after being interrogated, Hesketh was executed.

Unfortunately, the whole affair reawakened Elizabeth's suspicion of the Derbys and she declined to make Ferdinando Lord Lieutenant of Lancashire or appoint him to Leicester's old office of Chamberlain of Chester. It also aroused the hostility of many Roman Catholics. The young earl's death six months later in April 1594 looked like a revenge killing by poison. Whatever the cause of his illness, for ten days he suffered violent stomach pains and nausea which nothing could relieve. Chadderton, his spiritual adviser, prepared him for the inevitable end. Conscious of his rank and with a fine sense of drama, Ferdinando refused all further treatment: 'I am resolved presently to die, and to take away with me only one part of my arms, I mean the Eagle's wings, so will I fly swiftly into the bosom of Christ my only Saviour.'[18]

Unsurprisingly, the magnificent lifestyle of both Henry and Ferdinando proved a heavy drain on the Stanley fortune. There was not only the cost of maintaining a hundred and more liveried servants. The men had to finance the upkeep of a large administrative staff with a steward of the household, grooms of the bedchamber and clerks of the kitchen recruited from the sons of leading families in the county. Two head cooks with a dozen helpers ensured that guests at Knowsley were entertained in princely fashion. The weekly consumption of food amounted to one ox, a dozen calves, a score of sheep, fifteen hogsheads of ale and a plentiful supply of bread, fish and poultry. In addition, there were the expenses both Henry and Ferdinando incurred in support of their own and visiting troupes of players, and by the generosity they felt incumbent on their rank (such as Ferdinando's gifts to the queen). Moreover, Henry's wife, the Countess Margaret, was a constant source of extravagance. On one occasion she borrowed £300 from her lady-in-waiting and as early as 1567 Henry had been forced to sell land to pay her creditors £1,500. Her recklessness with money led to the breakdown of their marriage, in the course of which she accused Henry of attempting to avoid honouring a bond for £8,000 made with her father.[19]

Henry found some comfort with his mistress Jane Halsall by whom he had at least four children. When he became earl, he decided to make proper provision for them. The eldest son, Henry, half-brother to Ferdinando, despite his illegitimacy was permitted to take the family name and, in 1578, was given the Manor of Broughton, near Manchester. This was land that had originally been granted to a collateral branch of Stanleys after the defeat of Richard III at the Battle of Bosworth.[20]

Margaret's debts continued to increase and Henry was forced to sell land to raise money to settle them. But not all his financial difficulties can be laid at his wife's door. The queen had appointed him to two diplomatic missions: to France in 1585 and to the Netherlands in 1588. Such embassies were the dread of every noble household, since the expense incurred had to be met by the ambassador himself. The cost could be ruinous. It was a convenient way for the monarch to exploit the loyalty of her wealthiest nobles while, at the same time, keeping them in check. Henry's mission to France was to invest the king, Henry III, with the Order of the Garter and, by its very nature, had to be lavish, but it was an expense he could ill afford. He sought to improve the returns from both his properties in Lancashire and from his rights on the Isle of Man, which the Stanleys had neglected for years. He was still struggling with these and other measures to boost his revenue when he died, leaving Ferdinando with all the problems. However, Ferdinando only made the situation worse. He had already borrowed heavily from London moneylenders and was in debt to his tailor and shoemaker. Creditors came forward, claiming they were owed nearly £6,000. That was not all. Having no son of his own, Ferdinando could not prevent his title passing to his brother. However, he attempted to ensure that all his lands were inherited by his wife, Alice, and after her, their eldest daughter, Anne. William challenged this, arguing that it contravened arrangements made in 1570 by the third earl for the Stanley estates to be held in trust for sixty years. In the presence of Francis Bacon and other witnesses, servants of Alice and William deposited with Sir Thomas Egerton a trunk full of family papers in evidence of their respective claims.[21] Thus began a lawsuit that lasted sixteen years. Egerton later became Lord Chancellor and, at the age of sixty, married the widowed Countess Alice, who, apparently, had lost none of her vivacity. She was persuaded to accept a settlement out of Court, but the compromise broke down over the ownership of the Isle of Man. Queen Elizabeth, ever ready to take advantage of the discomfort of ambitious nobles, stepped in to reclaim the island for the Crown.

Despite litigation and debts, the Derbys remained one of the most influential families in England, and we find them connected with Shakespeare in a number of ways. As patrons of theatre companies and playwrights, they were intimately concerned with some of Shakespeare's fellow actors and responsible for the presentation of some of his early plays. We have already noticed that Henslowe's diary includes *Henry VI* in a list of plays performed 'by my Lord Strange's Men' in March 1592 at the Rose. Which of the three parts of *Henry VI* was performed is not clear, but the takings show that it was a great success.

The play that depicts the final stage in the Wars of the Roses is *Richard III* and it sheds a certain light on the relationship between the Derbys and Shakespeare. At the end, Shakespeare shows Richard defeated in mortal combat at Bosworth by Henry, Earl of Richmond. However, he alters the facts of history for purposes not solely dramatic. Throughout the play he emphasises the role of Thomas Stanley, first Earl of Derby, at the expense of his brother, William, in the defeat of Richard in 1485. (It was to Thomas's son, Edward, Lord Monteagle, that the Broughton estate near Manchester was, in fact, given.) Moreover, although in reality William Stanley took a critical and positive part in events, at the end of the play Shakespeare shows Thomas Stanley placing the crown upon the head of the new king, Henry VII:

> Lo, here this long usurped royalty [i.e., the crown]
> From the dead temples of this bloody wretch
> Have I plucked off, to grace thy brows withal:
> Wear it, enjoy it, and make much of it.[22]

In this way Shakespeare was able to pay a handsome tribute to Ferdinando, Lord Strange, in particular and the Derbys in general.

The scene, coming at the triumphal conclusion of the play, is an effective reminder to all who see it of the debt the Crown owed to the Derbys for their part in the founding of the Tudor dynasty. Henry VII was Elizabeth's grandfather, and Earl Henry's wife was a descendant of Henry VIII. This relationship only increased Elizabeth's suspicion of Earl Henry, as was clear in the summoning of the young Ferdinando to Windsor. Anyone watching *Richard III* and aware of these undercurrents could not fail to hear uncanny echoes of recent history. For example, in act IV, scene 4, King Richard, mistrusting Thomas Stanley, takes his son George as surety with menacing threats:

> Go then, and muster men; but leave behind
> Your son, George Stanley: look your heart be firm,
> Or else his head's assurance is but frail.[23]

In the last scene of act 5, the first words of the newly crowned Henry VII could hardly be more pointed:

> Great God of Heaven, say Amen to all!
> But, tell me, is young George Stanley living?[24]

When one sees this scene and remembers, too, that Shakespeare goes out of his way to include favourable mention of earlier Stanleys in parts of *Henry VI*, one is forced to conclude that the playwright was commissioned to rewrite certain historical events in an attempt to re-establish the Derbys in the favour of the queen.

This is only one example of how the theatre was used for dynastic and political purposes. The fact that the Stanleys were able to exert this influence arises not simply from their status as powerful members of the aristocracy, but from their long-established links with the Elizabethan players, links forged in the earliest years of those companies. In my search to evaluate these links more precisely, I came across an unexpected piece of evidence which provides fresh insight into the intellectual/philosophical concepts behind the theatres.

THE LOST SCREEN OF LATHOM

The piece of evidence in question can be found in the rich archive of material published by the Chetham Society in Manchester since its foundation in 1843. The society has collated a mass of documents connected with the history of Lancashire and Cheshire, some at a local or regional level. Other data has a bearing on figures and events at a national level. The year 1576 is a landmark in British stage history because it saw the construction of the Theatre, the first purpose-built playhouse. The Chetham's volumes of Stanley papers show clearly that the earls of Derby may have been responsible for an important feature in the design of its interior and that of other playhouses.

We have already seen that the marriage of Earl Henry to Lady Margaret Clifford was fraught with difficulties caused in part by her unbridled extravagance. But that was not the only problem. She was not alone among the high-born or educated in taking a real interest in astrology. Even so, her contemporary, the historian William Camden, described this somewhat ungallantly as a 'womanish curiosity'. It was unfortunate for Margaret that in 1580 she fell victim to severe rheumatism and, finding the remedies of her resident doctor of little use against the constant pain, to his annoyance, turned elsewhere for treatment, seeking the help of 'wizards and cunning men'.[25] The doctor denounced her to the queen, and while Elizabeth herself was not averse to consulting astrologers when it suited her, she used the charge against Margaret to place her under conditions akin to house arrest. Margaret was too closely related for Elizabeth's comfort or her own good: her curiosity about the future might lead her to enquiries into the unmentionable subject of the succession. As we saw earlier, Elizabeth's later suspicions had repercussions for Margaret's son, Ferdinando.

Margaret's 'womanish curiosity' is reflected in an interesting poem connected with the Derbys which has survived in manuscript.[26] Dated 1576, it was written by Thomas Chaloner of Chester, a herald painter and genealogist by profession and also one of the players in the Chester cycle of secular plays. The poem is untitled and simply headed 'A Coppie of the demonstractiones of Parker's worke to the right honourable my good L. Therle of Derbie Jullie 23'. It is too long to quote in full, but Chaloner begins by explaining to Earl Henry that the Parker referred to was Henry, 'a man of lancashire', indeed an old retainer of the earl at Lathom, where he had been

5. Lathom House. Once an imposing home for the earls of Derby and host to several acting companies, it was destroyed in the Civil War.

born and had served as yeoman of the wardrobe for twenty-two years. As such he would have been in charge of the livery of the Stanley household, including the costumes for the earl's players. He also designed a magnificent screen for the great hall at Lathom which Chaloner was employed to paint in 1576 while staying at the house. Having done so, Chaloner wrote the poem to explain the design, the result of years of study by Parker. Evidently it unfolded a great astrological and astronomical layout of the heavens 'that parkers paines hath fownde'.

Th'erthe as how yt stands benethe with hills, and valleys, brave,
with towrs and townes, with trees, and brooks, and many a cave,
and next to it the Instrument that sailors have on sea,
whereby they know to goe, and how again to fynd their way,
and how to caitche, and faitche their course by compasse all ys shown
and how th'erth devyds itselfe, therby is known,
and next to that ys to be seene another thinge as strainge
which is, as howe and when the moone in everie moneth doth chaing
and how she dooth her lighte augmente, and how she fades againe
and how she quarterlie doth stand, heare maist thou see full plaine
The course of all the planets brought arisinge at the east,
By primum mobile being led to sitt againe at weast,
a deep designe it represents, a practice good also,
That with his pains on erthe the manner of the heavens doth sho
and how therwith the dozen signes are led, and brought about,
all [?] needfull things in sutch a place, and to effecte no doubt,
To shewe thee when the daie is long, and how it shortens night,
and when the night is longe againe, and how the daie doth light,
and length it gives to man, and beast, and comfort to all flowers
To joie the daie, and void the night, by greater somes of howres
Eitch daie that in the moonth their is to knowe, hee shewes the waie,
And how throughout the yeares about when comes a hollie daie
And how the stubborne Saturne steers the highest heaven above,
And next to him how gentle Jupiter takes course alike to move,
And how that Mars mercilesse is to follow on,
And how that solemp Sol in midst like king is also known,
And how dame Venus vaunts herself, and triumphs with her fire,
By whom is everie man inflamed, and burns with her desire.[27]

Lathom was destroyed during the Civil War and all trace of the original screen has been lost. This is a matter for deep regret, not simply as yet another example of the ravages of war, but because with the screen, we lost an important link with the Elizabethan playhouse. It was designed and painted in 1576, the year the Theatre was built in Shoreditch. Parker's screen stood in the great hall at Lathom and provided a richly symbolic background for the visiting companies of players to perform against. It showed a picture of the universe with the planets in their settled order and degree, the procession of the twelve signs of the zodiac, 'how therwith the dozen signs are led and brought about', the passing of time from day to night and on again to day. For educated spectators of tragic or comic events unfolding in front of it, it provided resonances which today we can only guess at. The screen was, I believe, the equivalent of, perhaps an inspiration for, the design of the 'Heavens' which decorated the roof overhanging the open stage of the playhouse. We know this roof was called the 'Heavens' from the contract for the Hope theatre (built 1614), which stipulates that the builder, Gilbert Katherens, 'shall builde the Heavens all over the saide stage'. That this was decorated with stars and signs of the zodiac is clear from textual references in plays of the time. Lorenzo in Act V of *The Merchant of Venice* is meant to point up to this roof when he says, 'Look how the floor of heaven is thick inlaid with patines of bright gold.' Dame Frances Yates was the first modern Renaissance scholar in England to appreciate the significance of that symbolism: 'The painting of the "heavens" in Burbage's Theatre, with the images of the signs of the zodiac and of the planets, would have been a matter of great importance . . . They showed forth clearly that this was a "Theatre of the World" in which Man the Microcosm, was to play his part within the Macrocosm.'[28]

We must remember that it was possible at this time to be a Christian and also believe in astrology. For example, in 1427, the Italian St Bernadino of Siena preached that planets and constellations governed the physical world and that medicines were more effective taken on days which were 'safe' rather than ones which were not. At the same time he taught that the spiritual realm of the soul was above all the physical world: 'The soul is above the realm of the Moon, of Mercury and Venus, of the Sun, of Mars, of Jupiter, of Saturn and of all the signs which are in them: it is above the 72 constellations.'[29] So, it is not surprising that most Tudor monarchs and their advisers consulted or made use of astrologers. The Earl of Leicester appointed an astrological doctor to his service. Lord Scrope, President of the Council of the North, (1619–28) employed another. In fact, many doctors used semi-astrological methods in their treatments, and it was customary for the nobility to have the horoscope of their children cast at birth.

CHAPTER 2

Astrology and Other Influences

In Elizabethan England the co-existence of astrology and Christianity was a fact of life and an important one. We can see this clearly in the work of the formidable scholar John Dee. Gradually, this all-embracing view of the world was replaced by one governed by fresh scientific laws. We should perhaps note that in his poem Thomas Chaloner treats 'astronomy and astrology' as equal. On the Lathom screen, he says, you will find: 'No triffling toyes for tickle heades', but 'a blossome brave/from out the garnisht grownde/astronomy and astrologie'. Little wonder, then, that Henry Parker's design included a sailor's compass alongside the signs of the zodiac.

Varying descriptions of the cosmos were now appearing in many quarters. By the sixteenth century, cosmography had become a highly developed science. Defined by one Elizabethan as 'the description of the whole world, that is to say, of heaven and earth, and all that is contained therein',[1] it embraced a wide range of subjects from theology and metaphysics to the natural sciences. Books on the subject began to appear, including *The Cosmographical Glasse* by William Cunningham, a 28-year-old physician, which was published in 1559. He dedicated the book to Robert Dudley, (not yet elevated to Earl of Leicester) who obtained the patronage of Elizabeth for the author. Dudley could see the practical aspects of the book for the country's mariners and commercial explorers. But its philosophical content – its view of man's place in the cosmos – was also a subject of profound importance.

Cosmographic ideas were increasingly popular and Lathom was not the only great house in the realm to incorporate them. William Cecil, Lord Burghley, Elizabeth's Lord Treasurer, whom she loved to call 'Sir Sprite', built for himself a country retreat, Theobalds, Essex, where he liked to escape the duties of his office. The Duke of Württemberg visited the house at the end of August 1592. His secretary described one of the halls:

The ceiling contained the signs of the zodiac with the stars proper to each, and by some ingenious mechanism the Sun was made to pursue its course across them. The walls were decorated with trees with bark so artfully arranged that it was impossible to distinguish between the artificial and the natural; the birds themselves were deceived, and, on the windows being opened, perched themselves on the trees and began to sing.[2]

In a government survey of the house in 1650 there is no mention of any rooms decorated in this manner, so it must have been altered in the interval, possibly after James I acquired it as a royal palace in exchange for Hatfield House – Ben Jonson wrote a masque to celebrate the departure of the Earl of Salisbury (as Lord Burghley's son had now become). The king made Theobalds his favourite country residence and died there in 1625. The survey of 1650 followed the execution of Charles I during the Civil War and the house was dismantled in 1651. The materials were sold for the benefit of the Commonwealth army and, thus, puritan zeal played its part in destroying yet another link in our theatrical and cultural heritage.

Another mansion, not as grand, but just as illustrative of the same philosophic and artistic ideas, was built at Gorhambury, Hertfordshire, between 1563 and 1568 by Sir Nicholas Bacon, Lord Keeper of the Great Seal of England. An interesting feature of the layout was the orientation of the chapel, where the altar was set at the west end instead of the east. In doing this Sir Nicholas had a deliberate intention:

> The whole layout, orientation and progression of this part of the house carefully echoes that of Solomon's Temple: moving from east to west, one entered the hall (or Holy Place) via the porch, then one passed through the hallway (the Veil) to gain entrance to the chapel (or Holy of Holies) with the altar (Ark of the Covenant) in the west.[3]

We should bear this in mind when we come to consider that the dimensions of the tiring house at the first Globe theatre reflected those of the Holy of Holies.

Gorhambury was a monument to the forces behind the English Renaissance. John Nichols in his *Progresses of Queen Elizabeth* describes one of the banqueting houses inside the orchard:

> A little Banqueting House adorned with great curiosity, having the Liberal Arts beautifully depicted on its walls, stood in the orchard, the pictures which adorned it being of such men as excelled in each. Under them were verses expressive of the benefits derived from the study of them as Geometry, Arithmetic, Logic, Music, Rhetoric, Grammar and Astronomy.[4]

One wall in the main hall showed the figure of Ceres teaching the sowing of corn with the motto 'Moniti Meliora' or 'Instruction brings Improvement'. Francis Bacon

6. Gorhambury, the St Alban's home of Sir Nicholas Bacon, Lord Keeper of the Great Seal of England. Its chapel was laid out to reflect the orientation of the Temple of Solomon.

grew up surrounded by this iconography. So, too, in their own homes did the Cecils, the Stanleys and other noble patrons of the Elizabethan theatres.

All this knowledge, culture and visual splendour was inspired by and centred upon the queen. Elizabeth had been well prepared for her role. She amazed her Court by rebuking the Polish ambassador in fluent, closely argued Latin. But her learning did not make her bookish. Her intelligence and quick wit had been sharpened in the uncertain shadow of her Catholic sister, Mary. When she finally emerged as sovereign, her subjects, rich and poor alike, were dazzled by the force of her personality. By a clever combination of charm, wit, cold logic and dire threats, she bent others to her will, driving ministers and courtiers to surpass themselves in the effort to satisfy her demands.

THEATRE IN A RURAL SETTING

In 1575, one year before the Theatre was built, Robert Dudley, Earl of Leicester, was busy preparing for the queen's third visit to Kenilworth in Warwickshire. On yet another 'progress'[5] through the countryside, Elizabeth, accompanied by her Court, expected to be entertained in the most extravagant manner. These displays of majesty were one of the ways by which the queen bound her subjects to her. Since she had

7. Robert Dudley, Earl of Leicester, 1533–88, favourite of Queen Elizabeth and a powerful champion of the actors. 'The Earl of Leicester's Men' performed frequently at Court and, from 1576, in the first purpose-built public playhouse, the Theatre.

given Kenilworth Castle to him in 1563, Leicester could hardly stint his hospitality. He called on the services of George Gascoigne and George Ferrers to write masques and verses for the occasion. Both men were products of the Inns of Court and now well advanced in years but each had been involved in the traditional Christmas Revels in their time as writers or performers. Leicester also summoned a company of actors, most likely his own under James Burbage, to perform at the castle. Finally, after all his elaborate preparations, Leicester was ready in July to receive no fewer than fourteen earls and seventeen barons with their wives, together with foreign ambassadors and privy councillors.[6] He was determined not only to dazzle the queen with a show of his devotion, but also to assert before the world his precedence in her eyes. Seventeen days passed in hunting, firework displays, dancing, tilting, music and plays.

Leicester was the supreme impresario, organising each event to flatter Elizabeth and keep her lively mind amused. The tableaux and masques cleverly interwove native British legend with classical myth. As the queen moved through the castle grounds, she was greeted by a solitary figure standing on a floating island. This was the legendary Lady of the Lake who hailed the queen as her protector. The Lady went on to describe how, after the death of King Arthur and the end of his Round Table knights, she had taken refuge in the lake at Kenilworth. When Elizabeth heard the lines:

> Pass on Madam, you need no longer stand
> The Lake, the Lodge, the Lord are yours to command

Her amusement was obvious and her answer set the tone for most of the stay: 'We had thought indeed the Lake had been ours, and you call it yours now? Well, we will herein commune more with you hereafter.'[7] Later in the celebrations there was another aquatic display. This time the sea-god Triton was seated on a mermaid and the Greek poet Arion, saved from drowning, according to legend, by a dolphin, appeared on the back of one, some 24 feet in length. Six musicians, hidden inside, accompanied the pageant. All these effects called for considerable engineering skills and stage management. It is not surprising that, from Easter to the beginning of July, Leicester concentrated his attention on the preparations at Kenilworth to ensure the success of the queen's visit.

Elizabeth enjoyed masques and plays and made frequent use of them at Court. She was accustomed to the conventions of dramatic allegory, and was perfectly aware when the 'plot' of a play was being used to influence her. In 1564 students from Grays Inn performed at Whitehall before the queen and the Spanish ambassador. After listening to Juno debate the virtues of matrimony with Diana, advocate of chastity, the queen commented wryly to De Silva: 'This is all against me.'

At the end of her visit to Kenilworth, Leicester could breathe a sigh of relief, for apart from one royal whim which led to the sudden cancellation of a play and a supper, all appeared to have gone well. As the queen rode away from the castle, one of the two elderly writers, George Gascoigne, appeared as Sylvanus, god of the woods, trotting alongside her horse on foot. He improvised by quoting lines from his play which had been cancelled. The queen 'stayed her horse to favour Sylvanus, fearing lest he should be driven out of breath by following her horse so fast'.[8] In reply, he declared that 'if hys rude speech did not offend her, he could continue this tale to be twenty miles long'. He then begged the queen to provide a happy ending to his play, and, as they reached a group of holly trees, an actor disguised as a bush stepped forward to address the queen:

> Live here good Queene, live here . . .
> Give eare, good gratious Queene, and so you shall perceive
> That Gods in heaven and men on earth are loath such Queenes to leave.[9]

After this slightly comic intervention, however, Elizabeth, continued on her way.

One further point of interest emerges from these festivities: among the dramatic representations was a romance – *Zabeta and Deep-desire*. This story of the love of Deep Desire for a woman, Due Desert, was clearly an allegory of Dudley's pursuit of the queen. Leicester, in fact, had asked George Gascoigne to rewrite the tale of Desire's love for Lady Bewty which had been staged at the Inner Temple in the earl's honour during the Christmas Revels of 1561/2. Leicester had intervened successfully on behalf of the Inner Temple in a dispute with the Middle Temple, and, as a result, had been chosen by the students as their 'Christmas Prince'. This later commission shows that Leicester responded to the emotional impact of drama, aware of its power as a medium of persuasion. Certainly James Burbage and his company of actors were very useful to the earl in the pursuit of his ambitions. This was an important factor in his support and protection of the players. The same can be said of other aristocratic patrons of the theatre as we have seen in connection with the Derbys and Shakespeare.

THEATRE IN A LEGAL SETTING

By the time Elizabeth came to the throne there was already a long tradition of dramatic entertainment at the universities and Inns of Court. The Christmas Revels at the law courts in particular encouraged a lively interest in drama. Francis Bacon, later to become Lord Keeper of the Privy Seal under James I, readily took part in the revels at Gray's Inn. Sir Nicholas Bacon had planned that his two sons, Francis and Anthony, should be instructed in the law as the way forward for their advancement. So it was that, shortly after Sir Nicholas's death in 1579, Francis, now eighteen, entered Gray's Inn. He applied himself to his studies although he hoped to find an accelerated way up the legal ladder through the influence of his uncle, Lord Burghley, Chief Secretary to the queen. Within a year he was asking Burghley to help him to obtain a post which would make him less dependent on practice at the Bar.[10] He had set his sights on a career higher than an ordinary advocate. That, however, did not stop him from enjoying the life of a law student, particularly the annual Christmas Revels. In fact he became very much involved. As late as the winter of 1594/5 he contributed to the revels at Gray's Inn, writing speeches for six 'Councellors' as part of the festivities built around the masque *Gesta Grayorum*. Despite the anxiety of his mother, who wrote on 5 December to his brother Anthony, 'I trust they will not mum nor mask nor sinfully revel at Gray's Inn',[11] Francis had the satisfaction of hearing his words declaimed before a distinguished audience of Privy Councillors. These included 'Lord Keeper Puckering, Lord Burghley, Lord Howard of Effingham, Lord Buckhurst, the earl of Essex, Sir Thomas Heneage, Sir Robert Cecil, the earls of Shrewsbury, Cumberland, Northumberland, and Southampton, and the lords Windsor, Mountjoy, Sheffield, Compton, Rich and Monteagle'.[12] The list is impressive evidence of how many of the great and the good enjoyed dramatic entertainment.

Fifteen years later, in February 1613, Bacon was responsible for the performance of a masque before James I by students from both Gray's Inn and the Inner Temple in celebration of the wedding of his daughter, Princess Elizabeth, to Frederick, the Elector Palatine. Frances Yates comments:

> That the author of *The Advancement of Learning* which had been published eight years previously, in 1605, took time off from his other studies to work for this wedding adds the final touch to the extraordinary galaxy of poetic, artistic and scientific genius whose united efforts made the Princess Elizabeth's last days in England a blaze of glory.[13]

However, we should not forget that Princess Elizabeth had continued the royal tradition of patronage of the theatre. She had had her own company of players – The Lady Elizabeth's Men – since 1611.

By 1613 Bacon was Solicitor-General and he must have gained a reputation by then for his theatrical skills to be asked to be the 'chief contriver' of this masque. His technical knowledge can be seen in his *Essay of Masques and Triumphs* with its awareness of scenic effect and the importance of incidental music as well as character. When the wedding masque was printed, Francis Beaumont, its chief author, dedicated it to Bacon in recognition of his support: 'Ye that spared no travail in the setting forth, ordering and furnishing of this Masque.'[14]

Twelve months later, Bacon was organising another wedding masque: *The Masque of Flowers*. This was performed by men from Gray's Inn on Twelfth Night 1613, at Whitehall as part of the wedding celebrations of the Earl of Somerset and Frances Howard, the divorced wife of the third Earl of Essex and daughter of the Lord Chancellor, the Earl of Suffolk. Bacon not only created the masque, but bore the entire cost himself, a staggering £2,000, refusing an offer of a contribution of £500 from Gray's Inn. John Chamberlain (1553–1627), accomplished letter-writer and scholar, observed wryly in a letter: 'Marry, his obligations are such, as well to his majesty, as to the great lord and the whole house of Howards, as he can admit no partner.'[15]

That same year, 1613, Bacon was promoted to Attorney General and by financing the masque he was repaying Somerset for helping him to the office he had first sought twenty years earlier. By an ironic twist of fate, in 1616, in his new legal capacity Bacon was called upon by the king to prosecute Somerset and his wife for complicity in the murder of Sir Thomas Overbury.

JOHN DEE'S STAGECRAFT

William Cecil, Lord Burghley, had himself studied at Gray's Inn. He was appointed Chief Secretary of State by Elizabeth immediately on her accession in 1558 and remained her most loyal councillor for forty years. In 1572 he became Lord Treasurer. More than any other man, Burghley shaped the destiny of the nation, privy to his queen's most private fears and wishes. One sure way to preferment in Elizabeth's reign was to gain his blessing.

8. William Cecil, Lord Burghley, 1520–98.

John Dee first met him in 1551 when Cecil was a junior secretary of state working for Edward VI. As a result of two treatises which he wrote for the king on religious reform, Dee was granted a pension and for a time was on the royal payroll. It is not surprising that he looked upon Cecil as his patron. It was to Burghley he turned when he sought further remuneration for his services to the Crown in 1563. Then, in October 1574, he approached Burghley again; this time with a request for an additional pension of £200 annually. In Elizabethan England £40 or £50 would purchase a substantial house, so, in today's terms Dee was asking for a considerable sum – Park Honan has calculated that in 1596 £1 was equivalent to £500 today.[16] The pension therefore amounted to £100,000 at today's value. Dee could hardly be seeking such a sum for personal services to Burghley. It was in return for services to the Crown and evidently Dee felt he deserved it.

In 1574 the Earl of Leicester obtained a royal licence from the queen to allow his company of players to perform, the first adult company to be allowed to do so since the passing of the Vagabond Act of 1572. Christmas 1574 and 1575 saw Leicester's men performing at Court. In the summer of 1575, they were most likely the company performing again before the queen at Kenilworth. In 1576 they found a permanent home in London at 'the Theatre' the first of the purpose-built playhouses. I believe that John Dee was part of the grand vision of the nine playhouses which started to appear in 1576. Who else would Leicester turn to but his old tutor whose mathematical and engineering skills had already been put to good theatrical use when he was a Fellow of Trinity College, Cambridge, in a production of Aristophanes' *Pax*? On that celebrated occasion Dee had invented a flying machine for the Scarabeus; it flew up to Jupiter's palace with a man carrying a basket of victuals on his back. Spectators remembered this *coup de théâtre* long after the event. No doubt these skills were also called upon for some of the elaborate set pieces at Kenilworth. Dee had already proved his worth to the queen and her favourite, Leicester, more than once. In 1574 Dee found himself on the threshold of a new and revolutionary undertaking and so was seeking payment not only for services rendered but also for the expense that undertaking would put him to if he were to work with the colleagues he would need – hence the request for a large pension. Elizabeth, however, was reluctant to dispense such largesse and preferred to reward Dee with occasional presents of £50 a time.

MASTER OF THE REVELS

One of the most important offices associated with the development of Elizabethan drama was that of the master of the revels. By June 1560 the encumbent was housed in the ancient buildings of the Order of St John in Clerkenwell, now owned by the queen. The longest serving master of the revels in Elizabeth's reign was Edmund Tilney, who held office from 1579 until his death in 1610. He has left us a description of his quarters, which, he says, 'consistethe of a wardropp and other severall Roomes for Artifficers to worke in, viz., Taylors, Imbrotherers, Properti makers, Paynters, wyredrawers, and Carpenters, togeather with a Convenient place for the Rehearshalls, and settinge forth of Playes and other Shewes for those Services.'[17] From here he licensed no fewer than thirty of Shakespeare's plays, commencing with *Henry IV* and ending with *Antony and Cleopatra*. Shakespeare must have known the building well. Entries in Tilney's accounts give a good idea of the work carried out at his premises. In 1573 for example: 'For the cariadge of the partes of ye well counterfeit from the Bell in gracious strete to St John's to be pformed for the play of Cutwell Xd.'

Gradually the storing of costumes made for Court entertainments and the construction of furniture and props became secondary to the 'calling together of sundry players and perusing, fitting and reformyng theier matter (otherwise not convenient to be showen before her Maiestie)'.[18] William Cecil, Lord Burghley, saw this as the chief value of the office and as a matter of policy emphasised the 'quasi-political functions given to the Master as stage censor by the commissions of 1581 and 1603'.[19] When the plays had been so 'adjusted' they had to be rehearsed and as a rule rehearsals went on 'in the presence of the officers at St John's'.[20]

Before the Reformation the Priory of Clerkenwell had been an impressive establishment. It was, after all, the headquarters of the Knights of St John in England and had been built over 5 acres of land given by Jordan of Bricett or Briset, a member of a Breton family that had settled in England after the Norman conquest. For centuries it stood as testimony to the power and wealth of the Order. However, the ravages of time and a succession of inhabitants have destroyed the grandeur of those origins, although some of its lost splendour can still be glimpsed in the two-towered St John's Gate, originally the southern entrance to the precincts, and the Priory Church of St John the Baptist.

The Order of the Hospital of St John the Baptist started as a small community of monks in Jerusalem organised by the Blessed Gerard (*c.* 1099) to tend wounded crusaders. It was re-formed in Jerusalem by Raymond du Puy in about 1120 with a military wing dedicated to defending Christians against attacks from muslims. Du Puy had been inspired by the example of the founders of another order of military monks, the Knights of the Temple of Solomon. After its formal sanction by Rome in 1127 the latter grew rapidly into the great international order of Templars, who eventually rivalled the Knights Hospitaller in wealth and power. The Templars had modelled their monastic life on the rule of St Benedict in order 'to fight with a pure mind for the supreme and true king'[21] and had gained the powerful support of one of

9. The Grand Priory, Clerkenwell. By 1560 it was the headquarters of the master of the revels. At the Gate House, Edmund Tilney licensed plays for public performance.

the great figures of the Church, St Bernard of Clairvaux. However, while the Templars remained a military order, the Knights of St John were never purely fighters. Raymond du Puy introduced a rule that they should never draw the sword except when the standard of the cross was displayed either in defence of Jerusalem or in a siege of an enemy city. Each knight took a vow of chastity, poverty and obedience and the power of the Order spread throughout Europe. The Templars reached Ireland in 1174 and set up their headquarters on land given them by the Earl of Pembroke.

St John's Gate in Clerkenwell is substantially the same as it was when it was built in 1504. However, towards the end of her reign, Elizabeth planned to sell the priory. In 1601 John Chamberlain wrote to Sir Dudley Carleton (1537–1632), diplomat and voluminous correspondent: 'The Quene sells land still and the house of St John's is at sale.'[22] Even so, it was not until 1607 that her successor, James I, sold the greater part of the property. The master of the revels moved his offices out the following year. Later the priory passed to William Cecil's grandson, the second Earl of Salisbury. His wife, Lady Catherine, according to Thomas Fuller (1608–61), Anglican clergyman and author of *The Worthies of England*, 'was very forward to repair the ruined choir' of the old Priory church.[23] It reopened for worship on 26 December 1623, St Stephen's Day.

When Dr Joseph Hall preached at the re-opening, he chose for his text a passage from the Book of Haggai, chapter ii verse 9, 'The glory of this latter house shall be greater than of the former', a reference to the rebuilding of Solomon's Temple. Hall was a puritan. Was he scornfully aware that *Twelfth Night* had been performed at Court in February that year and the First Folio of Shakespeare's plays had appeared in print as recently as November? If so, in choosing his text, Hall was not simply recalling the former glory of the Temple, but also asserting his contempt for the drama which had in his eyes debased the priory. The restored church would have a far better future now that it had been clearly set apart once more for worship. Many in the congregation at the solemn opening would remember the religious divisions of the Reformation and their consequences. Hall's sub-text would not have been lost on them.

Elizabeth had seen things differently. She had been fond of dancing and the theatre. For her the plays were undoubtedly a medium of propaganda and she used them as such when she saw fit. But she also wished her subjects to be able to share the pleasures of the play. To house the revels office at the former priory would have been very appropriate in her eyes because the ideas for the design of the eight 'round' playhouses came from the Middle East with the first knights of the Templar order and the Knights of St John.

The Templar legacy can be seen all over the country, even after the suppression of the Order itself. When Sir Nicholas Bacon built his fine new house at Gorhambury, he chose a site near St Alban's, where a Benedictine abbey had once flourished, built by the Hond Operative Masons. Stone was brought from the abbey and used in Gorhambury's construction. Since the Templars had modelled their order on the Benedictine rule, there was an additional and appropriate resonance to the name, 'The Temple', by which Gorhambury became known.

It is clear, then, that key families from the nobility and, chiefly, the sovereign herself were far more involved in the development of Elizabethan drama than has been realised hitherto. In the next chapter we shall look at more of these families, and we shall see one figure weaving his way in and out of their midst, linking them all in a common endeavour: that figure is John Dee. By June 1594 he was weary of waiting for the royal pension he felt he deserved:

29 June 1594. I went to the Archbishop [i.e. Canterbury] at Croydon. After I had heard the Archbishop his answers and discourses, and that after he had been last Saturday at Tybald's with the Queen and the Lord Treasurer, I take myself confounded for all suing or hoping for anything that was. And so, adieu, to the Court and courting till God direct me otherwise. The Archbishop gave me a pair of suffrines, to drink. God be my help, as he is my refuge. Amen.[24]

After he had waited some twenty years, Dee's note of disenchantment is understandable. As we will see, however, Elizabeth did not forget her 'beloved and faithful servant'.[25]

CHAPTER 3

John Dee

Peole keep diaries for different reasons and in different forms. Dee started his in 1577 when he was approaching fifty, and certain conclusions can soon be drawn from it. He was not writing with an eye on posterity nor with the intention of publishing its contents at some future date. It is neither an exhaustive account of his reactions to great occasions of state nor a detailed analysis of his personal development. Above all it was written for nobody's eyes but his own. It is a record of events and meetings that were important to him in his daily life and that affected his career and his family. Undoubtedly he was anxious to maintain secrecy about some of the people and events he mentioned, since he used a number of codes to obscure the entries. At times he wrote an entry in Greek, but not conventional classical Greek. He would transliterate the letters of English words into the phonetic equivalents from the Greek alphabet. The simplicity of such a device was perfectly adequate to deceive the prying eyes of all except the most scholarly. Some entries have been heavily scored through, others physically cut out. There was much Dee wished to record but felt he had to keep secret. Nevertheless, when entries from Dee's diaries are placed alongside other information, they provide fresh insights into the background of the theatres.

The diary is not a complete narrative, but a series of journals kept at different times. Part of it was buried in a field and was recovered by the book collector Sir Robert Cotton (1571–1631), who bought the land where they were said to be hidden and dug them up. The editor of the manuscripts, Meric Casaubon, confirms this story: 'The book had been buried in the earth, how long, years or months, I know not, but so long, though it was carefully kept since, yet it retained, so much of earth, that it began to moulder and perish.'[1]

The first sentence of the diary is characteristic, brief but loaded with meaning:

16 January 1577. The Earl of Leicester, Mr Philip Sydney, Mr Dyer etc.

The reason for this visit was Sidney's forthcoming visit to Bohemia. But behind it lay the deep and trusting relationship that Dee had built up with all three men. Each of them had enjoyed the special bond often established between teacher and pupil. Each of them retained a life-long regard for Dee, and the poet and diplomat Dyer later became godfather to Dee's eldest son Arthur. Nineteen years had elapsed since Leicester had consulted Dee about the most suitable day for the queen's coronation, and here Leicester was, bringing his favourite nephew, Sidney, for advice before he set out on a diplomatic mission to the court of the Holy Roman Emperor, Rudolf. Dee's opinion would have been welcome, for it was to Rudolf's father, Maximilian, that Dee dedicated the *Monas Hieroglyphica*.

By this time, Dee was living in his mother Jane's house at Mortlake. From there he was within easy reach by river of three of the queen's favourite palaces: Richmond, Hampton Court and Nonesuch. The waterway also made him accessible to visitors from London, of whom he had many. With sufficient land to build extensions to the original house, it was an ideal place for Dee to live and to study. From here, in 1575, he buried his first wife, Katherine Constable. Here, in 1578, he brought his second wife, Jane Fromond, and here with the birth of Arthur in 1579, he started to raise a family. In the normal course of events he would have expected to spend the rest of his days at Mortlake, and, apart from some breaks, it remained his home until he died. So much is clear from the diary entry for 15 June 1579 reads:

My mother surrendered Mortlake houses and land . . . and to me was also the reversion delivered by written contract, and to my wife Jane by me, and after to my heirs and asignees for ever.[2]

His mother died the following year on 10 October, at the age of seventy-seven, a good age for those times and an indication of the care she had received from him. A careful reading of Dee's diaries reveals that in addition to being a great scholar and innovative thinker Dee was a dutiful son, loving husband and father. It is important to remember this as a balance to his more esoteric pursuits. The entry for 10 October 1580 is highly significant:

At 4 o'clock in the morning my mother Jane Dee died at Mortlake. She made a godly end: God be praised therefor. She was 77 years old. The Queen's Majestie, to my great comfort (hora 5), came with her train from the Court and at my door, graciously calling me to her, on horseback, exhorted me briefly to take my mother's death patiently . . .[3]

The queen's condolences are indicative of her regard for Dee. He came into her circle of advisers with the best credentials. First of all, he had been tutor to her beloved Leicester. Then he had decided the most auspicious day for her coronation. It is not surprising that, in October 1578, Elizabeth summoned him to Richmond to confer with him privately. At this time her health was causing concern. Relief for her 'grievous pangs and pains' was beyond the competence of her physician Dr Bayly. Leicester intervened once more to bring in Dee and, together with Sir Francis Walsingham, arranged for Dee to go to the continent.

> My very painful and dangerous winter journey (about a thousand and five hundred miles by sea and land) was undertaken and performed to consult with the learned physicians and philosophers beyond the seas for her Majesty's health-recovering and preserving.[4]

There can be no doubt that Dee was privy to the most intimate details concerning the queen's health and, in the course of his duties, he met the woman who became his second wife, Jane Fromond, one of Elizabeth's ladies-in-waiting.

A careful look at the diary entries concerning Elizabeth tells us much about the closeness of this remarkable relationship. In September 1580 we see yet another occasion when the queen deliberately singled him out publicly for notice:

> The Queen's Majesty came from Richmond in her coach, the higher way of Mortlake field, and when she came right against the church she turned down toward my house: and when she was against my garden in the field she stood there a good while, and then came into the street at the great gate of the field: where she espied me at my door making obeisance to her Majesty. She beckoned her hand for me. I came to her coach side: she very speedily pulled off her glove and gave me her hand to kiss: and to be short, willed me to resort to her Court, and to give her to wete when I am there, etc.[5]

This was not the only time Elizabeth personally pressed Dee to visit her at Court and it implies an unusual degree of trust on her part.

DEE'S LIBRARY

On a previous occasion the queen had called to see Dee's library, a magnificent collection of books and manuscripts, probably the finest in the country. As early as 1556, he had tried to persuade Queen Mary to gather together the manuscripts and books in danger of being lost or destroyed after the suppression of the monasteries. His plea was unsuccessful, but he himself collected innumerable texts. The catalogue he compiled in 1583 amounted to 'neere 4,000, the fourth part of which were written bookes'.[6] Neither Cambridge nor Oxford had half that number. Drawn by the library's reputation the queen, unfortunately, chose to arrive only four hours after Dee buried his first wife, so, on that occasion, Elizabeth declined to enter his house.

The library has been described as 'the scientific academy of England during the first half of Elizabeth's reign'.[7]

The collection, however, was not simply nor solely 'scientific'. Dee possessed the works of the great Greek philosophers, Plato and Aristotle; the new philosophers of Renaissance Italy, Marsilio Ficino and Pico della Mirandola, advocates of a new form of 'white' magic; books on medicine, theology and music; collections of the great Latin poets Virgil, Ovid and Horace; and significantly the great Greek dramatists, Aeschylus, Sophocles and Euripides. More important for our purposes, Dee had a copy of the Roman Vitruvius's treatise *De Architectura*. Dee considered architecture the highest among the arts and sciences, and in his 'Mathematical Preface to *The Elements of Geometry* of Euclid, which was translated by Henry Billingsley and published in 1570, he summed up Vitruvius's view of architecture:

> An Architect (sayeth he) ought to understand Languages, to be skilfull of Painting, well-instructed in Geometrie, not ignorant of Perspective, furnished with Arithmetike, have knowledge of many histories, and diligently have heard Philosophers, have skill of Musike, not ignorant of Physike know the aunsweres of Lawyers, and have Astronomie, and the courses Caelestiall in good knowledge.[8]

This list of attainments may seem a tall order in an age when knowledge has become increasingly fragmented by rapid advances in science, but it is a fair summary of the expertise Dee himself brought to the study of architecture. Six years after he wrote this preface, the Theatre was standing in Shoreditch, followed a year later by the Curtain in the same parish.

THE CURTAIN AND THE THEATRE

The land on which the Curtain was built lay just outside the former priory of Holywell and, like so much Church property after the Dissolution of the Monasteries, had a swift succession of owners. By 1585 the profits from the playhouse were being collected by one Henry Lanman or Laneman.

A line in the epilogue of a play known to have been performed at the Curtain refers to 'some that will fill up this round circumference'.[9] A German merchant from Ulm, describing London playhouses in 1585, wrote: 'There are some peculiar houses, which are so made as to have about three galleries over one another'.[10] In other words the Curtain conformed to the same concept as the Theatre and its successor south of the Thames, the Globe. Indeed between the closing of the Theatre in 1597 and its reopening as the Globe in 1599, the Curtain was probably the home of the Lord Chamberlain's company of which Burbage and Shakespeare were members. This

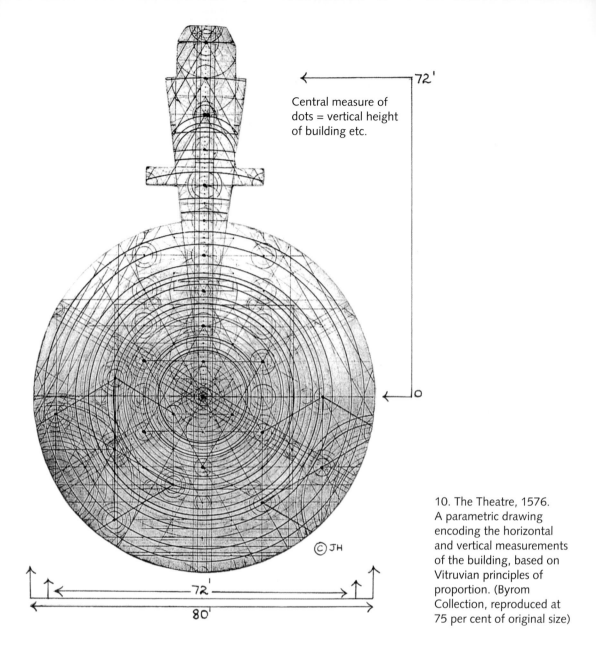

Central measure of
dots = vertical height
of building etc.

72'

0

72'

80'

©JH

10. The Theatre, 1576.
A parametric drawing
encoding the horizontal
and vertical measurements
of the building, based on
Vitruvian principles of
proportion. (Byrom
Collection, reproduced at
75 per cent of original size)

being so, *Henry V* and *Julius Caesar* may well have been performed there and it is the Curtain which Shakespeare refers to as a 'cockpit' and a 'wooden O' in *Henry V*.

The structure of the Theatre showed that Dee's theoretical concept, when translated into fact by contemporary building techniques, was flexible. The playhouse could be dismantled and carried across the Thames to be rebuilt. The Curtain showed that the idea resulted in buildings that were durable, for its structure lasted from 1577 to *c.* 1627. In 1583, however, alarm must have been expressed at the disaster at Paris Garden. On 13 January that year Dee made the following entry in his diary (one of only six for the whole month):

On Sunday the stage at Paris Garden fell down, all at once, being full of people beholding the bear-baiting; many being killed thereby, more hurt and all amazed etc. The godly expound it as a due plague of God for the wickedness there used and the Sabbath day so profanely spent.[11]

Paris Garden was the site of the Bear Garden, 'a round building three stories high',[12] which in later years was rebuilt and became the Hope theatre. It was one of the nine arenas in the canon of Elizabethan playhouses with which we are concerned. The news of this disaster was brought promptly to Dee, the source of the design concept. To the City fathers, always ready to promote their puritanical onslaught on the theatres, the catastrophe was heaven-sent. The Lord Mayor, Edward Osborne, wrote next day to Lord Burghley attributing the disaster to 'the hande of God for such abuse of the sabbath daie'.

WALSINGHAM AND THE HERBERTS

On 23 January, ten days after the Paris Garden disaster, Dee received a number of visitors at Mortlake. Two are of particular interest to us at this juncture:

Jan 23rd the Ryght Honorable Mr. Secretary Walsingham cam to my howse, where by good lok he found Mr Awdrian Gilbert, and so talk was begonne of North-west Straights discovery. The Bishop of St Davyd's (Mr Middleton) cam to visit me with Mr. Thomas Herbert.[13]

Thomas Herbert was the owner of the land on which the Curtain had been built and a member of the great Herbert dynasty headed by the Earls of Pembroke. They had been the first of the great noble families to employ Dee. When Dee returned to England after the success of his mathematical lectures in Paris, he entered the service of the first Earl of Pembroke in February 1552, at the age of twenty-four. He left the house to become tutor to Robert Dudley. Henry Herbert, the second Earl, was himself patron of a well-known company of players, and his third wife Mary Sidney, sister of Philip, became the patroness of many writers, turning the Pembroke family home at Wilton in Wiltshire almost into an academy for both arts and science. Indeed the house was likened to 'a little Universitie . . . a more excellent nurcerie for learning and pietie than ever it was in former time when it was an abbey'.[14] It was, of course, to Mary's two sons William and Philip, third and fourth earls respectively, that the First Folio of Shakespeare's plays was dedicated.

At Wilton, Mary Pembroke set up her own laboratory and employed Adrian Gilbert as her alchemical assistant. Dee had dealings with Gilbert over a number of years as his diaries show. Thomas Herbert would have wished to be assured during his visit that the Curtain, built according to Dee's specifications, would not suffer the same fate as the Bear Garden. He need not have worried. Dee had precisely the kind of knowledge that made him pre-eminently capable of the grand vision of the Elizabethan playhouse. In this he was helped by Theodore de Bry who translated that concept into ideal representations as well as more practical patterns for the builders. The whole scheme was endorsed and approved by the queen as an important element in her statecraft. For example, early in her reign Elizabeth had allowed the continuance of anti-Catholic plays to attack Philip II of Spain (1559). On the domestic front, it was against the known wishes of the City fathers that she licensed the Earl of Leicester's company in 1574. Again, it was her personal intervention in the 1590s that prevented the closure of the London theatres. Through the office of the Master of the Revels she developed a close control over the theatre.

DEE THE IMPERIALIST

At this point we should look at Dee's attitude to the history of Britain and his own pedigree. His father, Rowland Dee, had been a gentleman sewer to Henry VIII. Dee claimed he could trace his family back to Roderick, Prince of Wales, and so to distant kinship with the queen herself. The accession to the throne of the Tudor dynasty encouraged fresh interest in the historical origins of Britain and in the belief that the nation had been founded by the Trojan prince Brutus and consolidated by the heroic conquests of his 'descendant' King Arthur. One of the legends surrounding Arthur himself was that he had never actually died, but was waiting to return and lead England to fresh glory when a Welshman once again became king. As a man of Welsh extraction himself, Dee revered Arthur and named his first son after him. After all the upheavals of the Wars of the Roses and the Reformation, the Tudor monarchs were anxious to unify the nation. Arthur was an ideal rallying cry. Moreover, Dee believed in the idea of a British empire, free of constraints from Rome, a power to counterbalance the Holy Roman Empire and the rich conquests of Spain in the New World. So, he encouraged Elizabeth to see herself as an embodiment of all that Arthur stood for in chivalrous and temporal majesty.

A chief source for this Arthurian heritage was the chronicler, Geoffrey of Monmouth. According to him Uther Pendragon, father of King Arthur, defeated the Saxons at the old Roman city of Verulam, now St Alban's, in 512 and settled there until he died in 516. Verulam had been an important Roman city with its own open-air theatre. If, from his extensive reading of antiquaries, Dee knew of the theatre's existence and of the Welsh Roman amphitheatre at Caerleon in Monmouthshire (now Gwent), that awareness, linking both ancient Rome and King Arthur, might have given even more weight to his promotion of the classical concept for the Elizabethan playhouse.

What is certain is that, as a result of his studies into British history, he claimed Arthur's empire 'to have byn of twenty Kingdomes' and used these conquests to persuade Elizabeth of her right to 'sundry forreyn provinces'. The diary contains several entries which show Dee's attempts to influence the queen towards a policy of territorial expansion:

Nov. (1577) I declared to the Q. her title to Greenland etc., Estotiland, Friseland.[15]

On 3 October 1580 he noted:

On Monday at 11 of the clock before noon, I delivered my two rolls of the Queen's Majesty's title unto herself in the garden at Richmond, who appointed after dinner to hear further of the matter. Therefore, between 1 and 2 after noon, I was sent for into her Highness' privy chamber, where the L. Treasurer also was, who having the matter slightly then in consideration did seem to doubt that I had or could make the argument probable for her Highness' title so as I pretended.[16]

Elizabeth was more responsive to Dee's arguments than Burghley, but closer study of the documents Dee had prepared and further conversation with the queen won Burghley round. Elizabeth was so pleased, she rode out to Mortlake to tell Dee 'that the Lord Treasurer had greatly commended my doings for her title'. This was the occasion on which she also sympathised with Dee over his mother's death. Their shared imperial vision brought Dee even closer to the queen. He believed she was entitled to America, Greenland, all the isles between Scotland and Iceland and territories extending as far as the North Pole. Dee undoubtedly encouraged an expansionist policy on a spectacular scale to strengthen the queen's position abroad. He also encouraged Elizabeth's interest in the playhouses as a means to strengthen her power-base at home.

In the first diary entry we looked at we met three of Dee's former pupils – 'The Earl of Leicester, Mr Philip Sydney and Mr Dyer'. It is generally recognised that Dee played no small part in making Leicester one of the great patrons of learning in Elizabeth's reign. One aspect of that patronage, as we have seen, was his strong support of the theatre. When we learn that it was chemistry that Dee taught to Sidney and Dyer, we are introduced to another element in Dee's vast knowledge. Thomas Moffet, Chief Physician to the Pembroke family, described how Sidney, 'led by God, with Dee as teacher, and Dyer as companion', studied 'chemistry that starry science, rival to nature'.[17]

Chemistry, at this time was not the discipline we know today. It is more accurately described by the term alchemy, and, as such, covered a wide range of ideas, embracing the entire universe. For alchemy itself was not simply a 'scientific' study devoted to the attempt to transmute base metals into gold. By analogy, scholars and

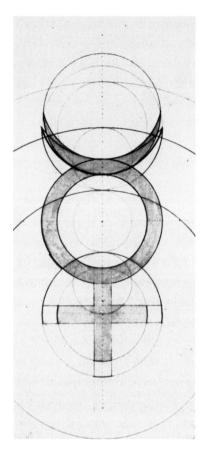

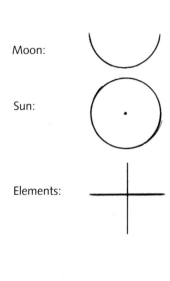

Moon:

Sun:

Elements:

11. *Left:* The Monad, original drawing in the Byrom Collection. (Reproduced at 75 per cent of original size.) *Right:* The component parts of the Monad.

philosophers reinterpreted the stages in this process as steps in a spiritual or philosophical development towards perfection.

Dee gives a detailed and complex commentary on this spiritual process in the *Monas Hieroglyphica*. In the treatise he attempts to devise a symbol or hieroglyph that can represent the entire universe. This he constructs from signs representing the heavenly planets: a crescent for the Moon, a circle with a dot in the centre for the Sun and a cross representing the four elements (earth, air, fire and water). He proceeded to write about these in twenty-four 'theorems' or commentaries in which he discussed the properties the geometrical shapes represent. These theorems are shown by different permutations of the constituent parts of the symbol. By contemplating them and studying Dee's commentaries, the initiate may be led to enlightenment. Here the illustration (one from the Byrom Collection) is taken from Theorem 13, which emphasises the importance of the planet Mercury and the properties it governs. Dee sees Mercury as equal in rank 'to the Sun himself' and as the 'greatly celebrated microcosm and ADAM'. Mercury is also 'the Messenger' who 'speaks to us very directly'. In doing so, he helps the soul to achieve the Beatific Vision. In formulating his theories, Dee drew on the ancient wisdom of the cabala. Each sequence of his theatre drawings contains an image of the Tree of Life. This is a diagrammatic representation of the attributes of God held in perfect balance. The pattern, by its very nature, becomes a path for spiritual enlightenment. The presence of both the Monad and the Tree of Life in the theatre drawings indicates a spiritual dimension inherent in the design, although, as we shall see later, it was not essential for everyone to be consciously aware of it. Like the cabalist, Dee considered that only the most learned were capable of understanding and experiencing such truths.

DEE'S SOJOURN ON THE CONTINENT

By the summer of 1583 Dee had decided to move to Bohemia in order to carry out extensive alchemical experiments. He left England with Albert Laski, the Count Palatine of Siradia, a Polish landowner who at one time aspired to the throne of Poland. Personable in appearance, princely in manner, he impressed many at the English Court. Dee first met him in the chamber of the Earl of Leicester at Greenwich Palace. Shortly after, Leicester informed Dee that he intended to bring Laski to dine with him. Dee pleaded poverty, saying that without selling some plate or pewter he would not be able to entertain them properly. Within an hour, the queen intervened to help. Dee explains in his diary:

> 31 July. The first gift from my Queen, hora 3. The Queen's gift of 40 angels sent by the Earl of Leicester his secretary Mr. Lloyd through the Earl his speech to the Queen etc. Mr Rawleigh his letter to me of her Majesties good disposition unto me.[18]

Dee was so far taken with Laski as to be persuaded to try his fortunes in Poland and left with him in September, taking 600 books and 100 manuscripts from his library, mostly works on alchemy and paracelsian medicine. Edward Kelly, alias Edward Talbot, who had earlier become Dee's scryer, joined him. Dee's relationship with Kelly is questionable, but I regard much of the recorded evidence as ambiguous. The views expressed on Dee's practice of speaking with angels depend very much on the standpoint of the reporter. For example, in Prague in 1586 Dee and Kelly were pressured to meet the papal ambassador to the court of the Holy Roman Emperor Rudolf II. He hoped to discover their views on the spread of heresy in Europe. He asked Dee, 'If you, to whom angels present themselves, have received any counsel, I beg you to share it with me.' Dee was polite but non-committal. He was aware that he would be praised for his activities only if they were useful to the Church. Kelly, not so shrewd, was more forthright, blaming heresy on the existence of so many bad priests. The ambassador replied civilly, 'These things are indeed well spoken by you', but afterwards told Rudolf's secretary that he would have liked to have Edward thrown out of the window. He made sure his views were known, for a week later Kelly was refused confession by a Jesuit priest and accused of lying or dealing with the devil. If Kelly had been more circumspect like Dee, the ambassador's reaction might have been less hostile. Yet, despite the aura of suspicion around them, both Kelly and Dee were repeatedly approached by Cecil and other representatives of Elizabeth to return home to work for the queen. Dee was away from England with his family for six years, not returning until November 1589. Meanwhile, his stature and repute suffered. The Queen, however, was not so fickle, as we shall see.

Unfortunately, Dee's six years on the continent were to prove a disappointment. In Cracow, Count Laski soon became disillusioned with both Dee and Kelly, and persuaded them to try their luck with Rudolf II in Prague. But there appeared to be no place for Dee even in that liberal and enlightened court. Rudolf was known to tire quickly of his protégés and courtiers. For a time Dee led a nomadic existence in search of a new patron, but in vain. In September 1586 he was invited by the Emperor of Russia, Fedor, son of Ivan the terrible, to take up residence at his court with the promise of a pension of £2,000 a year. Amazingly Dee declined the offer, no doubt still unwilling or unable to break away from Kelly's influence. (Years later, Dee's son, Arthur, became physician to the Emperor of Russia before returning home to be court physician to Charles I.)

By 1587 John Dee's relationship with Kelly had deteriorated so badly that there were now frequent, violent quarrels. A lasting separation finally came in the January of 1589. It was during this phase of his sojourn abroad, between 1587 and 1589, that the Rose theatre was built.

RETURN TO ENGLAND

During December 1588, Dee wrote to Queen Elizabeth accepting an invitation to return to England. We can only conclude that, whatever ill reports may have reached her about his life in Europe, Elizabeth still valued Dee's services. In March 1589 he set out from Bohemia for England. On his way he stopped at Frankfurt, the home of the De Bry publishing dynasty, a centre of alchemical philosophy and also the home of Michael Maier, Rudolf II's court physician. Towards the end of May, Dee was in Hamburg where he was visited by an occult philosopher, the physician Heinrich Khunradt. Finally, he landed with his family, and no Kelly, at Gravesend in England on 22 November.

On 9 December Elizabeth was gracious enough to receive him at Richmond. The brevity of the diary entry – 'At Richmond with the Queen's Majesty' – does not indicate the significance of this show of royal support so soon after his return and at a time when others were ready to disown him. Despite his genuine piety, despite the impressive range and the depth of his knowledge, Dee's attempts, with Kelly's help, to communicate with angels had been misunderstood by some and were a cause for concern. It is true that in England a number of senior courtiers were aware of these interests before he left the country. Ultimately, however, it was the disastrous pact he was duped into making with Kelly to exchange the sexual favours of their respective wives which called his probity and judgement into question. Even so, when Dee returned practically penniless to Mortlake to find some of his cherished possessions, including his quadrant and loadstone, worth in total about £400, had disappeared or been smashed to pieces, there were still Court officials, scholars and others in whom he confided, prepared to offer help.

After being back in England a full twelve months, Dee received the following message from the queen:

16 Dec. Mr Candish received from the Queen's Majesty warrant by word of mouth to assure me to do what I would in philosophy and alchemy, and none should check, control or molest me; and she said she would ere long send me 50 li more to make up the hundred pound etc.[19]

The queen's continued interest in and sympathy for Dee is evident, even if she chose (no doubt for prudential reasons) not to commit her assurances to paper.

But that is to anticipate. Not very long after his return to England, Dee received another visit from Adrian Gilbert:

19 Dec. Die ♀ Mr Adrian Gilbert came to me to Mortlake: and offered me as much as I could require at his hands both for my goods carried away, and for the mines.[20]

Earlier Gilbert had won Dee's confidence sufficiently to be allowed to take part in the experiments to summon angels. In the manuscript of *Mysteriorum Libri V, His Conference with angels*, written by Dee between 22 December 1581 and 30 May 1583, the question is asked:

Adrian Gilbert how far, or in what points is he to be made privie of our practice seeing it . . . was sayd 'That none shall enter into the knowledge of these mysteries with me, but only thir worker.' Truely the man is very comfortable to our society.

The answer is: 'He may be made privie to some things; such as shall be necessrie.'[21]

Passing into Mary Herbert's service, Gilbert was involved, among other things, in making medicines. He produced one remedy, 'Adrian Gilbert's Cordiall Water', which, it was claimed, could cure a veritable plague of diseases ranging from colic and consumption, to digestive problems, measles, pox, 'swouning' and fever![22] Little wonder that John Aubrey (1626–97), author of *Brief Lives*, described Gilbert as 'the greatest buffoon in the Nation'! Evidently Gilbert's dedication to alchemy had led him to break into Dee's house at Mortlake while he was abroad to 'borrow' books, papers or equipment which might be of help in his experiments. Hence his eagerness to put himself right with Dee on his return from the continent and offer 'as much as I could require at his hands' for 'my goods carried away'. The mines mentioned are examined in Chapter 8.

The six years abroad were not spent in isolation and inactivity. The discovery of what for convenience we will call Dee's 'angel diaries' gives us some idea of the topics and personalities which preoccupied him at this time, including his employment of scryers in an attempt to summon angels. It is a sobering thought that a learned and capable man of Dee's distinction could record such activities. But it has been said that: 'the records of the conversations in the Enochian language received by Dr Dee from the angels through the mediumship of Edward Kelly were also used to conceal secret messages relating to the magician's work for the Intelligence Service.'[23]

Whatever unrecorded service Dee may have done the state, his diary shows that certain figures in England knew his whereabouts on the continent and communicated with him, seeking his advice.[24] The queen herself wrote, urging him to return home.

GODPARENTS

Dee exercised his influence on the Elizabethan playhouse initially through the Earl of Leicester and then through his social and professional contacts with other members of the nobility. The clues are to be found in the choice of godparents for his children. This was an age when faith could still be a matter of life and death. Baptism was one of the two sacraments retained by the Church of England after the Reformation. In it godparents solemnly promised before God to 'renounce the Devil and all his works' on behalf of the child about to be baptised. No one undertook this duty lightly. Equally no one chose godparents lightly, least of all a man of faith such as Dee. The names of the godparents tell us much about Dee's social standing, the high rank of the godparents themselves and the matters of common interest which drew them to him. They show us Dee's intimacy with a circle of people close to the queen, at the centre of power, and in one way or another connected with the playhouses and the actors.

On 5 March 1590 he records:

The 5 of March (by old account) was Madimi Newton, my daughter, christened at Mortlake. Godfather, Sir George Carey. Godmothers, the Lady Cobham and the Lady Walsingham.[25]

Lady Walsingham was the wife of Sir Francis Walsingham. In 1573 he had succeeded Burghley as Chief Secretary of State and had inherited from him an intelligence network. We have already noted that Burghley had considered Dee's Monad to be of 'great value to the security of the realm'. It is also known that Dee discussed certain aspects of cryptography with Burghley. The Walsinghams lived at Barn Elms, not far from the Dees' house at Mortlake and the two families often visited each other. Codes were certainly one interest they shared. Dee and Walsingham gained a mutual respect and affection, as we can see from the simple entry recording Walsingham's death only a month after the christening:

6 April. Good Sir Francis Walsingham died at night hora 11.[26]

If we turn to the choice of Sir George Carey as godfather we are soon aware of its relevance to Dee's connection with the theatre. George Carey was the son of Henry Carey, the first Lord Hunsdon, cousin to the queen through his mother, a sister of Anne Boleyn. He was appointed Lord Chamberlain in 1585. Both Lord Hunsdons were important patrons of the Elizabethan theatre. By 1594, The Lord Chamberlain's Men were acting with The Lord Admiral's Men at Newington Butts. The former eventually became the most successful of all the theatre companies. An entry in the Court accounts of the Treasurer of the Queen's Chamber lists performances given by the Lord Chamberlain's Men before Elizabeth at Greenwich on 26 and 28 December 1595. It refers:

To William Kemp, William Shakespeare and Richard Burbage servants to the Lord Chamberlain . . . for two several comedies or interludes showed by them before her Majesty.[27]

After performing at the Theatre the Lord Chamberlain's men moved to the Globe where Shakespeare became one of the company's sharers.

When the first Lord Hunsdon died, he was briefly succeeded as Lord Chamberlain by Lord Cobham, whose wife was also a godmother of Madimi Newton Dee. Twelve days after Cobham died, Sir George Carey, now the second Lord Hunsdon, became Lord Chamberlain and continued as patron and protector of Shakespeare's troupe. They performed before the queen right up to February 1603, a month before she died. What we should note from the diary entry for 5 March 1590 is that Hunsdon, one of Madimi's godparents, is the first patron we can definitely claim for Shakespeare. He had an important and long connection with Shakespeare's company of players, the company for which the playwright acted and which produced so much of his work.

Despite the influence of Edward Kelly and the unfortunate effect he had on Dee's reputation, his closest friends did not abandon Dee. They still received him, still stood as godparents to his children, still sent gifts, even if these were sometimes trimmed to meet his more pressing needs. For example, the Lord Keeper of the Great Seal, Sir John Puckering, at one time Speaker of the House of Commons, was another godfather. He entertained Dee and members of his family at his home at Kew and gave him a horse, which Dee in turn gave to his scryer, Bartholomew Hickman. Similarly, on the 29–30 May 1590, Dee recorded:

> Good news about the efforts of Mr. Richard Candish, with the Queen and the Archbishop and Sir George Carey about obtaining the agreement for Eton College etc.[28]

As far back as the 1560s the provostship of Eton had been mentioned as a suitable appointment for Dee, one in which he would be able to pursue both his personal studies and others on behalf of the state.

Another daughter, Francys, born 'at the Sun rising exactly' on 1 January 1592, was given her name in memory of 'Good Sir Francis'. Nine days after the christening, she was taken by her nurse to be shown to Lady Walsingham at Barn Elms. Dee's last child, Margaret, was born on 14 August 1595. She was baptised on 27 August:

> Margaret Dee baptised hora 4½ a meridie. Godfather, the Lord Keeper his deputy Mr. Chowne. Godmothers, the Countess of Cumberland her deputy, Mistress Davis; and the Countess of Essex her deputy Mistress Beale.[29]

Margaret, the Countess of Cumberland was the daughter of Francis Russell, second Earl of Bedford. Her marriage to George Clifford, third Earl of Cumberland, in 1577 brought her into a family that claimed descent from Henry VIII's sister, Mary, and also allied her to Henry, fourth Earl of Derby, whose wife (also called Margaret), as we saw earlier, was also a Clifford and who now became her sister-in-law. More to the point, the Cumberland Cliffords kept a company of players in the provinces early in the reign of James I.

If we turn to the other godmother, the Countess of Essex, the ramifications of her connections are just as widespread. She was Frances, the daughter of Dee's friend, Sir Francis Walsingham. Her first marriage had been to Sir Philip Sidney in September 1583. She was barely sixteen years of age at the time, and the union displeased the queen. Frances was a good catch for fortune hunters and men of ambition, and there is evidence that a legal betrothal had already been arranged which displeased Walsingham, for he imprisoned the suitor in question for two years. This may explain why Walsingham agreed to the Sidney marriage although it brought with it no money. It may also account for the entry in Dee's diary for 18 February 1583.

the Lady Walsingham came suddenly on me in my house very freely. And after that she was gone came Sir Francis himself and Mr. Dyer.[30]

Perhaps, as has been suggested elsewhere,[31] the Walsinghams wanted to discuss their daughter's forthcoming marriage with their good and trusted friend. The ceremony took place on 21 September and was attended by, among others, Count Albert Laski. Immediately after the wedding Laski, together with Dee and his family, left England for the continent. Dee does not record the wedding in his diary but given his friendship with the Walsinghams and the fact that Philip Sidney was one of his favourite pupils, his attendance can be taken for granted. Three years later, in 1586, after being wounded at Zutphen, Sidney died. Frances found herself a widow at the tender age of nineteen. Her husband left all his books to his close friends Fulke Greville and Edward Dyer. Shortly afterwards, Frances asked Greville for a corrected copy of *Arcadia* – evidently she did not possess one and reading it may well have been one way in which she coped with her bereavement. (As we shall see later, some of Sidney's literary ideas were shared by Dee.)

Frances appears to have been a woman of some sensibility. In 1590, at the age of twenty-three, she secretly married Robert Devereux, Earl of Essex, the handsome, insolent and intemperate favourite of the queen. This was certainly an affair of the heart for Frances, and the queen was even more furious at this marriage than she had been about Frances's union with Sidney. One member of the Privy Chamber commented: 'God be thanked she doth not strike *all* she threats.'[32] Regardless of Essex's philandering, Frances remained loyal and loving through all his changes of fortune. Shakespeare is thought by many critics to have based the character of Henry Bolingbroke, the man who usurped Richard II to become Henry IV, on Essex.[33] In this connection we should remember that Essex's fatal attempt at rebellion in 1601 was preceded by a special performance, requested by members of Essex's circle, of *Richard II* at the Globe. Frances Walsingham's readiness to be godmother to Dee's daughter can be seen as an affectionate acknowledgement of support to the man who had been such a good friend to her parents and to Sidney.

It seems that Dee was never short of well-connected and aristocratic friends. One is forced to conclude that even on the continent his great learning, his personal bearing and his character were such as to win him affection from the most distinguished members of the courts he visited. For example, on 22 February 1585, his son Michael was born in Prague. One of the boy's godparents was the Spanish ambassador to the court of Emperor Rudolf. The detail of the birth entry reminds us that Dee was an astrologer:

22 Feb. Natus Michael, Pragæ, hora. 3 min. 28, a meridie, ascendente ☉-ε. Locus ☉)(.3. 32'.39".[34]

He records not only the time and the place of the birth but also the astral conjunctions to enable him to cast his son's horoscope.

The first factor to look for in a birth chart is the sign rising on the horizon at the moment of birth, the Ascendant. Here it is Mars – O–ε. Then a calculation of the latitude is possible, as here. With this information Dee could estimate the characteristics with which his son would be endowed and the formative influences likely in the future. In July 1594 the boy fell ill and Dee noted the position of the stars at the time. They showed a conjunction of the planets Saturn and Mars. Since both planets were believed to be malevolent, the outlook for the sick child looked bad. Exactly one week later, at sunrise, Michael died at the age of nine, uttering the words 'O Lord have mercy upon me'. The day was Dee's birthday. Such a conjunction of events would be loaded with significance for him. Only the previous month, on 3 June, Dee had taken his wife and all seven of his children to meet the queen at Thistellworth.[35] Elizabeth was as kind as ever. 'My wife kissed her hand' – perhaps Dee thought that the sight of him as a family man would help in his suit for official recognition. It might help to counter any uneasy rumours circulating at Court, for he was still waiting patiently for the firm offer of a post. In the light of the entries about Michael's birth and illness, and of Dee's manner in recording other auspicious and inauspicious events, we can say that Margaret's arrival, nearly twelve months after the boy's death, was almost certainly planned.

Three weeks after his birth Michael had been baptised in Prague. At the time Dee was seriously short of money. Even so:

14 Mar, Thursday. A meridie, hora 2½. My son Michael Dee was baptised in the cathedral church of Prague Castle. His Imperial Majesty's chaplain conducted the baptism service.

The next part of the entry detailing the godparents raises questions about Dee's orthodoxy and aspects of his conduct when he returned to England:

The godparents were the most illustrious Don Gulielmo de Sancto Clemente (Ambassador from the King of Spain to the Emperor), and his magnificent lordship the Lord Romff (his Imperial Majesty's First Lord of the Bedchamber, and an intimate and eminent member of his Privy Council etc.) The godmother was her most noble ladyship the Lady Dittrechstain, most beloved wife of the Lord Dittrechstain, who is his Imperial Majesty's High Steward.[36]

Rudolf had turned Prague into one of the great centres of learning in Europe, and the city was the centre of Bohemian protestantism. Yet Dee did not choose protestants as sponsors for his son. The ambassador of Spain's 'Most Catholic Majesty' would hardly have taken part in a protestant ceremony. Dee goes on to explain that 'the infant was named Michael, in grateful memory of the blessed Michael, who (by God's mercy) was, is and will be such a benefactor, helper and guardian to us'. Such a sentiment, together with entries recording his taking confession, he and Kelly taking communion in Catholic churches in Prague, and he and his wife taking the 'Eucharist' when in Manchester ('not a term used then in Anglican circles', according to the Reverend N. Barker Cryer) all indicate that Dee had converted secretly to Rome while on the continent. Elias Ashmole recounts the story of the discovery in a chest of fine workmanship, once owned by Dee, of a secret drawer 'full of books together with a rosary'.[37] If Dee remained a Roman Catholic on his return to England, he would have been compelled to keep it secret while still outwardly conforming. It is difficult to believe that his links with Catholicism did not become known and they may have been one of the difficulties in the way of finding him a placement.

Before Dee left for the continent three of the nine polygonal outdoor theatres had been built, namely the Theatre, the Curtain and Paris Garden (or Bear Garden). The Rose was the only one erected during his time abroad and it was constructed on an ill-chosen piece of marsh land. The next theatre to be built, the Swan, appeared four years after his return. At the time Dee was still living in Mortlake, waiting in hope of an appointment to some office worthy of his service to the Crown.

RESTRICTIONS ON PATRONAGE

The right to maintain a company of professional entertainers had been originally a royal prerogative which over the centuries had been extended to courtiers, nobles and gentry.[38] The Vagabonds Act of 1572 removed that privilege from baronets and gentlemen. Legislation in 1597–8 limited the right even further and: 'From then until the end of Elizabeth's reign only those companies licensed in the name of the sovereign, and of a few great nobles of sufficient consequence at Court to warrant the privilege, were legally free to perform plays in England.'[39]

As the theatre matured into a dominant cultural influence, the struggle to control it became a struggle between the sovereign, whether it be Elizabeth, James I or later Charles I, and 'representatives of extreme reformist and democratic opinion in Church and Parliament'.[40] In other words the attacks on the depravity of the theatre came from Puritan preachers who denounced them as dens of iniquity or from the magistrates and city fathers who deplored the damaging effect they had in keeping apprentices from their work. One of the chief means of survival, apart from the power of a company's patron, was the siting of the theatres themselves outside the jurisdiction of the city – hence the colony of playhouses south of the River Thames.

Building a playhouse within a 'liberty', an anomaly in the local government of a town or city, also helped. A 'liberty' was, historically, part of a former monastic settlement which had acquired certain privileges of self-regulation within its own precincts. These privileges survived the closure of the monastery itself, so that a particular area remained an 'exempt place or "liberty", an enclave within the walls of the City, but not part of it, and with a somewhat loose and ill-defined organisation of its own'.[41] Thus, it escaped the jurisdiction of the City. This applied already to the Theatre, the Swan and the Rose. It was also to apply to the Globe.

With the concentration of the privilege to maintain an acting company into the hands of the most important nobles, the physical siting of the playhouses was quite properly a matter of concern to them. After all, they were constantly being called on to protect their players from the Puritan onslaught. Significantly, the land on which the Swan was built in 1595–6 was Crown property, part of the dissolved monastery of Bermondsey. The official appointed to nominate suitable owners of this land was none other than George Carey, second Lord Hunsdon, whose importance as a patron of the theatre we have already noted. It must be admitted, though, that Hunsdon's love of the theatre had its limits. When James Burbage planned to re-open Farrant's 'private' theatre at Blackfriars in 1596, Hunsdon was one of the signatories to a petition of objection presented to the Privy Council. As E.K. Chambers comments: 'Playhouses had just been suppressed in the City, and a number of the more important inhabitants of the Blackfriars disliked the idea of one being opened in their select residential precinct.'[42] They feared the noise and the crowds.

A SUITABLE APPOINTMENT

Modern students of John Dee are indebted to the work of Edward Fenton, for in his edition of the diary he restored the astrological signs and other symbols which earlier editors had chosen to omit. Such private and intimate matters as his sexual activity and the times of his wife's monthly cycles were regularly recorded by Dee as matter for serious study. Dee was a very virile man, even after mid-life. (All his eight children were born after he had passed fifty.) His decision to record these activities is understandable in the light of his belief in the importance of astrological influences. However, putting aside Dee's own purpose in noting these events, Fenton's restorations are important in other ways, for they enable us to see Dee's life in a new perspective.

The major section of the diary covering the years 1577 to 1605 embraces the building of all but the last of the playhouses. It is in the study of this final record of Dee's life, with Fenton's additions, that clues to the theatre history have been found.

Other entries enable us to look with a fresh eye at Dee's long, drawn-out search for a royal appointment, which led ultimately to his move to Manchester.

On the 25 May 1591 he wrote:

Sir Thomas Jones, Knight (unasked) offered me his castle of Emlyn in Wales to dwell in so long as he had any interest in it (whose lease dureth yet 12 years) freely: with certain commodities adjoining unto it: and also to have as much mow land for rent as might pleasure me sufficiently.[43]

The castle contained about twenty rooms, a chapel, prison and brewhouse, large enough in all conscience for Dee, his family, his books and assistants. On the 27 May Sir Thomas:

confirmed the same his offer again before Mr John Herbert, Master of Requests, in his hall in Mortlake: which his offers I did accept of. God be thanked etc.[44]

Despite accepting the offer, Dee remained at Mortlake. In December of the same year, he received two separate assurances from Burghley of the queen's kind intentions towards him. Then in March 1592 Dee makes two of his most cryptic diary entries: '9,10 Mar The Privy Seal' and '16 Mar Great Seal' to indicate that he had dealings, social or otherwise with the holders of both these high offices. Sir John Puckering, Keeper of the Great Seal, was to be godfather to Dee's last child, Margaret, in 1595 and these two men may have been involved in finding him a suitable appointment. By the 6 August things looked more promising:

6 August I went to Nonesuch to the Court: where the Countess of Warwick sent me word by Mr. Ferdinando of the Queen's gracious speeches for St Crosses. And the L. Archbishop told me the like.[45]

The Mastership of the Hospital of St Cross at Winchester would have been ideal for Dee's purpose, bringing with it premises where he could establish his own private research centre. There he would, in his own words, be able to 'enjoy the commodious sending over into divers places beyond the seas for things and men very necessary; and for to have the more commodious place for the secret arrival of special men to come unto me there'.[46] Shortly after this come two related entries for 9 and 10 August:

9 Aug. The Lord Treasurer invited me to dinner at Mr. Maynard's at Mortlake, where Sir Robert Cecil and Sir Thomas Cecil and his lady were also . . .[47]

10 Aug. He invited me to dinner also the tenth day, where the L. Cobham came also to dinner, and after dinner he requested the L. Treasurer to help me to St Crosses: which he promised to do his best in. Etc.

Sir Robert and Sir Thomas Cecil were the two sons of Lord Burghley, the queen's Lord Treasurer. At the time, Sir Robert Cecil was employed as secretary to Henry Stanley, fourth Earl of Derby, and shortly afterwards the Derbys began to impinge on Dee's life. Secondly, Lord Cobham, who supported Dee's wish for the Mastership of St Cross, was well acquainted with Dee, for it was his wife who had stood as godmother to Madimi Newton two years earlier.

However, the Mastership of St Cross did not come to Dee, so the search continued. This time, in 1593, it was the Countess of Warwick who came to his help. She was the widowed sister-in-law of Robert Dudley, himself now deceased. She had married Robert's brother, Ambrose, who died in 1590; between 1562 and 1580 Warwick had kept his own company of players who often performed at Court. Much loved by the queen, Lady Warwick was ready to intercede on Dee's behalf, arranging crucial meetings for him. First of all, she was instrumental in getting Elizabeth to agree to send Crown Commissioners to visit him at Mortlake. This was important because Dee had carefully prepared the case for recompense for his services to the queen. In what had been his old library he placed three tables: one for the commissioners, one laid out with letters and evidence of his years of study, and the third with books he had written.[48] The visit was successful in that one of the commissioners, Sir Thomas Gorge, a groom of the privy chamber, 'dealt very honourably for me in the cause', and the queen speedily granted Dee 100 marks. Lady Warwick sent a member of her household from Hampton Court the same day, 1 December, to bring him the good news. Judging by the queen's reaction on this occasion and on others when she sent gifts of money, Elizabeth was fully sensible of her debt to Dee. The problem which exercised her was how best to reward his wide range of abilities and service. In February, the countess was still acting as the intermediary, delivering Dee's letter of thanks to the queen before Elizabeth moved to Somerset House. Twelve months later she was present with Lady Robert Cecil at a meeting between Dee and the queen in the privy garden at Greenwich, and she continued to deliver his letters to Elizabeth.

JOHN DEE AS WARDEN

Five months later Dee's search for a permanent position had still not borne fruit. On 28 October 1594 he wrote a letter in his wife's name to the Lady Skydmore – she was another godparent, this time to his daughter Katherine. Mary Skydmore, a cousin to the queen, was one of Dee's most loyal friends, and had strongly supported his claim for the Mastership of St Cross at Winchester. Now, not surprisingly, Dee's patience was wearing thin and he wrote as if from his wife, hoping for an opportunity to address the Privy Council on his desserts. His request came to nothing. On 8 December his wife was driven to presenting a letter of supplication to the queen as she was being carried from Somerset House. This extreme behaviour appears to have had some effect on the royal dilatoriness, for the very next day Elizabeth suggested that Dee should be the next Chancellor of St Paul's. Ten days later she sent him £40. While no small sum, it was hardly compensation for the lack of a permanent position. Finally, a little over two weeks later, on 3 January 1595, mention of Manchester is made in the diary for the first time:

The Wardenship of Manchester spoken of by the Lord Archbishop Canterb.[49]

Again, there appeared to be some hitch. Two days later Dee notes:

5 Feb. Afore dinner my bill of Manchester offered to the Q. by Sir John Wolly to sign, but she deferred it.

Two months later, after years of delay and disappointment, Dee received his reward.

18 April. My bill for Manchester Wardenship signed by the Queen, Mr Herbert offering it to her.[50]

John Herbert was Master of Requests from 1586 to 1600 and as such was the appropriate Court official to present the formal submission of Dee's appointment to the queen. He was a member of the far-flung Herbert/Pembroke dynasty and great-uncle to the poet George Herbert. He had been on visiting and dining terms with Dee for a number of years. Indeed, Dee was on intimate terms with several members of this Wales-based family.

By the end of May all the legal formalities connected with his appointment had been completed and Dee turned his attention to the most powerful noble in Lancashire, with whom he would now be working:

11 June. I wrote to the Earl of Derby his secretary about Manchester College.[51]

This secretary was none other than Sir Robert Cecil, who left Derby's service the following year to become secretary of state. Ten days later on 21 June, the earl was busying himself with Dee's appointment, informing a trusted member of staff in

Manchester (after all, the earl would be Dee's landlord in Manchester). The fellows of Manchester College also started to write in anticipation of his arrival. There was much to be done. It was already July and Jane Dee was expecting her eighth child in August. Dee's faithful friend, Lady Warwick, made sure all the proprieties were observed and formally thanked the queen on Dee's behalf:

> 31 July. The Countess of Warwick did this evening thank her Majesty in my name, and for me for her gift of the Wardenship of Manchester. She took it graciously: and was sorry that it was so far from hence: but that some better thing near hand shall be found for me. And if opportunity of time would serve her, her Majestie would speak with me herself. Etc.[52]

In August his daughter Margaret was born, and Dee was consulting with the Earl of Derby about his future position. He dined then with him on 22 September in London and again on 9 October, hearing about the state of affairs in the North, their joint interest in the theatre already a bond between them. Then it was time to pack up his goods and send them on ahead to Manchester. By 26 November Jane Dee was sufficiently recovered to travel with her brood of children, and set out by coach for Coventry. Dee himself finally reached Manchester on 15 February 1596 'a meridie hora 5', and on the 20 February he records:

> Installed in Manchester Wardenship inter 9 et 11 ante meridiem.[53]

Dee's appointment to Manchester raises a number of interesting questions. We looked earlier at some of the evidence which indicated that he was now a secret Catholic, and had thus joined that band of subjects which his predecessor, Bishop Chadderton, and Henry, the fourth Earl of Derby, had been instructed to root out and punish. Henry, of course was now dead. So, too, was Ferdinando. After Ferdinando's death, Lord Derby's players had been taken over by Lord Hunsdon and renamed The Lord Chamberlain's Men. Dee's new landlord, William, the sixth Lord Derby, was a mysterious figure, enmeshed in legal disputes over his inheritance for fifteen years. In his youth he had spent three years travelling on the continent and legends grew up about his adventures during that time. In the late 1580s he appears to have divided his time between Lathom and the Court, and, when at home, he seems to have involved himself with the family company of players. Perhaps it was the expense of the litigation over his father's will that forced William to withdraw from continuing as patron of these same players in London, who then, as we have seen, were taken over by Lord Hunsdon. Even so, William was still able to keep a 'lesser' company in the provinces for some years with appearances at Court as late as 1599–1601. An undated

THE · CHETHAM · HOSPITAL ·
· MANCHESTER ·

View from the North premises to the arching over of the River Irk.

12. Manchester College. This sketch, drawn in 1882, is an impression of what the medieval buildings of the College (largely still standing) might have looked like before the arrival of the railways.

letter has survived from William's wife to Sir Robert Cecil in which she speaks of her husband 'taking delight' in his players, which delight, she hoped, 'will keep him from more prodigal courses'.[54]

In June 1594 William Stanley had married Elizabeth de Vere, daughter of the Earl of Oxford. Her poor health, combined with her husband's notoriously quick-temper, made for a somewhat stormy start to their marriage, but they settled down happily together. His wife's mother was a sister of Lord Burghley and it was inevitable that Burghley, Sir Robert Cecil and the queen were fully conversant with Derby's financial and marital problems.

After Richard Hesketh's abortive attempt at conspiracy in 1593, the previous earl, Ferdinando, had lived under a cloud of suspicion and had never regained the queen's confidence. Dee, we should remember, had been employed as an agent for the Crown earlier, on visits to the continent. It would have been in keeping with the queen's practice to expect Dee, as warden, to keep an eye out for signs of disaffection in the North and to report back to Burghley even on Lord Derby, just as Chadderton had done on the fourth Earl. By 1598, Elizabeth was sufficiently reassured to reinstate William Stanley to the Derby's traditional seat on the Chester Ecclesiastical

Commission. In the contract for the wardenship it was stipulated that Dee was to be paid his salary even when absent from his post, so it is obvious that the queen did not expect him to remain in Manchester all the time. He was to have freedom to leave his post, a freedom he was to exercise when the time was ripe.

As warden, Dee found much waiting to be done. There were a number of legal disputes over college land which had been encroached on by unscrupulous neighbours. It was prudent of him to insist that his duties were purely administrative, for in that way there was less risk of his Roman sympathies being detected. For the next two years he applied himself energetically to the tasks ahead. Then, after a diary entry for 11 March 1598 in which he notes that he borrowed £40 from one George Kenyon of Kersall, to be repaid 'as soon as I can conveniently', there is a break in the journal until 1600. Silence descends and Dee is nowhere to be found. All he tells us is that on 10 June 1600, he set out 'from London' to return to Manchester.

What could have caused him to return to London with his family in 1598? He must have known it would be for a long time. I reviewed the aspects of his career described earlier in this chapter and I noted the names of his friends, particularly the godparents. One of these, Lord Hunsdon, was the patron of the most successful of all the acting companies of the day. Lady Warwick was related by marriage to his first patron, Leicester himself. The Derbys, with whom Dee was now officially involved, had produced three generations of patrons. Later on, the Cumberlands kept an acting company of their own under James I. Every one of Dee's aristocratic circle, by virtue of being close to the queen, would have regarded theatrical performances at Court an important form of regal entertainment. After considering all these facts, I came to the conclusion that Dee had been urged to return to London to oversee an important development directly concerning the playhouses.

In 1598 the long, drawn-out negotiations between James and Cuthbert Burbage on the one hand and, on the other, Giles Allen, owner of the site on which the Theatre stood, came to an abrupt end. The playhouse was taken down, beam by beam and plank by plank. Under the supervision of Peter Street, it was removed from Shoreditch across the Thames to Southwark, where it opened as the Globe in 1599. Then, in January 1600, Peter Street contracted to build the Fortune as a square version of the Globe. The two projects followed close on one another, and it is particularly significant that there are drawings in the Byrom Collection which show details concerned with both the Globe and the Fortune; they can, therefore, be studied together and compared with each other. The Fortune was up and running by the autumn of 1600, by which time Dee and his family were back in Manchester.

The Rose had been erected in Dee's absence on the continent. Its siting and construction had revealed limitations in the size of the stage and the audience

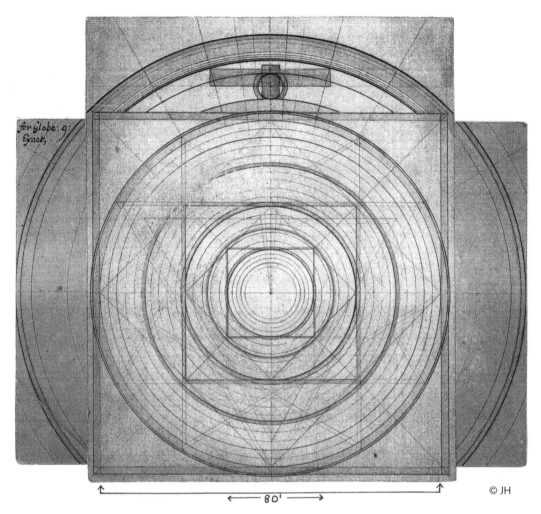

for globe: 9:
Exact;

←——— 80' ———→   © JH

13. The Globe and the Fortune. A pair of drawings to be worked together. The top one, well used, includes the pencil markings of the geometry underpinning the Roman amphitheatre. (Byrom Collection, reproduced at 75 per cent of original size)

capacity, and major revisions were soon necessary. Accordingly, when it came to moving the Theatre, Dee himself would have been anxious to see the exercise carried out satisfactorily. Its removal also provided an opportunity to correct any features that called for improvement. Lord Hunsdon, the Lord Chamberlain, whose company was to take over the Globe would have wanted Dee to be on hand. The Earl of Derby, in keeping with the family tradition and his own keen interest in the theatre, would have nodded at Dee's absence from Manchester.[55] Above all, the queen, upon whom ultimately the survival of the acting companies depended, would agree. She had, after all, permitted Dee's salary to be paid *in absentia*.

CHAPTER 4

The Third Globe

The design of the Elizabethan playhouse, and the dimensions of individual theatres, their estimated capacity and the nature of the Elizabethan stage area might have remained simply subjects in the academic syllabuses of students of theatre history or the performing arts, receiving, where appropriate, separate but brief notice in courses on English literature. Might have, but for the unexpected intervention of Sam Wanamaker, a man of incalculable energy and determination who had the strange idea of building a replica of the original Globe as near as possible to the site of Shakespeare's playhouse. From that moment all academic theorising had to be tried and tested to produce practical answers for the benefit of twentieth-century architects, builders, theatre technicians, actors, musicians and last, but far from least, theatregoers.

Looking back at the history of the English theatre, it is not surprising that all physical traces of the Elizabethan playhouses were erased. The extreme Puritans had their way, and just as they destroyed much of great beauty in the churches and abbeys of the realm, they wiped out the cradle of English secular drama. They acted out of genuine religious zeal and showed, once again, that good intentions, even if they do not lead to hell, can lead to barbarism.

Admittedly there were many other influences at work which led to the demise of that first burst of theatrical glory, not least the politically inept conduct of Charles I, the intervening Commonwealth and, with the restoration of Charles II, a fashion for a different kind of play to amuse a different kind of audience in a different kind of playhouse.

But when, 400 years later, in the last quarter of the twentieth century, the Byrom drawings were discovered, it seemed to me perfectly natural that there would be people interested in them and able to understand and explain their meaning. This, however, proved to be a mistake. The drawings undoubtedly aroused interest wherever I took them, but that interest was not matched by an ability to interpret them. Experts too numerous to mention readily admired the precision, skill and beauty of the drawings, but their connection with the Elizabethan theatre remained an enigma, a challenge to me personally, which I felt compelled to meet. There were undoubtedly clues, but clues to a method of working and a corpus of knowledge alien to the modern Western mind, trained as it is in analysis and specialisation. The drawings, I discovered, belonged to an altogether different discipline, one that emerged from the East and was more concerned with synthesis, with holistic unity than fragmentation.

SAM WANAMAKER

It is perhaps the result of a happy synchronicity that the drawings came to light at the time Sam Wanamaker was attempting to translate his dream of rebuilding Shakespeare's Globe into reality. To Wanamaker, Shakespeare's theatre was the greatest that Western culture had known. Yet in Shakespeare's own country there was nowhere the plays could be performed as his own audience would have seen them. Throughout the eighteenth and for most of the nineteenth century, the works of Shakespeare were studied as plays, if at all, with many attendant perceptions and absurdities of interpretation. It is not a coincidence that during this period the presentation of the plays on the stage, despite the greatness of some of the actors, was at its worst. It was the gradual rise of the status of theatre studies during the twentieth century that finally reunited the playwright with the poet. With the reminder that Shakespeare wrote for the stage not the study, it became possible to appreciate his skills as a playwright and to dismiss some of the more erudite explanations of the texts. If an idea was not demonstrable on the stage, it was more than likely to have been imposed on the play rather than to be an organic part of it. Gradually the importance of the actual theatrical context – the stage itself, the physical relationship between actor and audience – were recognised. The need to see Shakespeare performed in the conditions of his own day grew. Even so, it was to be 1949 before a figure emerged who was determined to make the idea a reality. And that figure was no scholar from academe, but, significantly, an actor and not even an English one.

Sam Wanamaker's boldness in determining to rebuild the Globe close to the site of Shakespeare's original playhouse needed to be matched with similar exceptional gifts in others. When the architect Theo Crosby offered his help Wanamaker found a worthy companion in arms. However, both men were dependent on the academics, legions of honourable Shakespeare scholars who had spent years amassing an impressive amount of expertise on the nature of the Elizabethan playhouse. Inevitably they had their differences which they did their best to sort out in order to arrive at a consensus of instructions for the architect and his builders.

The academic programme was ordered and logical, carried out within a structure of international meetings and discussions. However, since I was never part of that structure, I cannot comment on the interactions between scholars while these discussions were under way. All I can comment on are the decisions that were made public or that affected me. I was fortunate in that, after I had personally introduced the Byrom theatre drawings to Theo Crosby, I was able to establish a positive and ongoing relationship with him until he died in September 1994.

THE PROVENANCE OF THE DRAWINGS

My relationship with Crosby was valuable for, ironically, the actual provenance of the drawings gave rise to problems. They were and remain in private ownership. The owners wished and still wish to remain anonymous. They are perfectly entitled to do so and their reasons are eminently sensible. However, there is no doubt that this anonymity caused some problems in bringing the collection into the public arena, especially for the academic researcher. There is a long history of literary hoaxes and frauds, not a few connected with Shakespeare. However, it has to be stated at this point that not every artefact of an original nature belongs to a national institution or public archive, where it is readily accessible, with certain provisos, for public inspection. The rider to this is that because a manuscript or work of art is not in public hands, the scholar's natural caution leads to suspicion. It is a regrettable fact that the healthy scepticism necessary for objective investigation has a negative side which can operate to its own detriment.

The responsibility for looking after such a cache of original material is not insignificant. Perhaps it is another concomitant of the private provenance of the drawings that there have been times when even the most scholarly individuals have not been mindful of the proper care and handling necessary. I have witnessed instances of an almost cavalier manner in the curiosity of scholars, very different from the extreme care rightly expected by keepers of national institutions in the handling of artefacts. However, I also recall the late Sir John Summerson, the doyen of English architectural historians in his day, expressing the hope that the drawings might be kept permanently as part of a national archive. Yet once in an institution they would have to become identifiable in a different way: during my investigations, I came across a small group of similar drawings in the British Library. These had been mounted and stamped with a library stamp to deter theft, thus obscuring what might prove to be vital details from proper analysis. While I would not suggest such a practice would happen today, storage and accessibility remain problematic. Private ownership with all its associated difficulties will continue, and scholars will have to accept the terms private owners lay down.

Within the terms set out by the owners of the Byrom Collection it was perfectly possible for me to share the information I gleaned from the drawings with those responsible for reconstructing Shakespeare's Globe. I did this initially through Theo

14. The first bays at the new Globe, photographed by the author in 1992. The dome of St Paul's can be seen on the north side of the Thames.

Crosby, but the academics had a standing invitation to visit me to study the drawings themselves. Apart from one all-too-brief visit by one academic, unfortunately sickening with influenza at the time, no attempt at a serious study of the Byrom drawings was made during the period the new Globe was being built. It is irrelevant now that letters remained ignored, appointments were not kept and that my offers of help met with silence. Undoubtedly the demands of normal university commitments continued for the academics as the Globe enterprise grew. There was, also, the constant problem of funding (met generously from around the world). Time itself weighed heavily on advisers and builders alike, urging the completion of a project so long in gestation. Further consultation would have meant further delays. Above all, there was the unusual nature of the collection itself which arose out of another discipline alien to many Shakespeare scholars and raised fundamental questions about the exact nature of the Elizabethan theatre. It is not surprising that the drawings received no further attention after the death of Theo Crosby. It was the arrival of Mark Rylance on the scene that made it possible to resume a meaningful dialogue about work on the reconstruction of the Globe. Before he was appointed Artistic Director, Rylance invited me to share a platform with him at the Globe Centre to give the first Spearshaker lecture in April 1995. Since then he has ensured that channels of communication have remained open.

The first bays at the Globe were erected in 1992 only months before *The Byrom Collection* appeared and introduced the public at large to a selection of the drawings. I was heartened by the reception of the book, both by critics and readers. One gratifying consequence of publication was that I began to hear from the very people I had been searching for while I was preparing the text. They came from a variety of disciplines – doctors, scientists, architects, actors, and, yes, even university professors – and all had something to offer towards a fuller understanding of the drawings.

They wrote, from all around the world, not just about the Globe or the other theatre drawings, but about the collection as a whole, displaying in the process an enlightenment and sensitivity which for me justified the whole venture. They confirmed my belief that the book had to be written and that there was still much to be done. After the Spearshaker lecture, I continued to inform the authorities at the Globe, through Mark Rylance, of any relevant progress on the collection as the work on constructing the new Globe moved towards completion. One thing did surprise me and continues to do so: the media remained strangely indifferent to any suggestion of new material which might be of value to the enterprise. Perhaps they were suffering from Globe fatigue. Perhaps there is another explanation. Whatever the case, I found it perplexing.

THE SITE OF THE FIRST GLOBE

Part of the Globe's academic remit is to carry on research into the theatre of Shakespeare. In this connection the site of the original playhouse has always been a factor of prime importance. An archaeological investigation might provide valuable clues. The site had at one time been part of Courage's brewery bottling plant and in 1989 belonged to Hanson plc. Fortunately, unlike some other property developers, Lord Hanson showed exemplary patience and even funded the archaeological project. The aim was to investigate the whole site, not just to look for the Globe, but any clues to design features would be helpful. Archaeologists from the Museum of London Department of Greater London Archaeology led by Simon McCudden carried out their first investigations between 3 July and 16 October 1989 and uncovered remains thought to be associated with Shakespeare's Globe theatre.[1] These were 'part of the north-eastern circumference of the polygonal building'. They consisted of a series of chalk and brick foundations, one of which 'could be interpreted as forming the base of a stair-well'. The most exciting find suggestive of a theatre came on 11

October: a layer of 'crushed hazelnuts within a matrix of dark brown silt', similar to the deposit of hazelnuts at the Rose. It was believed that hazelnuts were used to cover the surface of the floor to help with drainage and, possibly, with the acoustics.

Unfortunately, only a small area was discovered, just enough, in the words of Theo Crosby, to be irritating.[2] Worse still, 10 per cent of what could be reasonably defined as the site of the Globe had been destroyed by building work in the nineteenth century, 20 per cent was a 'narrow strip of land', 30 per cent lay under Anchor Terrace, a row of listed, if empty, Georgian buildings, and the rest stretched under the irremovable approach to Southwark Bridge.[3] The situation was fraught with difficulties. The remains of the Globe that had been uncovered lay in the north-west corner of the Anchor Terrace car park site. Most of the remaining area had been badly disturbed by previous development. With a preservation order on Anchor Terrace, there was little chance that the Georgian buildings might be removed to reveal traces of the Elizabethan layer beneath. After various attempts at finding a solution, it was decided to conduct a sub-surface sonic scan over the findings and over the basement of Anchor Terrace. The result of that scan was promising.

It seemed that there were further remains worth investigating. The problem remained how that work could best be done. Between July and October 1991 a team of archaeologists, led this time by Simon Blatherwick, funded again by Lord Hanson, were allowed to dig a limited number of 'test pits' under numbers 1–15 Anchor Terrace and examine what little might be seen of the Globe beneath. However, there was another shock in store: the excavators discovered that the entire Anchor Terrace construction had been built on a concrete 'raft' to compensate for the instability of the clay of the Thames riverbank. Nevertheless, the three test pits revealed signs of the original Globe. Immediately beneath the concrete raft foundation was a dark grey clay containing occasional charcoal, mortar and brick flecks. Situated within this clay was 'an archaeological feature provisionally interpreted as a pier base'.[4] However, because of legal constraints on any excavation below the Anchor Terrace foundations, it was not possible to determine accurately the purpose of this feature. During this dig a Nuremburg token with a date of 1580 to 1630 was discovered in the dark grey clay around the pier base. German brass counters used, it is thought, to supplement Tudor silver coinage had been found on the site of the Rose.

The information the pits produced prompted varying interpretations. The archaeologists themselves stated in their report that 'we would be the first to advise you that we can't prove this goes with that'.[5] Even so, the Globe enterprise had learned enough to realise that the twenty-four-sided building they were planning would have to be altered. Wanamaker, now seriously short of funds, was quite happy for further construction to be delayed in the hope that more information would emerge.

15. Hollar's *Long View*, London 1647. The unique contribution of the playhouses to the skyline of Elizabethan London is clearly evident.

Much work had already been done by the academics on the design of the new Globe. What effect did the findings of the archaeologists have? They certainly appeared to confirm the general accuracy of the Globe as seen in Hollar's panoramic *Long View* of 1647, although Hollar's picture is of the second Globe and in it the playhouse is mistakenly labelled 'Beere bayting'. Secondly, the findings at the Rose had suggested a polygonal shape, yet Hollar's drawing depicted the Globe as round. The excavations helped to end this age-old dispute. The apparent paradox was resolved by the realisation that a structure with many sides can appear circular, especially from a distance. This 'optical illusion' theory was used to explain why both Norden and Hollar drew a round building in their engravings of the Globe because from a distance it looked round. The question now facing the new Globe's architect was how many sides did this particular polygon originally have. While the debate continued on a theoretical level, sufficient money continued to come in to enable a practical experiment that might help resolve the problem: two trial bays were erected in the summer of 1992. After prolonged deliberations, it was decided that the number of sides of the new Globe should be reduced from twenty-four to twenty, and be erected round a diameter of 99 feet.

The other great piece of evidence that Theo Crosby and the team of academic advisers had was the original contract for the construction of the Fortune theatre (1600). As we noted earlier, the builder, Peter Street, was the man who transported the timbers of the Theatre across the Thames and rebuilt it as the first version of the Globe. Some theatre historians have been very dismissive of him: one authority said: 'The Globe was put up by an illiterate carpenter who couldn't write'.[6] The remark is, in fact, misleading. Street was no jobbing builder, but a respected member of a long-established craft. He had been elected a warden of the Company of Carpenters in 1598. By that time the company, like other guilds, had developed into an organised hierarchical structure with a master and three wardens. Election to these offices was attended by ceremony and ritual which had evolved its own regalia. The master and wardens wore crowns or garlands and by 1611 used ceremonial silver gilt cups of handsome and elaborate workmanship. To dismiss Street as 'illiterate' does no justice to his abilities. His rank within the Company of Carpenters suggests he was more than capable of building the Globe to the specifications of the theatre drawings.

Peter Street's contract for the Fortune stipulated that it should be constructed to the same specifications as the Globe, but square. To some it may have seemed a simple matter to work backwards from those dimensions to arrive at the size of the Globe, but the problem was not quite so straightforward. The contract gave the exact height of each gallery level and specified that the stage should jut out from the tiring house to the middle of the yard, but the major question that remained for the builders was whether the tiring house itself was a separate structure from the gallery

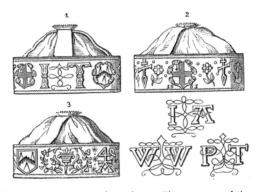

16. The Carpenters' regalia. *Above:* The crowns of the three wardens, dating from 1561. The initials worked on them indicate they were the gifts of John Abbott, Wolstone Wynd and Thomas Pecoke, then three members of the court. *Left:* Warden's Cup presented by Thomas Edmones.

bays. The Fortune contract stipulated this should be so and later evidence, such as the portable stage and tiring house at the Hope, confirmed it.

The academic discussions continued to be steered by Professor Andrew Gurr, Chairman of the Academic Advisory Council for the Globe project, detailed technical help was provided by John Orrell and the enterprise also called on the expertise of the project carpenter Peter McCurdy, the twentieth-century equivalent of Peter Street. Most of the decisions on the principles involved in the structure had been made before the untimely death of Sam Wanamaker at the end of 1993. It was then possible to turn attention to other matters such as the stage and the decoration on the front of the tiring house wall. Gradually the completion of the theatre became simply a matter of time and money and it was finally opened on 12 June 1997.

THE OPENING OF THE NEW PLAYHOUSE

The opening of the Globe could not be confined to one single day – there was too much to celebrate, too many to honour. The reconstructed Globe theatre opened to a Festival of Firsts lasting from 8–23 June. This celebration was necessary to acknowledge the wide range of patrons, private individuals, public bodies, single and corporate sponsors and countless others who had given voluntary help and moral support. The festival embraced performances of the two plays chosen for the opening season, *Henry V* and *The Winter's Tale*; a masque specially written in honour of Sam Wanamaker; a pageant *Triumphes and Mirth* to celebrate the completion of the theatre; a concert of songs from Shakespeare's plays and Elizabethan music performed by the Musicians at the Globe; a founder's day feast and a festival ball. The first full performance of *Henry V* was dedicated to the memory of Sam Wanamaker and his wife, Charlotte, and the first public performance of *The Winter's Tale* was in honour of the first architect, Theo Crosby, and his wife, Polly Hope, who was responsible for the mural on the Bankside Tower. Appropriately for an enterprise that includes a large educational element, the festival ended with children from eighteen schools taking over the stage to act, sing, dance and also watch, on this occasion a special production of *Julius Caesar* by staff from Globe Education. But the highlight, the event marking the official opening, was the evening of 12 June when Queen Elizabeth and Prince Philip, Patron of the Shakespeare Globe Trust, attended the celebration of *Triumphes and Mirth*.

The first Queen Elizabeth had summoned Shakespeare and his players to her Court. The second was more accommodating and arrived on the Royal Barge to be received at the Bankside Gates, once the audience was seated. Her entrance into the theatre itself was greeted by a solemn fanfare. After the national anthem, the Red Company's performance was ushered in by a compelling roll of drums rising to a crescendo and bringing the audience to rapt attention before Zoë Wanamaker, daughter of Sam, stepped forward to deliver the prologue to *Henry V*. This was followed by a performance of the fourth act. The second half consisted for the most part of *Triumphes and Mirth*, a pageant celebrating the universality and timelessness of Shakespeare's genius.

The evening ended with a display of fireworks over the River Thames. The delicate blue of the evening sky was lit by a succession of starbursts and sudden rockets of fire. Repeatedly, trails of brilliant light shot heavenwards, unfolding into fresh and unexpected patterns before falling back to earth. Even as they fell the colours changed, a dazzling feast of visual magic. The spectators watched spellbound. Of this, I felt sure, John Dee would have approved.

The opening season was an undoubted commercial success. The two companies of players, the Red Company in *Henry V* and the White Company in *The Winter's Tale*, performed to capacity audiences. The International Shakespeare Globe Centre became the top tourist attraction in London. A visit to a performance, whether standing as a groundling or seated in one of the galleries, is a unique opportunity for theatregoers in this country. Spectators can enjoy something close to the experience of the audiences in Shakespeare's own day but without the attendant discomforts of Elizabethan hygiene and sanitation. The novelty of that alone, regardless of the unaccommodating bench seats, guaranteed a constant stream of sightseers and spectators for many years to come.

However, from an aesthetic point of view, from the point of view of the theatre as the most rewarding venue in which to watch and listen to Shakespeare's plays, then I have regrettably to offer some serious qualifications to the word 'success'. I find a number of features disconcerting.

FIRST IMPRESSIONS

Visually, everything at the Globe is too large, and the spaces between parts of the building are too great. As a consequence, instead of dominating the setting the actors are dominated by it. Against the two massive pillars supporting the stage roof they look diminutive. This has a damaging effect on their ability to communicate with the audience. If not inhibited, they seem intimidated and the actor's natural assertiveness becomes aggression. Only the most experienced actor survives in these circumstances. As I watched them perform in that auditorium, it became clear to me that the actors were involved in devising some survival strategy – their voices became unnaturally stretched, the timing of lines and the rhythm of speeches seemed difficult for most of the performers. Another result of too much space is the loss of intimacy between actors on stage and between actor and much of the audience. This was surely one asset that could have been expected from the attempt at creating an authentic setting. It was particularly noticeable that some women playing on this stage encountered vocal problems and were happier in roles where masquerading as men allowed them to alter their pitch and force their voices somewhat. The problem is endemic in the size of the theatre. To counter it, the argument has been put forward that today's actors will have to be trained to 'use' their voices in this setting in order to be heard without loss of quality. Time will tell whether such adjustments can be achieved naturally.

But, of course, the size of the theatre has another serious drawback. It is not just that the actors are dwarfed, have difficulty in projecting and have to cover too much ground to position themselves effectively. The stage is too big, the roof above it is consequently too large, and, worst of all, the pillars supporting that roof are far too thick. They were widely criticised when the theatre opened, because they have a disastrous effect on the sight-lines.[8] Large portions of the stage are obscured from the audience, places where any significant action or symbolic interplay must be avoided because one section of spectators or another will miss it. The delight expressed by some actors at seeing every member of the audience 'in a way that's unlike any other theatre'[9] is not reciprocated by that audience. Indeed this has been such a glaring fault from the start that booking forms had to include the phrases 'limited view' and 'restricted view' in details of the seating plan. In the booking programme for 1999, these phrases were replaced by the following statement: 'All seats are priced according to a pillar rating. The roof of the stage and the galleries are held up by pillars, there is nowhere in the theatre from which the action is not masked, at some point, by pillars.'

It has been suggested by some that the Elizabethan theatres suffered from the same fault, that, in other words, it is inherent in the design. However, from the vantage point of the Byrom theatre drawings, I see things differently. While some people have expressed approval of the new Globe and its space, I am not alone in having reservations about its 'success'. For me the wording on the booking forms was an admission on the part of the theatre's administration of a serious weakness in the present design. As for the facilities for performing musicians, these leave much to be desired. The company has superb musicians but the natural acoustic is unkind to their excellence. The effectiveness of their contribution is hindered, and I cannot believe that the original musicians in Shakespeare's Globe suffered in the same way. One further problem arises out of the reconstruction: the orientation of the entire building. The academics decided that the stage should be positioned in the north-west of the theatre and face south-east. The result is that on a sunny English afternoon (and the Globe performances were always in the afternoon), the audience is forced to sit with the Sun in its eyes. Perhaps Shakespeare's original stage was positioned differently. We shall be looking at the argument for that later. These observations are not offered in a negative spirit, but in an attempt to define those areas of the reconstructed playhouse that give rise to dissatisfaction in the discerning spectator and to seek out the underlying cause.

Professor Gurr is not alone in misunderstanding the origin of the unique design of public theatres. In an issue of the Reading University newsletter published in May 1995 he described the Globe as 'at most a second-best option' for Shakespeare's company and 'very old fashioned by 1599'. But this is to ignore the impact the Renaissance was beginning to have in England and the relevance of Vitruvius to the design of the Theatre, the earlier incarnation of the Globe. Vitruvius's treatise, as we have seen, was well known to Dee. It contained clear instructions on how to lay out the geometry of a classical theatre. Examples that survive today in Greece and elsewhere in Europe demonstrate beyond doubt an amazing acoustic quality. Moreover, if the new Globe had been built precisely in accordance with the laws of proportion and harmony, then, I am convinced, many of the problems outlined above or mentioned elsewhere in this text would not have arisen.

The academics' determination to reach a consensus opinion from among their own conflicting views seemed to leave little room for the initiative of a private researcher, and an opportunity to join their number did not present itself. I had made what I considered discreet and helpful representations to Theo Crosby. His own enthusiasm and belief in the Byrom drawings were sufficient for him to consider them seriously. But this was not enough for them to be taken on board in the later planning stages, particularly after Theo's death. The Globe academics were perfectly entitled to disregard the work I was able to offer. However, I felt that the drawings had yielded sufficient clues to deserve a second and more prolonged examination. Fortunately, my own continued researches began to yield further corroborative evidence to strengthen the case, and, as I have said, favourable reactions from other quarters encouraged me. Throughout, the pioneering work of the late Dame Frances Yates has been invaluable. She was among the first to recognise the relevance of Vitruvius to the design of the Elizabethan playhouse and the importance of John Dee's 'Preface' to Euclid. She also displayed an admirable academic rigour in dealing with areas of study which appeared quite alien to many less adventurous researchers. I could only hope that I would eventually reach a stage in the elucidation of the drawings when the burden of evidence would make it impossible to ignore them any longer.

GEORGE MURCELL

One of the people who got in touch with me after the publication of *The Byrom Collection* was George Murcell, actor and artistic director of St George's Theatre, Islington. He wrote to me in August 1993. He had been part of a group of actors and directors formed in 1967 who were eager to set up an 'authentic Elizabethan playhouse in London'. Their search led them to a decommissioned church in Tufnell Park which seemed an ideal site for conversion. This nineteenth-century building was designed by

George Truefitt and was modelled on a fifteenth-century crusader church in Salonika. What had impressed Murcell and his colleagues was the proportions of the inner space and fine wood-frame ceiling. He showed the interior to Dame Frances Yates who immediately recognised its suitability for conversion and its echoes of ancient architecture. An advisory board was appointed to help with the project, consisting of such distinguished figures as Sir Tyrone Guthrie, John Neville, Christopher Plummer, Michael Benthall and Tanya Moiseiwitsch. The building had distinct potential as a venue for the performance of Shakespeare's plays as his contemporaries might have seen them but with one major difference: this playhouse would be roofed in and, in George Murcell's own words, there would never be a danger of rain stopping play.

It was inevitable that the paths of Murcell and Wanamaker would one day cross. This is not the place to rehearse what happened when they did. Those interested can read an account in Barry Day's book *This Wooden O*. From what might have been a mutually beneficial joint enterprise, the two men went their separate ways. By 1993, when Murcell first wrote to me, his vision of St George's, of which he was now the owner, was beginning to crystallise into a re-creation of the first Elizabethan playhouse, the Theatre itself.

Anyone visiting St George's cannot fail to be moved by what the *New York Times* has described as its 'magical space'. The acoustic is excellent and the setting and atmosphere enhance the quality of musical performances. Truefitt's design is full of resonances: the site is triangular, the shape round, the interior octagonal.

17. St George's, Islington. The excellent acoustics of the central 'round' of the church persuaded George Murcell to form a theatre company here in 1967.

George Murcell embodied all the idealism of his cause. Passionate, energetic and inspirational, he dedicated the last years of his life to translating his vision into a reality. His enthusiasm was exhilarating; his conversation an endless flow of hilarious anecdotes and heart-rousing determination. However, against the more audacious aspirations of Wanamaker's wish to rebuild the Globe, George's plan to adapt a church may have seemed pale to those with the money to dispense. Ultimately there should have been no need to see the two projects as mutually exclusive, but in an era when public funding became increasingly restricted it was the idea of the Globe, with all the international pull of building a replica near Shakespeare's original, that opened purses, private and public. Murcell, however, believed firmly in the pioneering work by Frances Yates on the origin of the Elizabethan theatre, outlined in her seminal work *Theatre of the World*. He also believed in the Byrom theatre drawings. They came from the same tradition as Truefitt's circular church: they spoke the same language as his building, the 'Vitruvian' language of harmony and proportion which originated even further east than Rome and which Frances Yates had also recognised when she entered the church for the first time.

George Murcell and I had many meetings in which we discussed his plans. He felt, rightly I believe, that London could accommodate both his indoor version of the Theatre and Wanamaker's Globe. He had already done a considerable amount of educational work with London schools, and the idea of concentrating on early English theatre had much to offer. After years of battling with bureaucracy and a mounting series of disappointments, he was afraid that I, too, might be dazzled by the glamour of the Globe enterprise and ignore St George's. To reassure him I drew up a statement of intent in which I carefully and clearly laid down the ways in which I thought I could be of most use to his aims. This provided a sound framework for our discussions and was still in operation when George decided to commission a radar scan of the site of the original Theatre in Shoreditch. In the event the scan was funded by George himself, Hackney Council and John Gleason, Professor Emeritus of San Francisco University. It is a matter of deep regret to many of his supporters that George died suddenly before he had chance to complete his contribution to the search for authenticity in the world of Elizabethan theatre.

DR MCCANN SURVEYS THE SITE

Certainly the radar scan George Murcell commissioned has its place in this story, but, before we look at it, we should first review further scans on the site of the Globe. After the initial attempt at a sub-surface radar survey and Simon Blatherwick's investigations by means of test pits in 1991, consent was given for further evaluation by another scan. This investigation was carried out by the Clark Laboratory of the

Museum of London Archaeological Service (MoLAS) under its Director, Dr W.A. McCann on 30 November 1995. The trial was designed: 'to determine whether the technique was capable of identifying known archaeology in the car park and possible features beneath the 1.5–1.7m thick concrete raft of Anchor Terrace.'[10]

When the Globe approached MoLAS, Dr McCann was admirably modest about the hopes he had for any significant success. His advice was that ground penetrating radar (GPR) 'had so far failed to produce realistic and consistent results in central London'.[11] Indeed he was not happy about the accuracy of the initial GPR survey on the site. Ellen Barnes of English Heritage made the same observation. However, in the event Dr McCann was able to report that 'the trial survey did produce accurate and repeatable results, with the radar accurately detecting the known archaeological features and anomalies located beneath the concrete raft of Anchor Terrace.'

For the enlightenment of the interested layman, Dr McCann explains in his report that ground penetrating radar

produces an electromagnetic (radio) pulse or continuous wave from a customised transmitter antenna which lies across the ground and which can be moved across it. The pulse (or wave) interacts with the immediate surroundings and a second, receiver, antenna provides indirect information about the form of this interaction over time. Any object or interface that involves significantly contrasting electromagnetic properties, and has sufficient physical dimensions, will cause a partial reflection of the impinging electromagnetic energy.

It was essential for the Clark Laboratory to be able to show that any correlation between its findings and known archaeological features was not the result of a simple coincidence of unrelated factors outside its control. Accordingly tests were done to ensure the repeatability of the results and these proved to be excellent. The findings were not merely coincidence. One caveat is important, however. GPR does not enable the investigator to identify the nature of a feature which has been discovered underground. Its strength lies in accurately locating areas where 'anomalies' are caused by changes in electromagnetic pulses, but it cannot distinguish between different structural features. This is normally done by following up the GPR with some form of limited excavation to confirm the precise nature of what has been found.

One of the major questions about Shakespeare's Globe that remained unresolved was its diameter. Finding the answer was made more difficult by the fact that the first version was burned down in 1613 and rebuilt the following year on the same site. Using the 1989 evaluation of the position of the exterior wall of the Globe, various projections were made of differing diameters across the entire site including under the standing building of Anchor Terrace. For the purpose of the exercise it was assumed that the exterior of the second (and larger) version of the Globe would be no more than 102 feet (31.09m) diameter, and the majority of the radar investigations were made within this limit. A succession of polygonal template overlays ranging from 54 feet (16.46m) to 102 feet (31.09m) at 5 feet (1.52m) intervals were constructed. These were oriented on the site with the help of the known archaeology, the easterly 'spar' and what was considered to be part of the second Globe's outer wall providing a good deal of accuracy. The calculations used to determine the size of the projections were based on the assumptions that the bays within the Globe were uniformly 16 feet (4.87m) at the external wall. This would obviously lead to a reduction in the number of bays as the templates decreased in size. Common sense dictated a minimum diameter for the template of 50 feet (15.24m).

It was thus possible to examine any concentrations of anomalies in a number of locations across the site in areas defined by individual alternative diameters. The recurrence of clusters of anomalies at locations defined by one alternative rather than another would be indicative. The greater the number of locations thus identified, the greater the reliability of the findings. In his interim report Dr McCann concluded:

an optimum correspondence between the anomaly plots and areas of potential structural elements associated with the theatre is found for the diameters of 77, 82 and 87 feet. It is significant that these diameters also give the best fit, for both inner and outer walls, with the archaeological features observed in 1989.[12]

A map plotting the anomalies in relation to the archaeological finds of 1989 was distributed by Dr McCann to various interested groups studying 'the problems associated with the Globe theatre'. The intention was to produce a final report embracing as large an input as possible from archaeological, geophysical and historical resources collated by the Clark Laboratory at MoLAS. However, representatives of the Globe decided that the data produced by the survey did not merit such treatment, and funding for further analysis was not forthcoming. Dr McCann and his team felt that this decision was based on 'non-archaeological and non-scientific considerations'.[13] In fact, the final recommendation of the interim report states that a phase 'of limited excavation should be carried out in advance of any detailed analysis of the survey data'. This was in keeping with the normal practice of recommending that all GPR work should be so followed up 'in order to confirm the presence of the identified anomalies and to determine their precise nature and provenance'.[14]

And there for the time being the matter rested until two other important factors came into play. Hanson plc sold Anchor Terrace. The new owners, Hollybrook Ltd, in redeveloping the site, undertook extensive renovation of the property and a late change in the proposed use of part of the basement provided an opportunity for another sub-surface survey in that particular area. The site owners were agreeable and

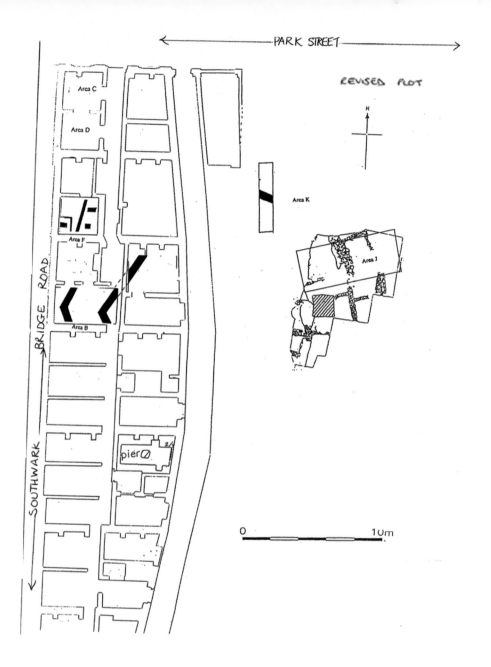

18. Geophysical survey, Anchor Terrace, Globe site. ('Revised Plot' © The Museum of London, The Clark Laboratory, Dr W.A. McCann, November 1998)

ready to provide every assistance. At the same time, there had been advances in the GPR technique itself and in the application of the three-dimensional software used to process the data generated. This meant that the Clark Laboratory felt confident that the improved technique and processing software could now provide data to replace the incomplete and unsatisfactory conclusions drawn from the earlier survey in 1995.

The survey took place on 25 February 1998. For practical purposes the site was

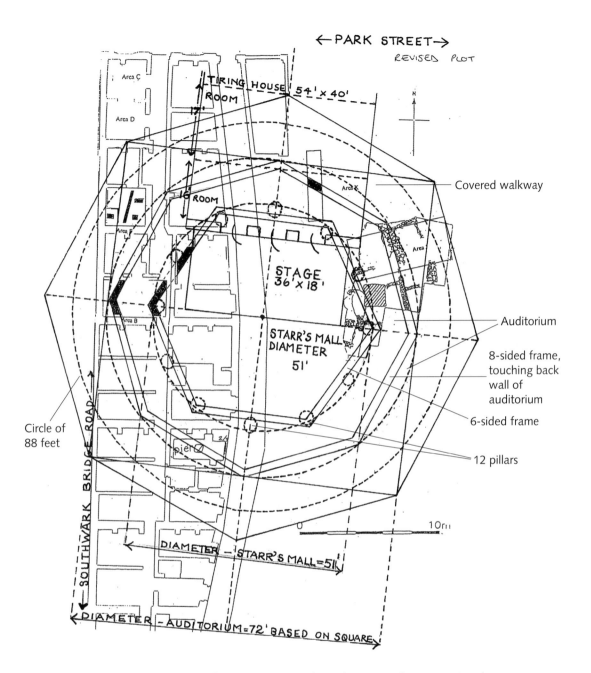

←PARK STREET→

REVISED PLOT

Area C

Area D

TIRING HOUSE 54' × 40'
ROOM
17'

ROOM

Area

Covered walkway

Area F

STAGE
36' × 18'

Area

Auditorium

Area B

STARR'S MALL
DIAMETER
51'

8-sided frame,
touching back
wall of
auditorium

6-sided frame

Circle of
88 feet

pier

12 pillars

SOUTHWARK BRIDGE ROAD

10m

DIAMETER — STARR'S MALL=51'

DIAMETER — AUDITORIUM=72' BASED ON SQUARE

19. Site of the original Globe, Anchor Terrace. A geophysical survey with a composite of measurements extracted from the Globe theatre drawings in the Byrom Collection. ('Revised Plot' © The Museum of London, The Clark Laboratory, Dr W.A. McCann, November 1998. Composite © Joy Hancox, February 1999)

divided into ten areas designated by the letters A to K. The survey, commissioned by the Globe, was to concentrate on those areas A, C, D, E and H in the basement of Anchor Terrace which might be expected to contain remains of a theatre with a diameter between 86 to 100 feet. Unfortunately the areas chosen by the Globe executive did not produce any significant 'anomalies' from the scan, so it was logical to conclude that (a) either no remains survived or (b) the diameters of both the first and second Globe did not lie between 86 and 100 feet. However data from area B (identified as to be looked at if time permitted) was much more illuminating. This was the area that had produced the most significant cluster of anomalies in the previous survey. Areas F and G also produced interesting clusters of anomalies. Finally, area K produced the best data of all. When the evidence from these four areas – B, F, G and K – was analysed with the evidence of the excavations from 1989, Dr McCann concluded:

> These data are consistent with the preliminary conclusions from the previous survey which suggested an external diameter between 72 and 82 feet and would, in fact, suggest that it lies towards the lower end of that range. It is therefore the general conclusion from this survey that possible significant remains of the Globe have been identified beneath Anchor Terrace and that these are more likely to have been associated with a structure whose external diameter was close to 72 feet rather than anything larger.[15]

In my capacity as one of the interested parties studying the problems associated with the Globe, I received from MoLAS copies of both the Interim and final reports of the two geophysical surveys. I must confess to feeling concern over the conclusion that the anomaly plots which had been uncovered did not warrant further examination, and, after studying the evidence presented in the interim report, agreed that the findings did warrant further excavation of the site. I therefore looked forward with great interest to the findings of the Clark Laboratory's later survey in February 1998. I should state at this point that long before either of these surveys was undertaken, I had come to the conclusion from my interpretation of the Byrom drawings that the first Globe playhouse was based on a frame of 72 feet and had said so in *The Byrom Collection* in 1992. To see the figure of 72 emerge out of Dr McCann's scholarly analysis of his survey was, to say the very least, significant. Indeed, when Dr McCann saw the degree of compatibility between the geometry of the Byrom drawings of the Globe theatre and his own findings, he agreed that an overlay of his work on mine showing the compatibility should be included in the paperback edition of *The Byrom Collection* in 1997.

THE SITE OF THE THEATRE

It is relevant at this point to look at results of the geophysical surveys undertaken by the Clark Laboratory on the site of the Theatre in Curtain Road, Shoreditch, at the initial behest of George Murcell. The first survey took place in May 1998 in the basements of the properties at 86–92 Curtain Road, at 3–15 New Inn Road and on the larger of two car parks situated behind 96a and 98 Curtain Road. The site, originally part of the Augustinian priory of Holywell, had been intensively developed since the priory was dissolved at the Reformation. As a result the ground penetrating radar technique was unable to detect any likely archaeological remains. The results of the investigation below the car park were equally unpromising.

However, a second survey was carried out in November 1998 in the properties 3a–6 New Inn Broadway, in the small car park north of 6 New Inn Broadway and on the pavement to the east of these sites. The overall results of this survey were, in Dr McCann's view, excellent. The radar scan identified what are thought to be traces of buildings

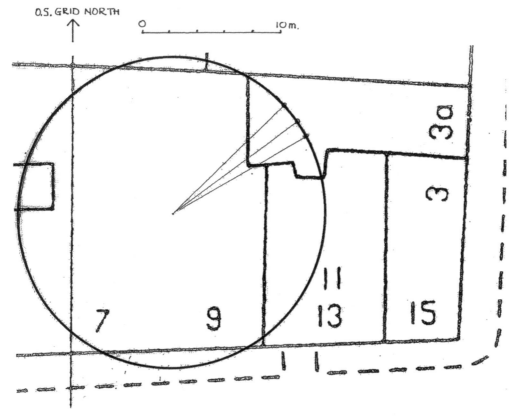

20. Radar scan of the Theatre site. (Geophysical survey © Museum of London, The Clark Laboratory, Dr W.A. McCann, February 1999)

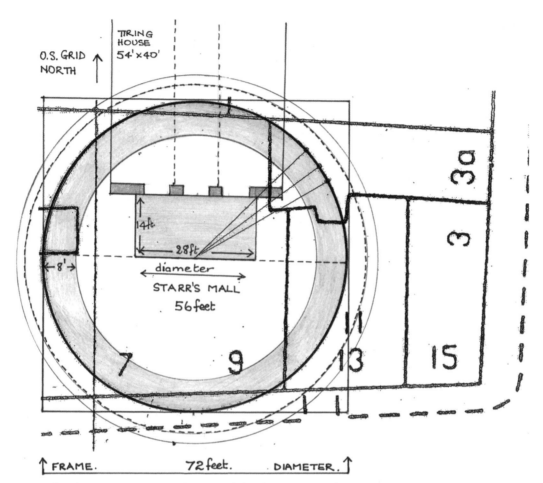

O.S. GRID NORTH

TIRING HOUSE 54'×40'

3a

3

14ft

28ft

8'

diameter

STARR'S MALL

56 feet

7   9   13   15

FRAME.   72 feet.   DIAMETER.

21. The Theatre composite. Radar scan of the Theatre site with measurements superimposed from the Byrom Collection. (Geophysical Survey © Museum of London, The Clark Laboratory, Dr W.A. McCann. Composite © Joy Hancox, February 1999)

associated with the original priory. Moreover, in two of the grids prepared for the survey significant clusters of anomalies were seen. In his conclusion Dr McCann states:

> From one set of these it is possible to construct a circle with a diameter of 22 metres or 72 feet. This is a significant figure and raises the possibility that these anomalies are the remains of The Theatre, which is known to have stood on the site. The other anomalies lie within the circle thus described and could represent remains of internal structural features. The circle occupies the approximate area which has been suggested as the most likely position of The Theatre by a number of scholars.[16]

So a diameter of 72 feet is discernible once again, this time from fresh evidence emerging about the Theatre. I felt even more reassured to have the dimensions of the

Byrom drawings thus vindicated. For, of course, all the scholars knew that the first
Globe had been built by reassembling the timbers of the Theatre in a different place.
The diameters of the two buildings should therefore be the same. I had given George
Murcell the dimensions of the Theatre in 1994. Unfortunately, he died before the
report was published.

THE SITE OF THE ROSE

We now had separate radar scans on separate sites which were mutually supportive.
I could hardly contain my delight. It was all the more necessary now that I should
examine again the archaeological evidence from the excavations carried out at a third

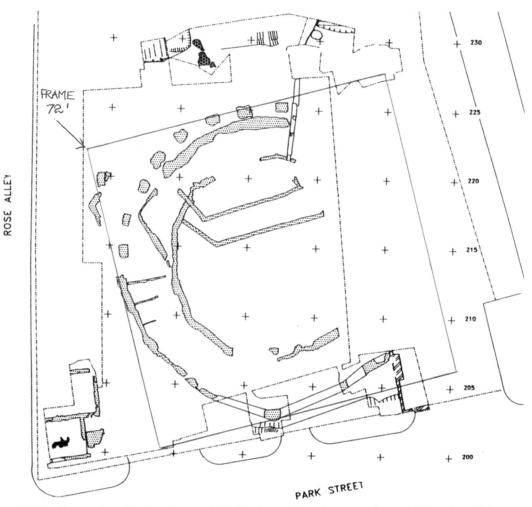

22. The Rose archaeology in a frame of 72. The imposition of a square frame of 72 on top of the
archaeological findings demonstrates the compatibility of the layout of the Rose with the concept
underlying the sequence of open-air playhouses.

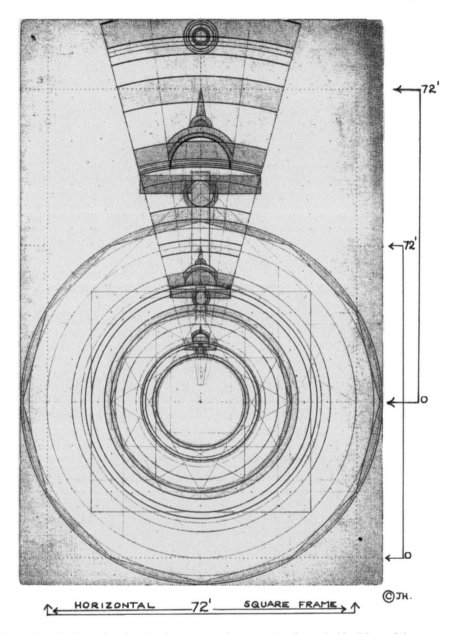

23. The Rose ideal. Horizontal and vertical measures showing a twelve-sided building of three levels. Underpinning the drawing is the geometry of the Roman amphitheatre. (Byrom Collection, reproduced at 75 per cent of original size)

site – that of the Rose theatre. These, as we have seen, had been conducted by the Museum of London archaeological staff between 19 December 1988 and 14 May 1989 under the leadership of Julian Bowsher. The publicity surrounding the dig and the danger of the loss of such an important historical site led to a public outcry. A further, small excavation was undertaken in June and July 1989 by the Central

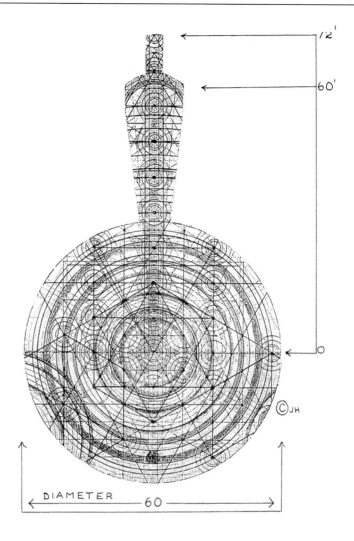

24. The modified Rose parametric. The master parametric template allows for different-sized buildings to be cut according to requirements. The entrance is indicated by the small circle near the bottom, coloured pink on the original. (Byrom Collection, reproduced at 75 per cent of original size)

Excavation Unit of English Heritage. The remains have been carefully preserved and the new building development at the site, Rose Court, completed in June 1991, incorporates a basement space specially built over the remains of the theatre. In 1998, the Museum of London published Julian Bowsher's fascinating account of the archaeological discovery of the Rose. To date the excavations have shown that the theatre went through two phases of building. On page 33 of Bowsher's account I read the following: 'The evidence revealed so far suggests that this phase [i.e. the original construction of 1587] was a simple but irregular polygon *with an external diameter of 22m (72ft).*'[17] The italics are mine: once again the Byrom drawings had been corroborated by external scientific fact. There is in Byrom's collection a sequence of drawings connected with various alterations undertaken at the Rose. From my interpretation of the geometry of all these drawings, I had already concluded that the Rose, too, had been built on a frame of 72 feet.[18]

CONCLUSIONS

At this point it will be helpful to list the latest scientific findings which have been published on the sites of three major Elizabethan playhouses. These are:

1. *Final Report on the Geophysical Survey of the Globe* by Dr W.A. McCann, May 1998.
2. *Final Report on the Geophysical Survey of the Theatre* by Dr W.A. McCann, February 1999
3. *The Rose Theatre, an archaeological discovery* by Julian Bowsher, 1998.

Each of these three reports gives a suggested diameter of 72 feet to the ground plans for the playhouses under investigation. The findings are the culmination of ten years work from 1989–1999 by fully trained professionals. Quite rightly, all three documents will be lodged as indispensable archive material for future researchers.

But what of the Byrom Collection? The drawings relating to the three theatres mentioned in these accounts had been identified years earlier (together with others), and the measurement of 72 for the diameter of each of them had already been deduced from information they contained. Nevertheless, that interpretation was deemed unacceptable to those making decisions on the new Globe, even at the planning stage. If there is any justification for commissioning archaeological and geophysical surveys, then it must lie in the application of their findings, where appropriate, to other known data from any and every available source. The Elizabethan playhouses are part of our cultural heritage, and so are the Byrom drawings. Those who executed the drawings in the first place knew the measurements, and I had been able to interpret them.

My most recent work in applying the data from the radar scans to my own work on the drawings at last seemed to justify my inclusion in the latest conference at the Globe theatre to be held in February 1999. Through the good offices of Dr McCann and Mark Rylance I was able to draw the attention of those present to the compatibility between the Byrom drawings and the radar scans. I was able to reiterate the need for a complete set of drawings to be made available in published form so that they can be studied at leisure. Unfortunately, such an undertaking will be expensive. Costs notwithstanding, a facsimile edition, or a catalogue raisonné has long been a necessity. In the meantime, I repeated yet again my offer to share the knowledge I had gleaned from the drawings with the assembled group. In June 1999, I received from Mark Rylance a formal letter sent 'with the approval of the Executive Committee of the Globe' which stated: 'We would like to express our support for the creation and publication of a Facsimile of the Byrom Collection drawings, back and front, and in colour.' As a result of the conference, one of the academics present, Rosalind King, of St Mary's College, London, came to study the collection over a period of four days. I arranged a series of private seminars which we both found invigorating and searching. It had taken ten years for such a dialogue to happen, and for me it was a new beginning – if only a beginning.

Apart from the undeniable compatibility between the 72 diameter in the physical investigations of the three sites and my work on the drawings, other important points emerged during our discussions. The excavations and radar scans by their very nature had been dealing with findings below ground. There were additional drawings in the collection relevant to those findings. It was necessary now that these should also be verified just as the others had been. What sort of support in the way of actual footings would the Globe theatre structure have required, given that it had three storeys? The drawings should be able to tell us.

In 1992, I had met Kenneth Peacock, then the master modelmaker in the School of Architecture at Manchester University and a man with an extensive background in engineering. He was also a wood pattern maker. He agreed to make a sequence of wooden models of the Elizabethan playhouses to the scale of the Byrom drawings. Now, it was through his good offices that I found someone suitably qualified with whom I could discuss particular issues from the archaeological finds. Peter Howcroft is of mixed British and German extraction and graduated from the School of Architecture at Sheffield. He has a special interest in the traditional tools and techniques of craft workers in wood. Since setting up his own workshop he had continued to research design and the craft as it was practised as far afield as Scandinavia and Japan. His family background on both sides is that of traditional craft workers. He was invited to take part in a special exhibition in Munich in 1998 where he demonstrated traditional English cabinet-making skills, using historic handtools from his own collection. He has, therefore, the academic background of an architect and the practical experience of a craftsman using traditional methods of working in wood. I considered these attributes qualified him to assess the methods and approaches which I thought had been used in the construction of the Elizabethan playhouses.

I had lengthy discussions with both men, and together we spent many hours studying the theatre drawings, particularly those connected with Dr McCann's findings from his radar scan. I began by explaining how I had arrived at the dimensions for my version of the Globe in the first place. I demonstrated the concept of the parametric drawing which contained both horizontal and vertical planes. I noticed with interest that, like Kenneth Peacock before him, Peter Howcroft had no difficulty with this concept. Both his knowledge of the European tradition of architecture and his own practical experience had shown him similar examples. Indeed, on his next visit, he brought a copy of a rare carpenter's manual: *The New*

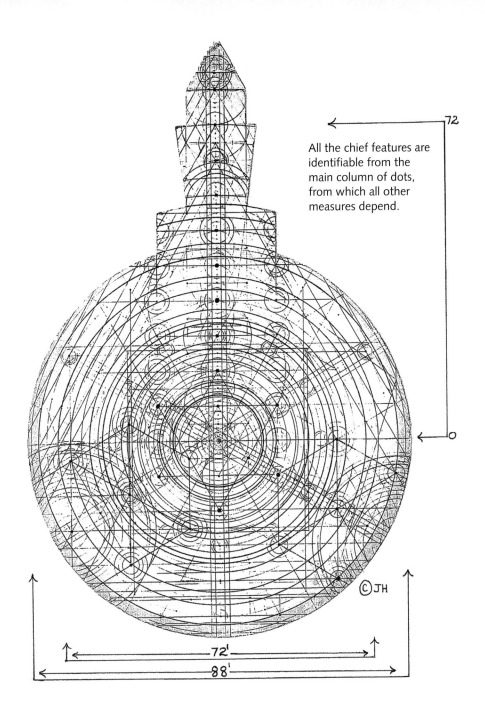

72

All the chief features are
identifiable from the
main column of dots,
from which all other
measures depend.

0

©JH

72'

88'

25. The Globe parametric with dimensions. The central column of the drawing includes details of
the height and design of the tiring house block. Key positions in connection with pillars and
gangways are also indicated. A sequence of other drawings was designed to be worked with this
parametric. (Byrom Collection, reproduced at 75 per cent of original size)

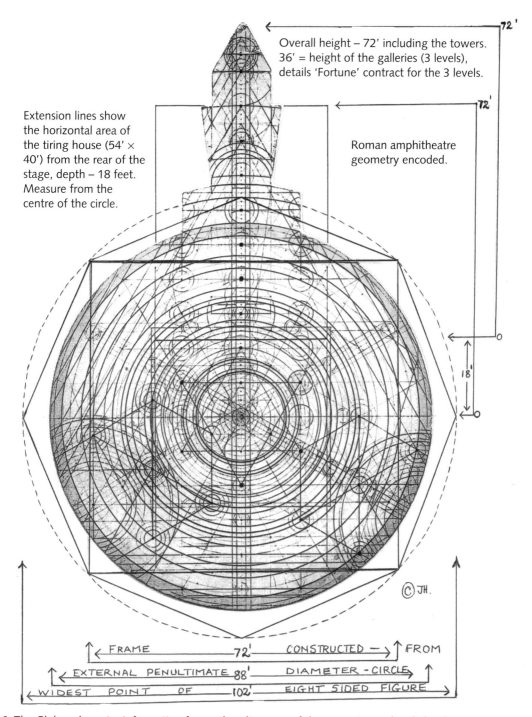

Overall height – 72' including the towers.
36' = height of the galleries (3 levels),
details 'Fortune' contract for the 3 levels.

Extension lines show
the horizontal area of
the tiring house (54' ×
40') from the rear of the
stage, depth – 18 feet.
Measure from the
centre of the circle.

Roman amphitheatre
geometry encoded.

72'

72'

0

18'

0

© JH.

FRAME   72'   CONSTRUCTED — FROM
EXTERNAL PENULTIMATE 88'   DIAMETER - CIRCLE
WIDEST   POINT   OF   102'   EIGHT SIDED FIGURE

26. The Globe schemata. Information from other diagrams of the same size and scale has been
superimposed to demonstrate the schemata. (Byrom Collection, reproduced at 75 per cent of
original size)

27. An hexalpha of the Globe. This can be used with parametric theatre drawings. This geometry was taken into account when constructing the Globe radar composite. (Byrom Collection, reproduced at 75 per cent of original size)

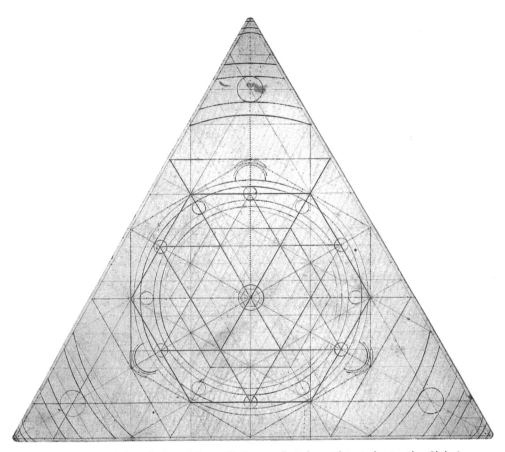

28. Triangle and hexalpha. The hexalpha, with the small circles within, indicates the Globe's supporting pillars. Their position is based on the design of a Roman amphitheatre, as shown elsewhere in the composite. (Byrom Collection, reproduced at 75 per cent of original size)

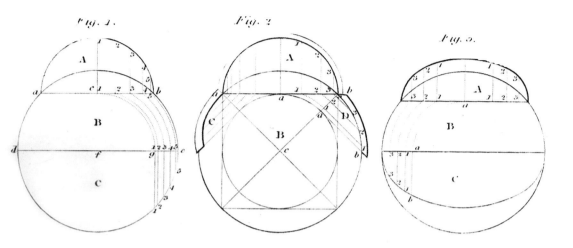

29. Cross-section of solids from *The New Carpenters' Guide*, Peter Nicholson, 1858. The two-dimensional geometrical drawing was intended for students of carpentry and shows both the horizontal and vertical planes, like the Byrom parametric drawings.

Carpenter's Guide by Peter Nicholson, published in 1858. At one point the author gives an abstract explanation of a sphere and its properties. He accompanies this explanation with an illustration showing sections of the sphere in both the horizontal and vertical planes. As a teaching method this appeared to be not only normal but necessary.

One matter of detail we discussed concerned the composite drawing which I superimposed on a plan of Dr McCann's radar scan and the earlier archaeological findings on the Globe site. This was the hexagonal drawing which indicated to me the position of what I considered were supporting posts at each corner to provide a frame of support for the general structure of the building. Peter Howcroft suggested that this pattern could indeed indicate the presence of what we called a 'structural matrix', a means of distributing the weight of a building above ground with timbers driven deep below the ground, an accepted practice in architecture. We all agreed that the proximity of the theatre to the River Thames would necessitate a structure with supports below ground to ensure firm and stable foundations. After all, the building was three storeys high. Support timbers would need to be tied in and their place logically positioned to this end. The Globe drawings seemed to demonstrate an awareness of this, and the radar findings confirm the likelihood that these concepts had been understood and observed. One minor piece of information I owe to Peter Howcroft is that Johann Theodore de Bry drew copperplate engravings for a book on architecture by Daniel Speckle in Strasbourg in 1599, the year the Globe was built.

30. An elevation of a building showing a structural matrix, taken from a book by Johann Jacob Schubler published in Nuremburg, 1740: *Useful Instructions, Essential Ideas in the Complete Art of Civic Construction*. The matrix can be seen exposed in the foundations.

De Bry was the man whose knowledge of the hermetic tradition and skills as an engraver filled him to translate Dee's ideas for the playhouses into drawings.

We also discussed the question of the walkway which the Byrom drawings show around the outside of the auditorium at the Globe. The seating in the theatre stretches to the limit of the 72 feet diameter. That diameter is coterminous with the 72 feet frame, and most of the anomalies thrown up by the radar scans are to be found within that area. The addition of the walkway in my interpretation of the drawings would include the staircase fixed to the back of the wall of the auditorium but still within the envelope of the building. (This, incidentally, is compatible with Visscher's engraving of the Globe.) Since the walkway is a relatively empty structure (apart from the staircases) the outside wall of the theatre would not be required to be a main load-bearing support like the inner wall immediately behind the seating. Accordingly, it would need less support in its foundations. It might have been based on an enlarged sill. This would account for the fact that comparatively fewer anomalies have been thrown up by the radar scans in this part of the site.

Our discussions had been positive and fruitful. I felt heartened by the opinion of these two experienced and very practical men. In deducing a structure for the Globe from the Byrom drawings prior to our meetings, I had not been building a castle in the air.

CHAPTER 5

The Missing Dimension

It seems that in at least three of the Elizabethan playhouses there was one common feature, one uniform measurement. This did not mean that the theatres were identical, but it did point to an interesting possibility that there was a purpose in this uniformity. The use of the dimension of 72 in each of the theatres appeared to be part of the overall structural constraints. The Theatre, the Rose and the Globe were polygonal, although the Globe had a different number of sides from the Rose. Nevertheless, both had been built to a design where the principal frame number was 72. The archaeology showed this; the Byrom drawings showed it. The more I pondered this fact in relation to the Vitruvian influences in the concept, the more the measurement of 72 seemed to be essential – and not simply to ensure structural stability. It looked more like evidence of another dimension purposely invoked in the concept of the Elizabethan playhouse. I came to call this 'the missing dimension', because it comes from a tradition that for the most part has long since been replaced in modern architecture and has no place in the reconstructed Globe on Bankside.

That dimension is to be found in the mystical use of number. I use the word 'mystical' deliberately because we are now entering the realm of sacred geometry, where numbers have values apart from their simple arithmetical quantities. In discussing number symbolism, it is better to avoid the suggestion of 'magic' because that term can be confusing and open to distortion and to resonances associated with black magic or witchcraft. To the ancients, by whom I mean not only the Romans and Greeks but the Egyptians and their Babylonian precursors, numbers possessed a 'divine' or spiritual quality. The modern scientific view is, of course, that numbers denote quantities, nothing more. Yet even today a debased residue of ancient belief survives in the superstitious value people put on certain numbers such as Friday the 13th or the dates of family birthdays used to fill in lottery cards. Unless we are prepared to acknowledge the higher, more profound concepts attached to number, not only in our own civilisation but others as well, we will never appreciate the full intent of the originators of the Globe design.

NUMBER AND ORDER

A useful starting point may well be the Greek mathematician and philosopher Pythagoras (fl. 530BC). Perhaps the first point we should note is the coupling of mathematics with philosophy embodied in his work. Right down to the present day, the two disciplines have often gone hand in hand. One of Pythagoras' tenets was 'All things are number'. He had studied the beliefs of the ancient Egyptians who witnessed a very practical and life-giving justification for the primacy of number and geometry in the annual flooding of the Nile and the need to measure out afresh the boundaries of peasants' land holdings after the waters receded. This rich soil fed the country, and the survival of the Egyptian race depended on the regulation and order imposed on the land. The word 'geometry' originates from a combination of the Greek words 'ge' for 'earth' and 'metrein' meaning 'to measure'. Geometry therefore enabled the Egyptians to impose that order. In addition, the study of the annual procession of the heavenly constellations brought further proof of regularity in the workings of our universe. Regularity is reassuring: with it you can plan; without it there can be only chaos. So the prime mover of the universe, according to Pythagoras, was a geometer, and God or the Gods were revered as embodiments of number and order. The nature of each god had a planetary equivalent and both could be represented by number.

LETTERS AND THEIR ATTRIBUTES

It is not surprising, therefore, that the quality above all others which distinguishes man from the rest of creation, the gift of language, should also give rise to numerical equivalence. For speech, too, displays regularity and order. Accordingly, in the early civilisation of the Middle East, each letter of the alphabet represented a particular type of universal energy or god. It also corresponded to the other attributes of the god it symbolised. It followed, therefore, that the number associated with that letter was also an attribute of the same god. So, the letters of the ancient Greek, Arabic and Hebrew alphabets all had numerical attributes. This became known as gematria. Today the Hebrew alphabet still holds deep religious significance for the faithful and each letter is studied with profound reverence.

For the Gentile and agnostic at large, the ideas we are about to consider may lead us into unaccustomed ways of thinking. But we must address them nevertheless. Our culture has its roots in the Judaeo-Christian system of beliefs. It will be helpful, therefore, and relevant at this point to look a little closer at certain aspects of the Jewish alphabet. Rabbi Michael L. Munk explains: 'The twenty-two sacred letters are profound, primal spiritual forces. They are, in effect, the raw material of Creation.

When God combined them into words, phrases, commands, they brought about Creation, translating His will into reality, as it were.'[1] Rabbi Munk continues: 'There is a Divine science in the Hebrew alphabet . . . The letters can be ordered in countless combinations by changing their order within words . . . Each rearrangement of the same letters results in a new blend of the cosmic spiritual forces represented by the letters.' He makes an analogy with chemistry. One combination of hydrogen with oxygen produces water, another arrangement of the two produces hydrogen peroxide. So, for the Jew, letters have a creative quality. In certain combinations in prayer, they can arouse spiritual forces of great power. But they must be articulated because the sound has an important part to play in arousing that spiritual potential. According to the Bible, the builder of the Tabernacle (the tent that contained the Ark of the Covenant as the Israelites journeyed to the promised land) was a man called Bezalel. He knew the combination of letters that created heaven and earth. He was thus able to utilise the spiritual forces needed to build the Tabernacle.

BUILDING THE TEMPLE

The same principle applied to the building of the permanent Temple in Jerusalem once the Israelites had reached the promised land and to the construction of temples in other religions in other Middle Eastern cultures. Each of the buildings was designed to invoke the divinity of the god to whom it was dedicated, to attract sacred powers. The names of various deities were based on the sounds which were considered most effective in evoking their presence. So the dimensions of a temple were an integral part in summoning those divine powers. So, too, were the furnishings, the areas and patterns enclosed in the building. We have evidence of this from the specifications for the Ark and the Temple in the Book of Exodus and First Book of Kings in the Old Testament. Important, too, were the name and number of the god to whom the temple was dedicated. For example, the Temple of Athena the Virgin was laid out at Athens in units of the 'virgin seven'.[2] Bezalel was fully instructed in this art and King Solomon, who followed his example by building the first permanent Temple, also understood the sacred letters and knew which powers they represented. Solomon, of course, is a proverbial figure of wisdom. In the Second Book of the Chronicles we are told: 'And all the kings of the earth sought the presence of Solomon to hear his wisdom, that God had put in his heart.'[3] Ezra the builder of the second Temple was a prophet and scribe. The knowledge and understanding of the sacred letters at this level was limited to a few holy men. Already we have the beginning of a secret tradition in building – a few chosen initiates who alone have the insight.

This tradition was carried on in the building of the great cathedrals of Europe. Tools and techniques predominated in the medieval guilds, but behind these was the figure of the Sage with his sacred knowledge. John Dee was part of that tradition, using his knowledge in the service of his patrons. In his 'Mathematical Preface' he refers to Moses in a very significant phrase: 'Moses was instructed in all manner of wisdom of the Egyptians and he was of power both in his words and works.'[4] This to Dee explains the miracles Moses performed in leading his people to freedom. He concludes: 'You see this philosophical power and wisdom which Moses had, to be nothing misliked of the Holy Ghost.' Here we have an example of the crucial accommodation made by the devout Christian with mystical or magical powers. It occurred repeatedly in the Renaissance with the rediscovery of lost traditions of knowledge. Dee strove to achieve the philosophical power exemplified by Moses in the *Monas Hieroglyphica*, as well as in his angel-magic. Similarly, he attempted to endow the design of the Elizabethan playhouse with something of that power. It may be difficult for scholars brought up in a different orthodoxy to accept that there was a philosophic or religious dimension to the quaint wooden playhouses with their thatched roofs. However, I believe that Dee convinced certain Elizabethans (the patrons, including the queen) of the importance of this dimension if a public playhouse was to be fully effective, aesthetically, emotionally and spiritually.

He realised, in building a temple, the special significance of numbers in their relation to letters. In addition, he believed that by observing the laws of proportion, as demonstrated by Vitruvius, a building was literally a harmonious whole, set out in numerical ratios. The analogy with music is important because of the acoustic qualities produced in such a harmonious structure. Certain numbers were evidently critical to a building because they corresponded to specific letters and sounds.

We may appear to have travelled a long way in our search, but we are now able to look with more understanding at the intriguing recurrence of number 72 in the dimensions of the Theatre, the Globe and the Rose. There are other drawings in the Byrom Collection that clearly show the same design concept running through the entire canon of public playhouses. I choose to concentrate on these three because the evidence from the archaeological and geophysical investigations seems to go some way in providing corroboration for the Byrom drawings.

AS ABOVE SO BELOW

The ancient Egyptians believed the god who gave man the art of writing was Thoth. He was also known by the Greek name Hermes Trismegistus – 'Thrice Greatest Hermes' – because he was believed to have been a king, priest and prophet. Whether or not he ever existed, he was regarded as the founder of magic (it is impossible to avoid the term altogether in this discussion), and by magic I mean an accumulation of knowledge that gave the 'magus' an understanding of the interrelated forces which held the universe together and which the magus was able to bring into play. This corpus of beliefs became known as the hermetic tradition. Hermes Trismegistus' most famous pronouncement, 'As above so below', is a fundamental tenet for all those who follow that tradition: the belief that the natural, physical world surrounding us all is a reflection of the Order of a higher invisible, spiritual world. Man is the microcosm, a miniature representation of the entire universe, which is the macrocosm. It follows from this that there is a basic unity running throughout all creation, a natural harmony between man and the universe. The Judaic version of the hermetic idea is to be found in the opening chapter of the Book of Genesis: 'So God created man in his own image, in the image of God created he him, male and female he created them.' This is not to say that the Judaic and hermetic traditions were the same. Far from it, but there were points of convergence which Renaissance scholars found particularly illuminating.

Hermes was believed to have been contemporary with Moses, whose special 'philosophical powers' we have just looked at. Moses had held high office in Egypt under the pharaohs, and understood the Egyptian mysteries. Pythagoras the Greek philosopher was believed to have lived in Egypt also and to have studied the same mysteries. Plato, the greatest of all the Greek philosophers, was conversant with the same tradition. Thus with the discoveries of the Renaissance came an awareness of what seemed to be a continuum of wisdom stretching back from Plato to Pythagoras, from him to Egypt and further back still to the seventh century BC and Zoroaster, the founder of the ancient religion of Persia. Many scholars of the Renaissance and later, including Dee, adopted a syncretistic approach to these different philosophical traditions, combining them into a system of belief compatible with Christianity.

72

When we turn back to look at the recurrence of the number 72 we find it holds a special significance in different civilisations. John Michell, in *The Dimensions of Paradise*, draws attention to Plato's views on the origin of names in his dialogue *Cratylus*. In it Cratylus claims that names have a divine origin and are not simply the result of random choice. The objection is made that things have different names in different languages, but Plato turns the argument to the sound of words and suggests that certain sounds have consistent connotations. These might be archetypal and when the wise men of each nation came to name things they might have drawn on the same source, but with different results. Plato also seems to be aware of the cabalistic belief that letters have a numerical value which is important for the meaning of a word. Michell notes that in gematria the numerical equivalent of the Greek letters for the word 'truth' (*aletheia*) is 72.

Other religions produce other resonances from the symbolic use of number. According to the Hebraic tradition there are seventy-two names for God. In the eleventh chapter of the Book of Numbers verse 26, Moses is commanded by God to summon seventy elders to be given the spirit of prophecy and then God added two more: 'the name of the one was Eldad and the name of the other Medad: and the spirit rested upon them.' Thus in deliberately raising the number of prophets from seventy to seventy-two, God Himself endows the number 72 with mystical, almost sacred, resonances. In the second century BC the Greek astronomer Hipparchus observed the stars from the island of Rhodes and made a catalogue of some 850, dividing them into six classes according to their brightness. They formed seventy-two constellations. He was the first astronomer to discover the precession of the equinoxes. There are two equinoxes – the vernal, which occurs about 21 March, and the autumnal, which occurs about 21 September, when day and night are approximately the same length. Hipparchus discovered that the position of the Sun in the sky at an equinox is slightly different each year. The complete rotation of the earth around its polar axis through all the signs of the zodiac takes about 25,000 years. At present the earth is moving out of Pisces, where it has been for 2,000 years and is about to enter Aquarius, where it will stay for the next 2,000 years. These transitions have been known and revered for thousands of years as major moments in the history of mankind. What is interesting for us is that with the precession, the terrestial globe moves approximately one degree every seventy-two years.

From all this we can see that there were biblical, cabalistic and astronomical associations with the number 72. For scholars following a syncretistic approach to the hermetic tradition the number 72 would be filled with such resonances. In Dee's mind, when he was drawing up the design of the Globe, it was undoubtedly a measurement he chose deliberately to invoke qualities he wished the Elizabethan playhouse to possess. If he had further thoughts on that concept, the opportunity to give them expression came when it was necessary to rebuild the Theatre on the south side of the river. The change of name to the Globe was hugely symbolic and the playhouse itself, though built from the timbers of the Theatre, would have displayed that symbolism in a number of ways. Its shape was a regular octagon with all its properties and an outside diameter of 102 feet.

ARCHITECTURAL SYMBOLISM

From the foregoing pages it is easy to see that Dee took his ideas for the concept of the playhouse from a tradition stretching back through Vitruvius to the Middle East. The buildings of Islam were invested with symbolism on several levels – in number, in shape, even in decoration. The decor on the interior of a dome in a mosque was often based on images of the Sun and the stars to reinforce the association of the dome with heaven above, an idea replicated in the 'Heavens' above the stage of the playhouse in conjunction with symbols from the Lathom screen. Moreover, Islamic symbolism was not confined to sacred buildings, but is to be found in secular ones as well. According to Professor Robert Hillenbrand

> some types of secular architecture developed their own distinctive symbolism. Thus the city of Baghdad was, it seems, self-consciously conceived as *imago mundi*, its concentric circular walls broken by four equidistant gates (one of them roughly aligned to Mecca). It is a concept of immemorial antiquity found alike in Europe, China and the Middle East.[5]

If, at this point, readers begin to feel nervous at the suggestion of Eastern symbolism in the Elizabethan playhouses, they may be reassured by another insight from Professor Hillenbrand:

> It is entirely likely that detailed research into other popular Islamic architectural forms will also disclose a stratum of symbolic significance – a significance which was perhaps never intended to be apparent to the populace at large.

He concludes that there is in Islamic architecture a 'refined symbolism' which, from the first, 'was not bruited abroad but was intended for the cognoscenti alone'. The same is true of the great gothic cathedrals of Western Europe. Unfortunately, we know very little about the internal decoration of the Elizabethan playhouses, but I believe the same holds true for them, too. There would be aspects of the concept not revealed to the carpenters or obvious to playgoers but important to the Elizabethan *cognoscenti* – Dee and his patrons.

WESTMINSTER'S OCTAGON AND THE TEMPLARS

There is at least one national monument still standing in England which celebrates the inherent beauty of the regular octagon in stone. It is the Chapter House at Westminster Abbey. Built between 1246 and 1259 by Henry III, it was designed primarily for the daily meetings of the monks to discuss matters of business and discipline. But even from the beginning it was used by the king as well. One of its earliest secular uses was as a council chamber for the first representatives of the Commons, and from 1352 until about 1395, the Chapter House regularly resounded to debates. Delegates could sit as equals and deliberate in an intimate, acoustically kind setting. The diameter of the Chapter House is 60 feet, the same as the diameters

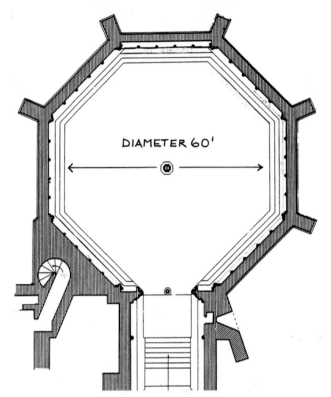

DIAMETER 60'

31. The Chapter House, Westminster Abbey. Octagonal in shape, it has a diameter of 60 feet (18m), the same as the Temple Church. Built between 1249 and 1259, it was part of Henry III's plan for the abbey to rival the splendid churches being built in France. From the beginning the Chapter House was intended as a council chamber for secular affairs as well as for the monks. The crypt beneath was to be a repository for royal treasure.

32. St John the Divine writing to the seven churches of Asia Minor, Chapter House mural, Westminster Abbey. The design of the churches resembles that of the tiring house tower on the roof of the Globe in Visscher's engraving.

of the Round Church that forms the nave of the Temple Church in the Strand
(*c.* 1185) and of the Rose theatre. It is significant that the Round Church was built
by the Knights Templar, who were one of the main channels of Islamic and hermetic
knowledge into Europe.

These warrior monks became the guardians of the Christian sites in the Holy Land
and in the process desecrated Islamic mosques. At the same time, like many
occupying forces, they fell under the influence of the culture around them. One
mosque, the Dome of the Rock, had been built on a site in Jerusalem sacred to both
Muslims and Jews. It was the site of Solomon's Temple, the place where God made
his solemn covenant with the Jewish people. But it was also the site of the rock from
which Mohammed was mysteriously taken up into heaven to converse with Allah.
The Dome of the Rock was taken over by the Templars and turned into their own
church: the 'Templum Domini', the Temple of the Lord. Another mosque nearby, the
Mosque of Al Aqsa, was renamed quite inaccurately the Temple of Solomon. Part of
this mosque became the palace for the kings of Jerusalem, and the rest became the
headquarters of the Knights Templar. The Templum Domini became the mother
church of the knights, appearing on the seal of their grand master and on their
armorial bearings.

The knights absorbed a great deal of the wisdom of Islam and with it the learning
of classical Greece: philosophy, arithmetic, science and, what is most relevant for us
at this point, techniques of building. Moreover, their experience of the Middle East
led them to believe in a God common to Christian, Muslim and Jew: God, the
architect of the world. We see this idea begin to appear in religious illustrations in

33. The Dome of the
Rock. The geometry
employed in building
the mosques was used
by the Templars for
their own churches.

sketch, R. Walker

Western art, in, for example, the illuminated depiction of Christ in a French Bible of about 1250, where he is shown holding a compass to re-enact the Creation of the universe.

Over the years the Templars amassed immense power and wealth, and this aroused great jealousy among secular rulers in Europe. Their unorthodox concept of the deity was used to bring a charge of heresy against them; the Order was suppressed and the knights systematically destroyed between 1307 and 1314.[6] Their influence, however, survived long after. It is significant that 150 years after the Order was disbanded, a chapel was built at Rosslyn in Midlothian, Scotland, which is filled with Templar symbolism. The words of the official guidebook to the chapel echo uncannily the comments of Professor Hillenbrand on the 'refined symbolism' in Islamic mosques: 'clearly recognisable Templar symbolism abounds half-hidden to all except the initiate, paradoxically in plain sight, yet overlooked by all.'[7] The profusion of carvings from many cultures has helped to make Rosslyn a place of pilgrimage. Here, for instance, in a church dating from 1446, we find the head of Hermes Trismegistus alongside the grinning features of the Green Man peering out of stone foliage. The imagery at Rosslyn is a testament to the readiness of the Templars to absorb fresh ideas.

After worshipping for ninety years in the Dome of the Rock, the Templars had experienced the full impact of the organic unity of a building based on the geometry of an octagon within a circle. There is little wonder then that the same geometry is found in many Templar churches. A regular octagon became the preferred design for chapter houses attached to Gothic cathedrals in the twelfth and thirteenth centuries. The typical design of the round Templar church is relevant to the origins of the Globe theatre because its geometry comes from the same tradition as that underlying the playhouses.

THE EARL OF LEICESTER

The role of Robert Dudley as patron to James Burbage was central to the survival of the actors' companies. No one questions this. Nor, interestingly, does anyone question his ennoblement by the queen: she simply wished to show her regard for her favourite. But is that all there was to it? Why, for example, did Elizabeth choose to make him Earl of Leicester instead of Birkenhead or any other place? Perhaps we are mistaken when we ignore the historic and symbolic significance of titles in an age when chivalry and heraldry were of solemn and deep significance.

The earldom of Leicester was an old creation with honourable associations. The earliest and one of the most famous holders of the title was Simon de Montfort. He summoned the first meeting of the Commons in the Chapter House at Westminster.

He married the sister of Henry III who created him Earl of Leicester in 1239 and this appears to have been a royal title even then, reserved for the king's closest associates. Simon was also godfather to Henry's first son, Prince Edward, and in 1240 he went on a crusade to the Holy Land. However, Henry III was a weak, extravagant ruler extorting money by ruthless taxation and wasting it in costly wars. De Montfort became a focus of opposition by the barons, and civil war broke out in 1258. In 1264 he captured the king and Prince Edward at Lewes and attempted to make Henry act only with advice from a council, or parliament. This was the origin of the House of Commons. In 1265, however, de Montfort was defeated by the king and his title was forfeited.

The earldom then reverted to the crown and merged with all the other royal honours. Significantly, the king then conferred it on his youngest son Edmund 'Crouchback', who held the two earldoms of Leicester and Lancaster. The two titles then descended through his line until the time of John of Gaunt, the son of Edward III. He inherited the Leicester earldom in 1362 and later the same year was created Duke of Lancaster. He was the 'old John of Gaunt, time-honoured Lancaster' whom we encounter in *Richard II*. John of Gaunt was the uncle of Richard II and father to Henry Bolingbroke, who deposed Richard and ascended the throne as Henry IV in 1399. On the death of John of Gaunt, the earldom of Leicester once more reverted to the Crown, together with all Gaunt's other honours. The title then stayed with the sovereign and it was over 160 years before another Earl of Leicester was created when Queen Elizabeth thought fit to honour Robert Dudley with the title as a particular mark of her favour.

In the play *Richard II* the character of John of Gaunt is a complete invention. Shakespeare portrays him not as the 'turbulent and self-seeking magnate' of history, but as a 'father and patriot of grandiose stature'.[8] Thus Gaunt is useful both as a dramatic foil to Richard II, and also as a mouthpiece of Tudor patriotism:

> This royal throne of kings, this scept'red isle,
> This earth of majesty, this seat of Mars,
> This other Eden, demi-paradise[9]

The famous speech has turned John of Gaunt into something of a star part, and, tapping into the Englishman's deepest loyalties, became an anthology piece as early as 1600. It has remained so ever since.

Robert Dudley was created Earl of Leicester in 1566. Ostensibly his elevation was to raise him to a rank fit for a man who had been suggested as a husband for Mary, Queen of Scots. That the choice of this particular earldom had symbolic implications can be seen in the fact that, although Elizabeth gave him lands in ten counties,

Leicestershire was not one of them. From the beginning it had been a title so closely connected with relatives of the reigning sovereign that its choice may have been an indication that Elizabeth was considering Dudley as a fitting consort for herself. The historical associations of certain ancient titles remain important even today, particularly those bestowed on royal princes. They were much more significant in an age when the nobility wielded real power.

THE EARLS OF PEMBROKE

The ancient title of another family of theatre patrons repays study. The earliest earls of Pembroke had connections with the Templar knights and their properties in London. The Welsh estates of later earls witnessed a commercial development in Elizabeth's reign which has its own relevance to the story of the playhouses.

The Knights Templar first settled in England in the reign of Henry I. Their headquarters were in Holborn, near Chancery Lane, and in 1185 they built their church, now the Temple, within the precincts of their monastery, the boundaries of

Left: 34. The Temple Church, London. The laws of arabic geometry are evident here on the north bank of the Thames. The 'round' is tiered and has fine acoustics. *Right*: 35. Temple effigies.

which extended right down to the banks of the Thames. The monastery, the New Temple, had grown with the power of the Order which for a long time was the recipient of bequests from rich and powerful benefactors. Among these were the first earls of Pembroke, the FitzGilberts, medieval lords whose lives were spent in vigorous combat either in the service of the king or in pursuit of their own ambitions. They were never averse to waging war in the very real hope of gaining a kingdom for themselves. At the same time, they were mindful of their duties to the Church. It is with the FitzGilberts that we see the first signs of a pattern which recurs in successive Pembroke dynasties, a pattern which binds together in a continuous frieze the names of Pembroke, Tintern and the Templars.

The first earl, Gilbert FitzGilbert, flourished during the reign of King Stephen, a notoriously weak monarch. Already the owner of baronies in Normandy, when he inherited the title to Nether Gwent in Wales, with the castle of Chepstow, near Tintern, he returned to England. The men of Gwent were famous for the size and strength of their bows and this is probably why Gilbert became known as Gilbert Strongbow. In 1138 Stephen made him Earl of Pembroke and he fought for the king against the Welsh rebels. Like many feudal lords, Gilbert changed sides to suit himself, but acknowledged his loyalty to the king before dying. Tintern Abbey was founded during his lifetime for a strict branch of the Benedictine order, the Cistercians, and, when the original founder died, Gilbert became the abbey's patron. He left endowments to it on his death and was also a benefactor of the priory at Southwark and of the Templars. His son Richard FitzGilbert, the second earl increased these bequests. Richard campaigned so successfully in Ireland that his conquests aroused the jealousy of Henry II. He died in Dublin, where he was buried in 1176. Almost 400 years later, Sir Henry Sidney, then Lord Deputy of Ireland, restored a tomb with an effigy thought to be Richard FitzGilbert's. Sidney's daughter, Mary, married Henry Herbert, the second Earl of Pembroke of the Herbert line, in 1577. No doubt Sidney's gesture was in honour of that marriage, a compliment to the hereditary rank his fifteen-year-old daughter was about to receive.

William Marshall, the fourth earl of the FitzGilbert creation, served four kings: Henry II, Richard the Lion Heart, John and Henry III. William was elected regent for the first three years of Henry III's reign. In his youth he was regarded as a model of chivalry and in old age a figure of unswerving loyalty. He continued the tradition of his forebears in supporting the abbey at Tintern and the Templars. He was buried in the Temple church beside the late master of the Temple who had received him into the Order. His widow was buried in Tintern Abbey. He was succeeded in turn by each of his five sons, none of whom had any issue.

William, the fifth earl, died in 1231 after a life spent campaigning in Ireland, France and Wales. He, too, was a benefactor of Tintern and buried in the Temple

Church. His widow married Simon de Montfort, Earl of Leicester. The sixth earl died of wounds fighting in Ireland. The seventh, Gilbert, continued the family tradition of bequests to Tintern and was buried alongside his father and brother in the Temple. Two more brothers, Walter and Anselm, were both buried at Tintern Abbey. The earldom then reverted to the Crown in 1245, halfway through the long reign of Henry III.

Henry III is remembered as the greatest patron of medieval church building in England. It was he who reconstructed Westminster Abbey as we see it today. Originally, it had been built by Edward the Confessor in lieu of a vow he had made to visit the Holy Land; he was buried in front of the high altar. Many miracles were attributed to Edward and in due course he was canonised. Henry II built a shrine to which Edward's body was moved in 1163 on his feast day, 13 October. Over 100 years later Henry III pulled down that part of the church and built a magnificent new shrine covered in marble and mosaic, surrounded by eleven gold images of saints and kings and decorated with jewels, while the abbot employed craftsmen from Italy and imported porphyries for a new pavement. When all was finished, on 13 October 1269 the Confessor's body was carried in solemn procession to its new tomb by King Henry III, his brother and his two sons. The feast day remained one of great ceremony at the abbey until the Reformation, with annual processions from many of the religious foundations in London.

The 13 October was also the date, in 1307, when King Philip the Fair of France launched his attack on the Knights Templar. In one day Philip's officers swooped to arrest 15,000 knights the length and breadth of France. The Master of the Order, Jacques de Molay, was imprisoned and tortured; later, in 1314, he was roasted alive over a fire of charcoal. Edward II was reluctant to join in the suppression of the Templars but did so under pressure from the pope who ordered that the New Temple lands be given to the Knights Hospitaller of St John. Edward refused and gave 'the New Temple and all other tenements and rents late of the Temple in the city and suburb of London' to his cousin Aymer de Valence, Earl of Pembroke in the Valence line.

De Valence died suddenly on an ambassadorial mission to France and because of his kinship to the king (his father was half-brother to Henry III), he was buried in Westminster Abbey. Earlier de Valence had given up any claim to the new Temple at the insistence of another cousin of the king, the Earl of Lancaster. Lancaster had let part of the property to the legal profession, the doctors of common law, as a place where aspiring lawyers could study, and thus the two large refectories of the former Templars became the centres of the Benchers of the Middle and Inner Temple. Like the two universities of Oxford and Cambridge, the Inns of Court developed their own tradition of hosting masques and plays. Church festivals, such as Shrovetide and Christmas, were the occasions for the students' elaborate revels.

The Temple Benchers were finally given the ownership of their quarters by James I in 1608. In return they agreed to maintain the Temple Church and its services for ever. The Hospitallers of St John had gained possession of the rest of the New Temple property in 1340, but lost it all when they were suppressed with all the other monastic orders at the Dissolution.

Aymer de Valence had no heir, but his nephew Laurence, Lord Hastinges, was created Earl of Pembroke by Edward III on, of all days, the 13 October 1339. The king granted Hastinges the prerogatives and honour of an earl palatine in the lands he inherited from Aymer. There appears to have been something symbolic in this act, a determined assertion of continuity on the king's part since Hastinges was descended not directly from Aymer but from his eldest sister. The king could have given Hastinges other honours but he deliberately revived the Pembroke title and choosing to affirm a renewal of the Pembroke earldom on the feast day of the Confessor *and* the day when the Templars had been disbanded was a remarkable act. Part of the Templar beliefs centred round the cabalistic doctrine of reincarnation, the idea of the transmigration of a soul through a series of lives as a learning process. As we have seen, the early Pembrokes had been Templars in sympathy and deed. By renewing the earldom while the memory of the suppression of the Order was still fresh, Edward III may well have been expressing a hope for a return to Templar chivalry and ideals. Was this why the king also made Lord Hastinges one of his Knights of the Round Table? The new earl fought alongside Edward against France at the beginning of the Hundred Years' War. He died at Abergavenny not far from Chepstow, the first home of the Pembrokes in Wales, and was buried in the priory there in 1348.

The first Herbert creation of the Earls of Pembroke began in 1468 with William. Appropriately a man of Welsh extraction, he was an ardent supporter of the House of York in the Wars of the Roses. When Edward IV became king in 1461 he appointed Herbert Chief Justice and Chamberlain of South Wales. That same year Herbert captured Pembroke castle and the king rewarded him with the town and the stronghold. Later, after capturing Harlech, he was made Earl of Pembroke, but he was defeated by the Lancastrians in 1469, beheaded, and buried in Tintern Abbey. His son, William, resigned the earldom in 1479 because King Edward IV wished to create his son (the future Edward V) Earl of Pembroke. In exchange he made William Earl of Huntingdon. On his death in 1491 he, too, was buried at Tintern. Once more the Pembroke title had reverted to the Crown – it was one of the honours held by Edward V until he was murdered by his uncle (Richard III) in the Tower of London.

The second Herbert creation, the longest and the most distinguished, began in the reign of Henry VIII with another William. He was descended by an illegitimate line from the first Earl William and he became the brother-in-law of the king when Henry married Katherine Parr, his wife's sister. John Dee entered his service in February

1553. With this Herbert, the Pembrokes' Welsh connection began to reappear. His son and heir was Henry Herbert who, at the age of forty, took for his third wife Mary Sidney, the young daughter of Sir Henry Sidney and sister to Philip. (It was in honour of this marriage that Henry Sidney restored the Pembroke effigy in Dublin.)

Earl Henry maintained a company of actors and in 1592–3 they were apparently performing in the provinces because the plague kept them out of London. The troupe, formed from members of an amalgamation of Lord Strange's and the Lord Admiral's companies, met with such little success that its actors were forced to sell their playing costumes and three of their plays appeared in print, two of them, it is thought, had been worked on by Shakespeare.[10] The appearance of the Earl of Pembroke's name on the title page of *Titus Andronicus* has led scholars to surmise that the play came to Pembroke's company from Lord Strange's and then passed on to the Earl of Sussex's Men. With it may have come Shakespeare himself. Pembroke's Men disappeared for three of four years but by the end of 1597 there was another company under Herbert's protection which signed an agreement with Francis Langley to perform at the Swan for the twelve months leading up to 20 February 1598. The last we hear of it is a note in Henslowe's diary about two plays performed in October 1600 'my Lordes of Penbrockes men begane to playe at the Rosse'.[11] The company no doubt disbanded on Earl Henry's death. He was succeeded by his two sons the third and fourth earls, William and Philip. These were the 'most noble and incomparable paire of brethren' to whom the First Folio of Shakespeare's works was dedicated in 1623.

In 1603, London was in the grip of another epidemic of plague and the acting companies were forced to tour once again. James I took refuge at Wilton House in Somerset and Shakespeare's company was summoned by Mary, the widowed Countess of Pembroke, to perform during the king's stay between 24 October and 12 December. According to one tradition the play in question was *As You Like It*. Whether this is accurate or not, the visit is testified to by an entry in the Chamber Accounts for 2 December 1603: 'John Hemynges one of his majesty's players . . . for the paynes and expences of himself and the rest of the company in comming from Mortelake in the countie of Surrie unto the courte aforesaid (at Wilton) and there p'senting before his majesty one playe.'[12] One of the company of actors, Augustine Phillips, had bought a house at Mortlake near the river and the company appears to have gathered there to rehearse until the plague abated.

At the time of the summons to Wilton, William, the third earl, a young man of twenty-three, had just been made a Knight of the Garter by James I. He had evidently inherited something of his mother's and uncle's literary tastes, since he aspired to writing verse himself and was a generous patron to several writers, including the dramatists Philip Massinger and Ben Jonson. To Jonson he sent £20 every year to purchase books. Aubrey described him as 'the greatest Maecenas to learned men of any peer of his time or since'. But he did not begin to shine until James I ascended the throne. In fact three months after succeeding to the earldom in 1601 he was thrown into the Fleet prison for getting one of Queen Elizabeth's favourite maids of honour, Mary Fitton, pregnant. He admitted responsibility but refused to marry the girl. Although he was released after a month he was banished from Court and any hope of advancement under Elizabeth was effectively lost. According to one source, William became Grandmaster of the Freemasons in 1618, succeeding Inigo Jones of whom he had been a patron.[13]

Shakespeare's monument at Stratford says he died on 23 April 1616 and, according to the burial register, was buried two days later in Holy Trinity Church. The King's Men, the company with which he had for so long been associated, continued to perform his plays. In May 1619 they were summoned to be part of the festivities staged at Whitehall in honour of the French ambassador. The play chosen for the occasion on the 20th, was *Pericles, Prince of Tyre*. That same day William, third Earl of Pembroke, wrote to a friend in Germany that 'being tender-hearted' he could not endure watching the play 'so soon after the loss of my old friend Burbage'.[14] The creator of so many of Shakespeare's leading parts, Richard Burbage, had in fact died two months earlier in March. But the memory of his performances, the impact he had had on spectators, was still painfully vivid for Pembroke. After Burbage's death, only two of the original members of Shakespeare's acting company were left: John Heminges and Henry Condell. They now undertook the task of gathering together copies of every play Shakespeare had written. For its day it was a most unusual act of homage and not an easy one to fulfil. Shakespeare critics point to the precedence created by Ben Jonson himself who collected his plays, poems and masques together in a folio edition of 1,000 pages – an impressive volume, handsomely prefaced with an allegorical title page in 1616. Even so a collection of plays was still unusual: Heminges and Condell, have earned the gratitude of posterity, for they saved from possible loss eighteen of Shakespeare's plays which had not appeared in print earlier. Shakespeare's biographer, Park Honan, describes the undertaking as follows:

> The volume was costly to produce; and its syndicate of publishers . . . faced a loss. The work was not undertaken chiefly for profit. Nobody knows who proposed it. The typesetting of thirty-six plays, some from printed copy but others from scripts in varying hands and in varying degrees of legibility, for double columned folio pages, was a colossal task.[15]

Yet the task was done. It is true that in their dedicatory letter to the two Herberts – William, Earl of Pembroke and Philip, Earl of Montgomery – Heminges and Condell refer three times to the plays as 'trifles'. Plays, as such, had little literary status. Only the previous year, in 1622, Henry Peacham published in his *Complete Gentleman*, a guide to what every aspiring gentleman should know, a list of contemporary poets that did not include Shakespeare.[16] Critics have thought that Heminges and Condell dedicated the First Folio to the Herbert brothers in order to gain the prestige of their aristocratic support. Whatever the case, the 'incomparable paire' were evidently happy to accept the dedication. As the dedicatory letter says:

> But since your L.L. have beene pleas'd to think these trifles something, heeretofore; and have prosequuted both them and their Authour living with so much favour: we hope that (they out-living him, and he not having the fate, common with some, to be exequutor to his own writings) you will use the like indulgence towards them, you have done unto their parent.

In other words, although other men's plays might be regarded as 'trifles', both the noble brothers and Heminges and Condell are perfectly aware that Shakespeare's are more than that. In a second letter the editors urge 'the Great Variety of Readers' to 'reade him, therefore, and againe, and againe'.

The two Herbert earls had not just enjoyed the plays, they knew and admired their author. As we have seen, their family was part of a literary and philosophical tradition that made them fully conversant with the role of the theatre in royal statecraft. The dedication's description of the plays as 'trifles' in no way conflicts with this: deference was duly paid in this way, as custom demanded, to the rank of two nobles, one of whom was already the Lord Chamberlain. The other would hold that office later. Both men supported the king's players and undoubtedly wished the finest examples of the Elizabethan theatre to be preserved. Heminges and Condell were fully aware of the Herberts' regard for Shakespeare. This diminishes neither the loyalty they themselves felt for him nor the magnitude of their achievement. It does, however, help to explain how such an unusual and daunting task as the First Folio came to be undertaken.

GIORDANO BRUNO

To make clearer the place of the two Herbert brothers in the cultural tradition we are examining, we must turn aside for a moment to look at the visit to England of Giordano Bruno in 1583. Bruno (1548–1600) was an Italian monk and an exponent of Christian cabala – a form of belief combining elements of hermetic or 'Egyptian' ideas, the cabala and orthodox Catholicism. Bruno cherished the hope of creating an all-embracing spiritual movement that could heal the divisions of religion throughout Europe. He came to England to lecture on his beliefs and promote new philosophical and religious tolerance. Then he followed John Dee to Prague where

Dee, too, had been preaching a similar if not identical gospel. The Roman church was horrified at what it considered to be the heresy of Bruno's beliefs, which included his support for the Copernican view of the universe that the Earth and the other planets rotated around the sun. As a result Bruno was burned at the stake in Rome in 1600. With him died his hopes for Europe's spiritual reunion.

While he was in England, he stayed at the home of the French ambassador and during his visit he wrote a poetic dialogue, *The Ash Wednesday Supper*, which was published in London in 1584. It recounts his visit to the house of Fulke Greville, close friend of Sir Philip Sidney, where he explained the Copernican system to his host and fellow guests. In fact the dialogue is an account of a visit to Oxford where his views met with stiff opposition. The poem describes how two men, John Florio and Matthew Gwinne, call for Bruno at the French embassy and make their way by street and river to the house where the supper party was to take place. Florio was Italian tutor to the Earl of Southampton, and had been introduced into the Southampton household as a government spy by Lord Burghley. He may well have been employed in the same capacity on this occasion, but he was bilingual and his presence at the supper was no doubt of great practical help. Matthew Gwinne was a leading physician and became the first professor of physic at Gresham's College in 1597. (Gresham's was a forerunner of the Royal Society.) There is a print with his name handwritten on the back in Byrom's collection.

When the three men finally arrive at Fulke Greville's, they find an unnamed knight sitting at the head of the table. From what emerges during the supper all commentators assume that this anonymous figure is Philip Sidney. Also present were two learned doctors with whom Bruno debated the theory that the Sun is the centre of our universe. In the ensuing argument the two doctors reveal not only their ignorance but also their hostility to Bruno.

When Bruno eventually returned to Italy he was interrogated by the Inquisition. He claimed that the famous supper party had taken place at the French embassy. Whether or not this was so, we do know that during his visit to England he travelled to Oxford in June 1583, where he disputed publicly with Prince Albert Laski and members of the English nobility. On his way back from Oxford, Bruno stayed at Bisham, the Berkshire home of Lord and Lady Russell. Dee, of course, had been introduced to Laski by Leicester soon after he had arrived in London, and Laski had known of Dee's reputation even before that, while he was still in Poland. On 15 June 1583 Dee wrote in his diary:

Lord Albert Laski came to Mortlake to me. About 5 of the clock came the Polonian Prince Lord Albert Laski down from Bisham where he had lodged the night before, being returned from Oxford whither he had gone of purpose to see the universities

where he was very honourably used and entertained. He had in his company the
Lord Russell, Sir Philip Sidney and other gentlemen.[17]

This entry corrects the assertion by Frances Yates that Dee left for the continent just
before Bruno arrived in England in 1583.[18] But she is right in her assessment of the
missionary programmes of both these advocates of an hermetic cabalistic philosophy in
which, as far as this country was concerned, Queen Elizabeth was to play a central role.
On his arrival at Mortlake, Laski was able to give Dee a full report of the debate. Dee
left for Prague in September 1583. Prague was a city noted for its religious freedom –
Jews were allowed to study the cabala openly there. Emperor Rudolf appointed a
noted cabalist as one of his spiritual advisers and displayed a wise tolerance to the
reformed church of John Huss. It is not surprising, therefore, that Bruno also made his
way to Prague, for Rudolf's attitude exemplified the beliefs he espoused.

In the course of *The Ash Wednesday Supper* Bruno praises Sir Philip Sidney as a
famous and cultured knight 'well known to me, first by reputation when I was first
in Milan and France, and now since I have been in this country through having met
him in the flesh'.[19] Bruno dedicated to Sidney two works published in England in
1585. Sidney, together with Edward Dyer and Fulke Greville, had earlier chosen to
study philosophy under Dee, and Bruno speaks highly of him in the dedications of
both the works, writing of Sidney as someone sympathetic to his beliefs. After
Sidney's death, his sister Mary, Countess of Pembroke, dedicated her life to the
completion of the *Arcadia* and the pursuit of Sidney's literary creed. Bruno's influence
on Sidney's circle continued through Mary's education of her own sons William and
Philip. The two brothers were brought up at Wilton, breathing in the atmosphere of
Mary Pembroke's literary academy and chemical laboratory. They imbibed a strange
and heady mixture of traditional Templar thought, the cabalistic and hermetic legacy
of Bruno and Dee, and fresh ideas arising from Copernican astronomy, as well as the
new science of chemistry which was now beginning to emerge from alchemy.

EDWARD DYER

Linked closely with Sidney was the poet and diplomat, Edward Dyer. On him, too, Dee
had a profound influence and Dyer was happy to be godfather to Dee's first-born child,
Arthur. Dyer has his own place in the Elizabethan involvement with the hermetic
tradition. He was eleven years older than Sidney, but that did not prevent the two men
from becoming very close friends. Dyer had long had a high regard for Sidney's mother,
who was the sister of Robert Dudley, Earl of Leicester, and that regard was enough to
recommend him to Sidney initially. Dyer found they had many interests in common
arising from the shared experience of studying with John Dee. Dee's mystical

conception of music – that it puts man in tune with the structure of the universe expressed in his 'Mathematical Preface' – influenced Dyer's and Sidney's views on poetry. Dee stressed the mathematical origins of music – the harmonic intervals based on quantity and proportion. Sidney expressed a similar belief with regard to human speech, and hence poetry, where 'number, measure, order, proportion' are vital. Both Sidney and Dyer wrote verse, and Dyer was instrumental in encouraging Sidney's attempt to write poems in classical metres. Ultimately these experiments were abandoned, but they were an important stage in Sidney's development as a poet. We need to realise that behind them was the authority not only of acknowledged classical poets like Virgil, but also the cabalistic tradition expounded by Dee.

At twenty-six Dyer had been appointed Steward of Woodstock, one of the queen's favourite estates. However, after only twelve months he displeased Elizabeth sufficiently for her to remove him from office. Later he regained her favour and was rewarded with the licence to 'pardon and dispense with tanning of leather'. In making this appointment did the queen quietly amuse herself with an implicit pun on Dyer's surname? When Dee tried to help merchant adventurers to found a British empire, Dyer joined with Sidney and his mother in investing in Martin Frobisher's attempt to open up a north-west passage to the legendary wealth of Cathay. Later, when the whole Court, including the queen, had been duped into believing that an Italian goldsmith had managed to extract gold from a base mineral brought back by Frobisher, Sidney and Dyer doubled their investment in the next voyage. Moreover, in 1588 Dyer was sent by the queen to Dee in Bohemia to try to persuade Edward Kelly to return to England so that she could avail herself of his alleged alchemical skills. When we review Dyer's life and interests, we can see that he, too, belonged to the circle of well-established Englishmen who were influenced by and ready to promote, in differing ways, the teachings of John Dee, whether it be in exploration, writing poetry, alchemy or the design of the Elizabethan playhouse.

MICHAEL MAIER

When we look at the life of the Rosicrucian, Michael Maier, we can see Dee's influence continuing beyond his death. Maier was born in Rendsburg, a small town not far from Kiel in Germany, about 1568. He studied medicine at Rostock University, soon attracted the attention of Rudolf II and was appointed his personal physician. Rudolf also made him a count and his private secretary. After the death of the emperor, Maier came to England in 1612. By that time James I had been king for nine years, and Dee had been dead for four. However, Dee had met Maier in Frankfurt in 1589, and Maier was obviously well acquainted with Dee's work, especially the *Monas Hieroglyphica*.

In 1614 Maier published the treatise *Arcana arcanissima* (the most secret secrets), which he dedicated to Sir William Paddy, physician to James and, later, President of the College of Physicians. This treatise and Maier's other writings show clearly the mind of an alchemist working within the hermetic tradition, with a thorough knowledge of all ancient mythology including that of Egypt. Some of his ideas can be seen, therefore, to be close to Dee's. He does appear to have believed in the possibility of the transmutation of metals. In this he shows his inferiority as a philosopher to Dee, whose alchemical beliefs led him on further to seek a spiritual level of awareness.

Maier visited England on several occasions, meeting and discussing ideas with the physician Robert Fludd, as well as Sir William Paddy and Francis Anthony, a fellow alchemist and the discoverer of a quack medicine called 'aurum potabile'. Significantly, James I does not appear to have been one of Maier's patrons. This may well have been partly because in 1614 Isaac Casaubon, a distinguished philologist, published proof that the hermetic texts written by the legendary figure Hermes Trismegistus, which Dee and many Renaissance scholars had believed were older than Plato's works, were actually produced by various authors between AD 100 and 300. Despite this attack on the source of Dee's philosophy the beliefs he and other hermeticists expounded continued to exert influence for some time. It was the young Prince Henry and his sister Princess Elizabeth who endorsed Dee's teachings.

JAMES I

Within three months of his accession James I began to take control of the English acting companies. In May 1603 Shakespeare's troupe, formerly the Lord Chamberlain's, was absorbed into the royal household as the King's Men. Not long after, the Admiral's Company became Prince Henry's Men and the Earl of Worcester's Company was taken under the patronage of Queen Anne. Their patents specified the theatres at which they were to perform: the King's Men at the Globe, Prince Henry's Men at the Fortune and the Queen's Men at the Curtain. Later James licensed two more companies under the patronage of his second son, Charles (1608) and his daughter Elizabeth (1611).

Moreover, in July 1604, the Act against Vagabonds was revised yet again and the privilege granted to 'any Baron of the Realme, or any other honourable Personage of greater Degree' to license a company of players to travel under his protection was withdrawn. Increasingly, the Lord Chamberlain directed the activities of the Master of the Revels who, from 1606, was responsible for licensing plays for publication in addition to performance. In this way the king and his closest advisers exercised control not just over the companies but also over the plays they presented. Inevitably the companies and their writers sought to please the tastes of the royal patrons on whom their existence depended rather than the wider public of the Elizabethan playhouses. In the words of Glynne Wickham, the Jacobean and Caroline theatre 'had dwindled to satirizing the quirks of men and manners or to refreshing the spirits of a leisured few with song, dance and costly spectacle.'[20]

The offices of the Master of the Revels moved further west up the Thames in 1608 and were housed next door to the Whitefriars theatre. Edmund Tilney remained nominally Master until his death in 1610. However, his nephew, Sir George Buck, appears to have carried out most of the duties after the succession of James, who in 1603 had effectively appointed him acting Master. By 1612 the office had moved yet again, this time to 'St Peter's Hill'. That same year Buck described the work of the Master of the Revels in a treatise he had written: 'I might add herunto for a corollary of this discourse the Art of Revels which requireth knowledge in Grammar, Rhetoric, Logic, Philosophy, History, Music, Mathematics, and in other Arts, (and all more than I understand I confess) . . .'[21] Perhaps the duties were too much for him, for he went mad.[22] In March 1622 he was removed by the Lord Chamberlain, the Earl of Pembroke. His successor almost immediately sold his position to Sir Henry Herbert, a kinsman of Pembroke. Herbert remained Master until the closure of the theatres in 1642.

It was the King's Men who performed *The Tempest* in 1611 and 1612. It was one of the plays chosen for the festivities celebrating Princess Elizabeth's marriage to Frederick, the Elector Palatine of the Rhine. The other Shakespeare plays performed at the celebrations were *Much Ado about Nothing*, *Othello* and *Julius Caesar*. The same company also performed (apparently for the first time) Ben Jonson's comedy *The Alchemist* in 1610. Jonson's play is a harsh satire on the alchemist as a charlatan; Shakespeare portrays Prospero (considered by many to be based on John Dee) as a magician using his powers to subdue the savage and to reconcile opposing forces, the usurper and the usurped. Each play seems to be drawing on opposing opinions of Dee. Whereas Jonson seems to be exploiting the notoriety that surrounded Dee's last years, the positive portrait of Prospero emphasises Dee's search for the harmony and unity characteristic of the Christian cabalist. From this standpoint, *The Tempest* was an apt choice of play, adding a rich spiritual resonance to the wedding celebrations.

James I disliked Dee and all he represented; Prince Henry was more supportive of his ideas. The prince had a keen interest in mechanics and hydraulics which found expression in the re-creation of Renaissance gardens with speaking statues and musical fountains. These were created according to the same Vitruvian principles of proportion, number and harmony that Dee extolled in his 'Mathematical Preface'.

Henry and his sister Elizabeth had grown up seeing Shakespeare's plays acted at Court by Shakespeare's company. They also experienced the magical illusion of the masque at its best, presented through the creative genius of Inigo Jones. It is not surprising that they were both passionately devoted to the theatre, each supporting an acting company. In 1612, the Lady Elizabeth's Men performed before James at

Queen of Bohemia.

36. Elizabeth Stuart, Electress Palatine and Queen of Bohemia (1596–1662). She was daughter of James I and patron of 'The Lady Elizabeth's Men'; a company of English actors performed at her court at Heidelberg.

Court and, in honour of her future husband, Frederick, appeared at the Cockpit as part of her wedding celebrations. In 1614 the company produced Ben Jonson's *Bartholomew Fair* at the Hope. Troupes of British actors were invited to appear before her when she moved to Germany and in 1626, after the death of James I, yet another company of which she was patron, the King and Queen of Bohemia's Company, appeared at the Fortune.

Elizabeth's journey with her husband to Heidelberg in 1612 was conducted with great ceremony and splendour. When she entered Oppenheim she was greeted with intricately decorated triumphal arches which had been erected in her honour. An impressive volume describing her progress and containing elegant engravings by Johann Theodore de Bry was published at Oppenheim. De Bry had moved his engraving and publishing business from Frankfurt to Oppenheim and during the brief reign of Elizabeth and Frederick (1613–19) he produced a flood of volumes on hermetic topics, all richly engraved. The Protestant leaders of northern Europe expected great political advantages to flow from this marriage. Many artists, too, looked for encouragement and patronage from the young couple.

When she left England, Elizabeth took with her the hydraulics engineer Salomon de Caus, who had designed gardens for Prince Henry. He was given the task of modernising the ancient castle at Heidelberg and designing a new garden. The latter he filled with mechanical marvels. In this way, the practical application of number and geometry expounded by Dee in his 'Preface' was tested. The skills Dee had first displayed in the notorious production of *Pax* at Cambridge were developed by Inigo Jones in the masque and by de Caus in the wonders of Heidelberg. What had originally been looked on as 'magic' and illusory provided the stimulus for a technological revolution.

Both in England and abroad Princess Elizabeth was effectively the last of the royal patrons of the theatre who was also deeply interested in the hermetic cabalistic tradition. After the death of her father, James I, England entered the troubled reign of Charles I and, as his conflict with Parliament grew, so did the strength of the Puritan opposition. To the end, the King's Men dominated the stage. Civil War broke out in 1642, and all the playhouses were closed. The second Globe was demolished in 1644. Soldiers partially dismantled the second version of the Fortune in 1649 and in 1656 the Hope was also razed to the ground. With the arrival of the Commonwealth, the public playhouses disappeared from the London skyline. The philosophical tradition that had inspired their design found a new form of expression in the group of scientists, mathematicians and philosophers who came to be known as the Invisible College, and led to the formation of the Royal Society. When the theatre returned with Charles II it was no longer a popular art form but an aristocratic, indoor theatre, seeking to please the tastes of an over-sophisticated coterie.

CHAPTER 6

Contributing Factors

At the end of the previous chapter we came to a watershed in the history of the English theatre. We must pause briefly to consider the influences at work which led to the decline of the hermetic cabalistic teachings of Dee, Bruno and their disciples. These influences were many and varied. James became king in 1604 and his reign was marred by a number of dishonourable acts, among them the execution of Sir Walter Raleigh in 1618 on a charge thirteen years old, simply to please the Spanish. Raleigh's *History of the World* was read and admired by Prince Henry and his sister, Elizabeth of Bohemia – she took a copy with her when she left for Germany. His own collection of books included seminal cabalistic texts, but to the Jesuits Raleigh and his disciples represented 'a school of atheism'. Raleigh's execution, like the death of Bruno, was a result of the Counter-Reformation instituted by Rome.

As the son of Mary, Queen of Scots, James I had grown up in a Court rife with plots, intrigue and murder. This left him, in Macaulay's words, a 'nervous drivelling idiot'. That he was also witty and well read did little to redeem his character. In 1597 he wrote his famous treatise on witchcraft, *Demonology*, in which he advocated the death penalty for all witches. As a consequence, the first half of his reign was one of the most intense periods in English history for persecuting witches, only equalled by the excesses of the Long Parliament (1645–7).

Belief in witchcraft in this country, as in Europe generally, was as old as human society. Sir Keith Thomas defines a witch as:

a person of either sex (but more often female) who could mysteriously injure other people. The damage she might do – maleficium as it was technically called – could take various forms. Usually she was suspected of causing physical injury to other persons, or of bringing about their death. She might also kill or injure farm animals or interfere with nature by preventing cows from giving milk or by frustrating such domestic operations as making butter, cheese or beer.[1]

In the late Middle Ages the Church introduced a more sinister charge against witchcraft: the idea that the witch was in league with the Devil. Henceforth witches on the continent were prosecuted as Devil worshippers rather than for the harm they were said to do people. This idea did not take hold in England at first, but it was certainly prevalent by the end of Elizabeth's reign. James I's treatise expressed the same belief that witchcraft implied a contract with the Devil. Three acts of parliament were passed against witchcraft in an attempt to destroy this imaginary evil – in 1542 (repealed in 1547), in 1563 (repealed in 1604) and finally in 1604 (repealed in 1736).

It is not surprising that the beliefs of the hermetic–cabalistic schools of thought, claiming authority from ancient, pre-Christian civilisations, helped to encourage a belief in demonology among intelligent people who should have known better. It was the corollary of the beneficient powers, the 'white magic' which Dee and Bruno believed in. It was a darker power or 'black magic' – the power exercised by Faustus as opposed to that of Prospero. In 1604, the year the final act against witchcraft was passed, Dee petitioned the king in an attempt to clear his name of being a sorcerer. So sure was he of his innocence that he asked to be put on trial and to be executed if found guilty. James, however, dismissed the petition, turning his back on Dee and all he stood for. Thereafter Dee, a man of undoubted vision and proven ability, was left to die in poverty. With the benefit of hindsight, we can see that his 'white magic' was essentially a bridge leading from religion to science.

Rudolf II, the liberal Holy Roman Emperor sympathetic to the ideas of Christian cabala, died in 1612. This led to the persecution of the Protestants in Bohemia. They rebelled, offering the throne to James I's Protestant son-in-law, Frederick of the Palatinate. Abandoned by James, Frederick was defeated by the Catholics at the Battle of the White Mountain outside Prague in 1620. This was a major disaster. The persecutions in Prague destroyed freedom of expression for the cabalists. The Palatinate was occupied, and the wonders of Heidelberg castle devastated. For a brief while Heidelberg had flourished as another centre of cabalist thought. Now, irreplaceable books and manuscripts in the city's libraries were destroyed. The elector's own library was taken to Rome. The technological inventions of Salomon de Caus in the castle and its gardens disappeared without trace.

After the divisions of the Civil War in England came the Commonwealth, and the English nobility were eclipsed until the Restoration in 1660. Lathom House, the home of the earls of Derby in the North-West, had been destroyed and with it the astrological screen. Bacon's house at Gorhambury, once a monument to the new learning, was the subject of a convoluted inheritance squabble for years after his death. Eventually the old Tudor house fell into decay and the owner, Viscount Grimston, built a new house in the 1780s. Long before then, however, John Aubrey visited the estate in 1656 only to see the parkland Bacon had considered a paradise reduced to 'a large ploughed field', the summerhouse defaced and the garden overgrown.[2]

Finally, the prevailing cast of thought during the Commonwealth was very different from that in the palaces of Elizabeth and the great houses of her nobles. All these factors caused much of the learning connected with the origins of the Elizabethan playhouses to disappear underground. What managed to survive openly did so in the new experimental sciences.

PHILOSOPHICAL ALCHEMY

Dee's ultimate ambition in the pursuit of knowledge was the attainment of a higher level of consciousness. One of the ways he sought this was through alchemy, not simply alchemy as the means of changing base metal into gold, but philosophical alchemy where the alchemist seeks a transmutation of spirit. The first Arabic treatise on alchemy to be translated into Latin for use in the West states:

> The foundation of this art is that whoever wishes to pass it on must himself have received the teaching from a master . . . It is also necessary that the master should have practised it in front of his pupil . . . For whoever knows well the order of this work and has experienced it himself cannot be compared with one who has only sought it in books . . .[3]

The personal oral tradition is strong in alchemy. A sixteenth-century French practitioner, Denis Zachaire, wrote:

> Above all I should like it to be understood in case one has not yet learned it that this divine philosophy far exceeds purely human power; still less can we acquire it from books, unless God has introduced it into our hearts by the power of his Holy Spirit, or has taught us through the mouth of a living man . . .[4]

The novice–master relationship occurs in the study of many mysteries. Often, however, the master lays stress on the importance of experience over study. The alchemist, like the cabalist, believes that the study of books in itself does not bring enlightenment. Indeed cabalists maintain that it is useless even to start studying the cabala until the student has lived for forty years. Similarly Zachaire reminds us here that there are limitations to learning from books. He is making the age-old distinction between knowing and understanding, an important distinction when we are dealing not simply with facts but beliefs; the acquisition of facts about a particular faith does not in itself convey the sense of fulfilment the practice of that faith may bring. Such an attitude, however, can invite scepticism in orthodox academic circles. Students today know full well that, even in theology, they are unlikely to obtain their degrees simply by the power of the Holy Spirit. Nevertheless, the corollary is still true – a degree in theology does not guarantee faith.

THEODORE DE BRY

Theodore de Bry was a Huguenot, in other words a heretic in the eyes of Rome, who had been forced to flee religious persecution in his native city of Liège. He settled in Frankfurt where he pursued the family calling of an engraver and goldsmith. His reputation was sufficient for him to gain two important commissions in London at the time of the building of the Theatre. That same year, 1576, he was employed in making a detailed engraving of the installation of the Knights of the Garter at Windsor. This ceremony was central to the chivalric propaganda deliberately created around the Virgin Queen by poets and courtiers. De Bry could only have been entrusted with such an undertaking on the basis of merit and repute.

In 1587 he was in England again to engrave thirty-four plates of Sir Philip Sidney's funeral procession. (In itself almost a state occasion.) Back in Frankfurt, he produced an illustrated edition of Thomas Hariot's account of his experiences in Virginia with engravings based on John White's watercolours. In fact his visit to England coincided with a decision to concentrate on engraving and publishing. The quality of his work survives for all to see in the volumes he produced. It was his son, Johann Theodore, who engraved the illustration of the ceremonial arch at Oppenheim built to welcome Princess Elizabeth to her new home. It is quite clear that the de Bry family publishing business became a focus and conduit for much of the hermetic writing of the age. Just as the famous Venetian printer, Aldus Manutius, gathered around him an academy of Renaissance humanists, so, too, the de Brys drew to them like-minded scholars and others sympathetic to the hermetic tradition, such as the aristocratic patrons of the theatre companies.

Moreover, as a trained goldsmith from a family of goldsmiths, Theodore de Bry was fully accustomed, through his own guild, to the idea of secret practices imparted only to the fully trained initiate. Earlier German goldsmiths had written on the design techniques of masons and the importance of geometry in their work. De Bry lived for several years in Strasbourg, the city where the first lodge of German masons was founded. In other words, he had worked with people to whom the ideas of Vitruvius would be part of the orthodoxy of the new learning, and was in a position to acquire the practical and technical knowledge required to set out the pattern and designs of the theatre. At the same time, as a victim of the charge of heresy in his youth, he would see the need to hide the knowledge from reactionary thinkers by using methods employed by guilds to protect their skills. One of these was the use of a code that could both conceal and convey information. Evidence from the

Compagnonnage guild of carpenters shows that a system of dots was an accepted code in this context. Such a system is employed in the Byrom theatre drawings.

WALSINGHAM AND CIPHERS

We noted earlier John Dee's close links with Sir Frances Walsingham, his neighbour at Barn Elms. Walsingham was one of the most powerful men in the kingdom. In the early 1570s he had served as ambassador to France and had been in Paris at the time of the massacre of the French Protestants on the eve of St Bartholomew's Day, 1572. The next year he was recalled and made Principal Secretary. Elizabeth was said to govern with the aid of seventeen councillors, but according to the Spanish ambassador in reality it was only three: Leicester, Walsingham and Burghley.[5] Walsingham had already gained the support of Burghley by providing him with information on foreign affairs. As Principal Secretary ('Mr Secretary', Dee calls him in his diary), he was at the centre of Elizabeth's foreign-policy making for sixteen years until he died in 1590. During this time he built up a network of agents. In the beginning he paid them out of his own pocket, but the network grew. It demonstrated its worth to the state and in 1582 public money was made available to meet Walsingham's expenses. In the eyes of some historians this marks the beginning of an official secret service. Its initial purpose was to gather information about the activities of Catholics both at home and abroad, who at that time were regarded as the main enemies of England's Protestant settlement, plotting against the life of the queen herself. Sir Francis had a large house in Seething Lane close to the Tower of London which seems to have been the London office of his spy network.[6]

In the early days of gathering and transmitting information everything depended on the agent carrying the intelligence on his person or in his belongings. Many of the subterfuges, such as secret compartments behind mirrors, in buttons or rings, were discovered. Hence it became very important to send messages in code. Treatises on ciphers such as Giovanni Battista della Porta's *De Furtivis Literarum Notis* were an invaluable aid in designing a cipher.[7] One of Walsingham's chief agents was Thomas Phelippes who specialised in devising codes. These could be based on numbers, symbols, or the use of jargon from normal business activities in which an apparently routine trade account was in reality a description of the size and whereabouts of enemy forces.[8]

In addition to Phelippes, Walsingham employed Dee to create a series of codes. Years earlier (1562) Dee had discovered *Steganographia*, a manual on ciphers by Abbot Trithemius of Sponheim, for which 'a thousand crowns have been offered, and yet could not be obtained'.[9] Significantly, he informed Burghley of his find. The book was not published until 1606, so Dee must have seen it in manuscript form. This was the work that helped him in the writing of the *Monas Hieroglyphica*. Another of the Abbot's works *Polygraphia*, published in 1518, contained hundreds of alphabets into which words or phrases could be substituted for individual letters. Moreover, in 1552, Girolamo Cardano, an Italian doctor and mathematician, visited London and stayed with Sir John Cheke, tutor to Edward VI and England's foremost Greek scholar. Dee visited him at Cheke's home. This is not surprising for, like Dee, the Italian was interested not only in mathematics but ciphers as well. He invented a device known as the cardano grille. Alan Haynes describes it as follows:

> This was a piece of sturdy material pierced with rectangular holes at irregular intervals. The same height as the script, they varied in width allowing access to whole words, syllables or letters. Each was randomly numbered and by placing the grille on a piece of paper the message was spelled out in the number order – at this point still a clutch of letters. These were further disguised by incorporation in an apparently innocuous message. A decoder with an identical grille placed it on top of this text to read the message in the correct order.[10]

Substitution was a favourite form of cipher in which the names of key personalities could be replaced by names from a totally different subject area. For example, days of the week could be used for people. Burghley was fond of using the signs of the zodiac. In one of his codes the queen was Aries, and Philip II, Scorpio.[11] Simpler and even more common was the use of numbers for personalities. Codes and ciphers, then, were far from unusual in the Elizabethan age. Indeed, in the transmission and preservation of certain forms of information they could be deemed essential.

THE THEATRE DRAWINGS DECODED

The evidence of the geometry in the theatre drawings from the Byrom Collection shows that there is a system of coding in which information concerning measurements and dimensions lies hidden both for secrecy and convenience. The design of the Elizabethan playhouse belongs to a tradition of architecture that carries in its measurements an expression of cosmic and microcosmic proportions. Christopher Butler in his book *Number Symbolism* draws attention to the design of the Church of San Francesco della Vigna in Venice. The Christian cabalist Francesco Giorgio, who commissioned the church, required the architect to produce a design which would use numbers to produce simple musical harmonies:

> Thus he asks for the width of the nave to be nine paces, 'which is the square of three, the first and divine number'. The length of the nave will be 27 paces, and

'will have a triple proportion which makes a diapason and a diapente' (that is an octave and a fifth). He means that 27 includes the proportions 9: 18: 27, which could presumably be marked by architectural features within the church, 9: 18 being the diapason (1: 2), and 18: 27 being the diapente (2: 3).[12]

Butler explains that Giorgio, basing his argument on Plato's dialogue *The Timaeus*, chose these proportions explicitly as being microcosmic. Giorgio links the thinking of Plato with ideas of Vitruvius and a belief in the divine precedent of the Temple of Solomon to show how, in architecture, 'human creation may correspond to the Universe as a whole in its proportions'. The natural beauty in God's universe is to be reflected in the man-made building: 'We being desirous of building the church, have thought it necessary, and most appropriate to follow that order of which God, the greatest architect, is master and author.'[13]

Similar thinking is behind the concept of the playhouse. Indeed one of the Globe drawings has written on it the proportions 3: 6: 9:, an echo of Georgio's 9: 18: 27. Dee, himself a Christian cabalist, possessed a copy of Giorgio's seminal text *De Harmonia Mundi*. The employment of these proportions would produce in Dee's eyes and ears the best visual and acoustic properties for the theatre. However, since the basic concept derives from the cabalistic–hermetic tradition which most ecclesiastical authorities, Catholic and Protestant alike, considered heretical, the measurements were concealed. De Bry had suffered persecution at first hand and had been forced to flee Liège. Dee was aware of how unorthodox some of his religious views were and the suspicion with which he was viewed. We should not forget that his first foray into the theatre with the design of a flying machine for his production of *Pax* at Trinity had led to 'vaine reports' being spread abroad 'of the meanes how that was effected'. Working together on a practical manifestation of some of their shared beliefs, both Dee and de Bry would be anxious to avoid incurring opposition from reactionary forces.

The original Globe was built in the spring of 1599. Today, at the distance of over 400 years, it should be possible to address the hermetic and cabalistic origins of the Elizabethan playhouse without provoking outcries of heretic or even crank. What we are going to do is to examine the way in which information about this unorthodox concept was encoded in the theatre drawings that came to be part of John Byrom's Collection.

The first drawing we should look at is Figure 37. The colour is in two tones: yellow being dominant against a more neutral background. This is relevant since many of the drawings containing information about the Globe are colour-coded to these two shades. At first glance it is easy to see that the drawing shows an eight-sided figure which contains within it a large square which touches four points of the octagon. The sides of this square are equally divided by what look like dots in the illustration but are in fact minute pin-pricks that pierce the card. On close examination, it is evident that the pin-pricks were used to mark out minute but regular intervals or units. Each unit is therefore a measure of distance. Each side of the large 'dotted' square contains exactly seventy-two units. Within the large square is another square, each side of which is made up of fifty-two units. Then, inside that smaller square is a circle whose diameter is equal to fifty-one of the same units.

Circumscribing the entire figure is a much larger circle. Its diameter is 102 units – double the diameter of the inner circle. This represents the external boundary from which the eight sides of the first Globe were produced. Other drawings in the collection prescribe this measurement, too. By this reckoning the smaller, inner circle with a diameter of fifty-one represents that part of the playhouse open to the stars. We can conclude, therefore, that the Globe playhouse required an external diameter of 102 units (in this case feet), although the main theatre structure was based on a frame of seventy-two units (feet).

On the reverse side of the card is a pattern based on the same geometry with additional features (Figure 38). The first we should note is a circle based on the square frame of seventy-two units (feet) and whose diameter is, therefore, seventy-two units (feet). The line of this circle indicates the position of the back wall of the auditorium. The second feature to note is the square within the smaller circle. The sides of the square are divided by the same units into thirty-six and the diameter of the smaller circle is fifty-one units. This square is connected with the dimensions of the stage. If we pause for a moment to consider the numbers thrown up by the geometry, we see an interesting fact emerge: thirty-six units are half of seventy-two and fifty-one units are half of 102. Significant measurements are in proportion with one another. This became even more apparent as other drawings concerned with the first Globe playhouse were examined. Although the drawings were not conventional architectural plans, close study led me to suspect that they were patterns of a building concept in which a hidden system of measurement followed laws of proportion with rigorous consistency, both in the vertical and horizontal planes. This consistency enables us to make further calculations about the area of the stage. Adherence to the same law of proportion dictates a stage depth of eighteen units. Thus we have a stage area of eighteen by thirty-six within a theatre whose auditorium has a diameter of seventy-two.

These two drawings are, of course, solely concerned with the horizontal plane. Others, like the parametric drawings included, are concerned with both planes. Once the eye has registered the element of proportion in the concept, the measurements fall into two broad categories: those that are proportionate and those that are not. It is the proportionate measurements that are dominant. We are dealing with information conveyed in diagrammatic form – in straight lines, curves and dots rather than words.

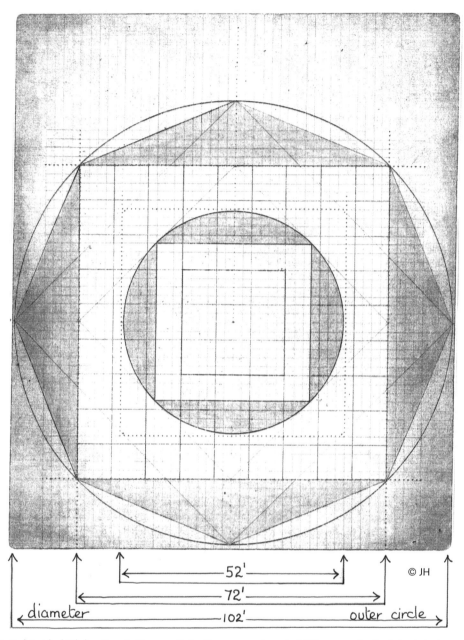

52'
72'
diameter   102'   outer circle

© JH

37. Eight-sided Globe, Front. (Byrom Collection, reproduced at 75 per cent of original size)

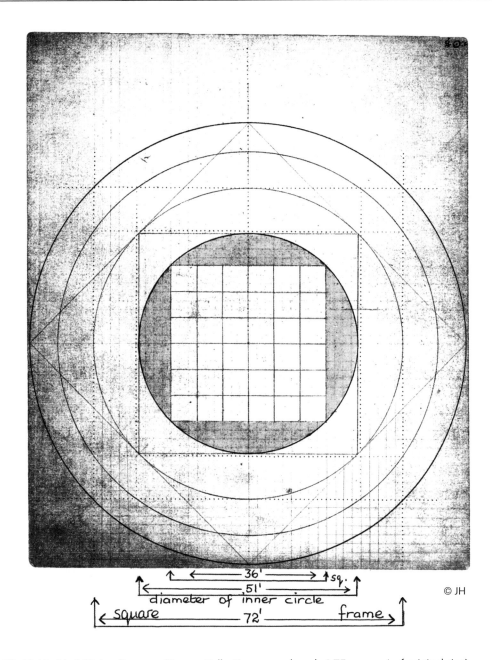

© JH

38. Eight-sided Globe, Reverse. (Byrom Collection, reproduced at 75 per cent of original size)

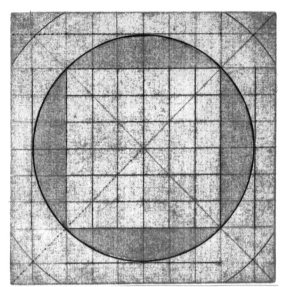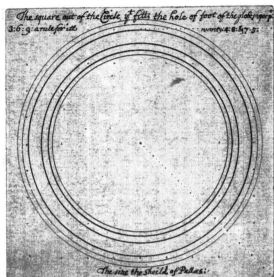

39. Part of the Globe sequence, '3: 6: 9: a rule for itt'. *Left:* Drawing A, Front; *right:* Drawing B, Back (Byrom Collection, both reproduced at 75 per cent of original size)

The artist responsible is addressing those who, like him, have pronounced visual perception and his method is not only economical and convenient but also secret.

We must now turn our attention to Figure 39. The reader will easily recognise its connection with two preceding drawings. Drawing A is in fact a close up of a view of the central portion of Figure 38. The four arcs in the corner, if completed, make up the circle with a diameter of seventy-two units. Within that we can see the complete circle with the diameter of fifty-one units, and inside that smaller circle the square with sides of thirty-six units, from which we were able to deduce the dimensions of the stage. The presence of dots in this drawing and in the one on the reverse is part of the code telling us how to proceed. Drawing B on the reverse contains further information about Figure 37, some of it written out this time. The lines of the concentric circles on the drawing differ in thickness. The third circle from the outside is much heavier, and delineates a circumference with a diameter of fifty-one. The writing at the top of the card speaks of 'The square out of the circle'. By this is meant the faint but straight rows of dots at regular intervals outside the third circle which, when joined together, form a square. The line of this circle, as mentioned earlier, is the circumference of the area open to the skies. At the same time it marks the beginning of the closed area, the seating of the auditorium, and as such marks the base or 'foot' of the Globe's galleries or 'uper part'. These words have been added to de Bry's original drawing, probably by John Dee himself, to ensure that the geometry of the concept would contain the number symbolism he wished to build into the playhouse. In this he would be following the practice of his cabalist predecessor, Giorgio, when he laid down the ratio 9: 18: 27 for the church of San Francisco in Venice. Moreover, if we look at the ratio stipulated by Dee for the Globe, 3: 6: 9:, we will recognise the mathematical relationship between the two.

The treatise *De Harmonia Mundi* helps us to appreciate the relevance of Dee's ratios to the concentric circles and dots of the theatre pattern. Giorgio explains the importance of his numbers in a memorandum which he wrote about the design of the church of San Francisco. For example, '9 was the square of 3, the first and divine number'. Moreover, his figures can be tested in the physical fabric of the church. Nothing of the original Globe remains above ground to help us, however. Dee was familiar with Giorgio's principles from his own copy of *De Harmonia* and certainly held similar beliefs. Accordingly, he simply chose the formula 3: 6: 9:, but took sufficient trouble to state this was a basic principle – 'a rule for itt'.

Giorgio was an Italian aristocrat and a Franciscan monk, not a reclusive scholar, remote from the world. He was entrusted with important diplomatic missions by the Venetian state. He did, however, believe fervently in the inter-related nature of the entire universe. As Frances Yates

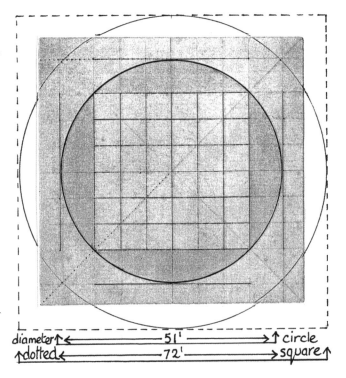

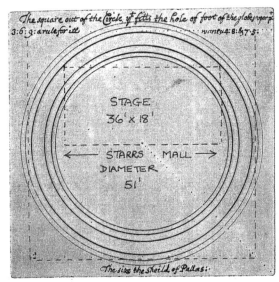

40. '3: 6: 9:' with playhouse dimensions highlighted. (Byrom Collection, reproduced at 75 per cent of original size, © JH)

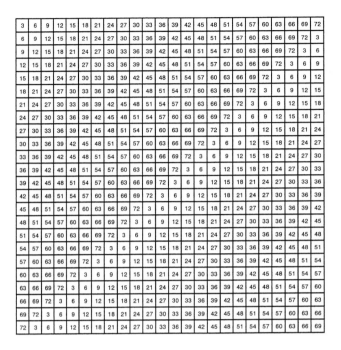

3	6	9	12	15	18	21	24	27	30	33	36	39	42	45	48	51	54	57	60	63	66	69	72
6	9	12	15	18	21	24	27	30	33	36	39	42	45	48	51	54	57	60	63	66	69	72	3
9	12	15	18	21	24	27	30	33	36	39	42	45	48	51	54	57	60	63	66	69	72	3	6
12	15	18	21	24	27	30	33	36	39	42	45	48	51	54	57	60	63	66	69	72	3	6	9
15	18	21	24	27	30	33	36	39	42	45	48	51	54	57	60	63	66	69	72	3	6	9	12
18	21	24	27	30	33	36	39	42	45	48	51	54	57	60	63	66	69	72	3	6	9	12	15
21	24	27	30	33	36	39	42	45	48	51	54	57	60	63	66	69	72	3	6	9	12	15	18
24	27	30	33	36	39	42	45	48	51	54	57	60	63	66	69	72	3	6	9	12	15	18	21
27	30	33	36	39	42	45	48	51	54	57	60	63	66	69	72	3	6	9	12	15	18	21	24
30	33	36	39	42	45	48	51	54	57	60	63	66	69	72	3	6	9	12	15	18	21	24	27
33	36	39	42	45	48	51	54	57	60	63	66	69	72	3	6	9	12	15	18	21	24	27	30
36	39	42	45	48	51	54	57	60	63	66	69	72	3	6	9	12	15	18	21	24	27	30	33
39	42	45	48	51	54	57	60	63	66	69	72	3	6	9	12	15	18	21	24	27	30	33	36
42	45	48	51	54	57	60	63	66	69	72	3	6	9	12	15	18	21	24	27	30	33	36	39
45	48	51	54	57	60	63	66	69	72	3	6	9	12	15	18	21	24	27	30	33	36	39	42
48	51	54	57	60	63	66	69	72	3	6	9	12	15	18	21	24	27	30	33	36	39	42	45
51	54	57	60	63	66	69	72	3	6	9	12	15	18	21	24	27	30	33	36	39	42	45	48
54	57	60	63	66	69	72	3	6	9	12	15	18	21	24	27	30	33	36	39	42	45	48	51
57	60	63	66	69	72	3	6	9	12	15	18	21	24	27	30	33	36	39	42	45	48	51	54
60	63	66	69	72	3	6	9	12	15	18	21	24	27	30	33	36	39	42	45	48	51	54	57
63	66	69	72	3	6	9	12	15	18	21	24	27	30	33	36	39	42	45	48	51	54	57	60
66	69	72	3	6	9	12	15	18	21	24	27	30	33	36	39	42	45	48	51	54	57	60	63
69	72	3	6	9	12	15	18	21	24	27	30	33	36	39	42	45	48	51	54	57	60	63	66
72	3	6	9	12	15	18	21	24	27	30	33	36	39	42	45	48	51	54	57	60	63	66	69

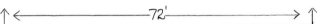

72'

41. Symmetry demonstrated by the Globe ratios 3: 6: 9:. Working diagonally across the square from left to right, the numbers are identical. Going in the opposite direction the numbers increase regularly by 6. Such patterning would have appeared magical when number was rediscovered during the Renaissance. (© JH)

explains: 'The secret of Giorgio's universe was number, for it was built, so he believed, by its Architect as a perfectly proportioned Temple, in accordance with unalterable laws of cosmic geometry.'[14] This may seem fanciful and eccentric to our modern scientifically attuned ears, but before we turn away smiling indulgently, we should, perhaps, note that in October 1999, Sir Martin Rees, the Astronomer Royal, published a book in which he explains how the universe depends on the precise accuracy of six highly complex mathematical calculations going back to the very instant of creation. Here is an extract from an explanatory article he wrote for the *Daily Telegraph*:

> The third number, referred to as script 'E', has a value of 0.007, and it defines how strongly atomic nuclei bind together, and how all the atoms on Earth were made. Its value controls the Sun's power, and how stars transmute hydrogen into all other atoms of the periodic table. If this number were 0.006 or 0.008 we would not exist.

Number, it seems, remains the key to the secret of the universe.

Dee, like Giorgio, was hoping to achieve a man-made harmony in the Globe which reflected the harmony of creation. The reader must accept that we are now moving from tangible, physical facts to intangible properties affecting both eye and ear,

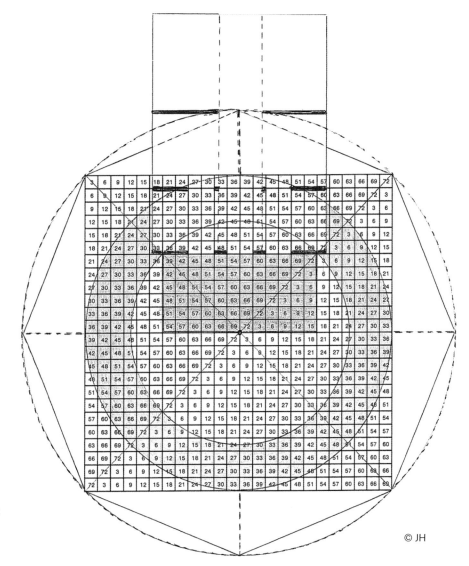

42. The magic square based on a frame of 72. '3: 6: 9: a rule for itt'. Superimposed on this is the ground plan of the Globe. The underlining at A shows the three entrances on to the stage.

© JH

produced by specific number combinations. If a difference of 0.001 dictates the Sun's beneficial power, perhaps it is not too difficult to accept that the number patterns which follow had a validity for the design of the original Globe.

In what follows I claim no special credit for myself. One day, while studying Figure 39B, I decided to construct my own version of a 'magic square' based on the digits 3: 6: 9 in ascending order to the number seventy-two. Figure 41 shows the result of that exercise. The numerical patterns that emerged were, in the true sense of the word, extraordinary. Working from the bottom of the square across from left to right, all numbers in the diagonal squares were the same as the numbers in the bottom row.

Working in the opposite direction from right to left, the numerical value of the diagonal squares decreased regularly by six. The symmetry was intriguing.

The next stage was to place the dimensions of the ground plan of the Globe on top of this pattern. The results seemed to confirm my deductions in a totally unexpected way. For instance, when we look at Figure 42 we can see immediately that the focal point of the whole stage and hence the theatre, namely the centre of stage front, falls towards the number seventy-two. We are pointed in this direction for that most important element in the Elizabethan play, the soliloquy, the moment of solitary communing between actor and audience. This position on the stage is the optimum spot for the spectator who is watching and listening. It is also the place at which an actor can achieve maximum dramatic effect. Similarly, the reader should look at the three openings at the back of the stage into the tiring house. In 1570, Andrea Palladio published designs for a Roman theatre produced in accordance with the instructions laid down by the Roman writer Vitruvius in volume five of his treatise *De Architectura*. In doing so, Palladio demonstrated how the geometry of Roman theatres (themselves derived from the theatres of ancient Greece) demanded that the position of the stage openings should be set for maximum visual effect. The eye should be able to take in the full impact of an entrance or exit. At the Globe, according to the Byrom drawings, each of these openings was generous – fully 6 feet wide. To conclude, the overall symmetry in the number square represents the attempt in the design to achieve a coherent acoustic and visual harmony.

HARMONY IN DESIGN

It is necessary here to define what we mean by harmony in this context. The theatre as envisaged by Dee and de Bry was viewed as a whole. Their concept was holistic in that the significance of the individual parts could only be grasped in terms of what they contributed to the whole edifice. The Globe was not built just to accommodate more people in order to take more money at the 'box-office'. Equally, its size was dictated neither by the sight-lines alone nor by its acoustical demands. All three of these very desirable properties were held in a tension mathematically calculated in keeping with the overriding purpose of the place. The playhouse was envisaged as a crucible in which a nation's spiritual and national identity could be refined. The Globe arena originated in the open-air Greek theatres. We should remember that in the city state of classical Athens attendance at the theatre was a religious duty for every citizen. English drama also had religious roots in the telling of the Passion story at Mass. By the time Elizabeth had ascended the throne the theatre was perceived as an aid to ensure her sovereignty. Hence the cluster of noble families determined to protect the theatre players, with the queen, against political and religious opponents in the City.

Dee was fully cognisant of this attitude to the theatre and saw the importance of creating an ambience akin to that of a temple in which the spirits of the spectators could be raised by both laughter and tears to a higher awareness. Accordingly, his choice of dimensions had both a spiritual and a practical basis. The harmony of the visual and acoustic properties was essential to achieve his purpose. For Dee harmony was an absolute. Because it was rooted in excellence, the theatre would ensure excellence. Plays can be performed in a Greek amphitheatre in any language under the Sun and that language will be heard. The same applies to musical languages as widely different as those of Europe, Japan or Bali. The playhouse was attuned to perfection, for that is what Dee sought to provide. Unfortunately acoustics has been a much neglected science. The lack of a decent concert hall in London since the loss of the old Queen's Hall is regarded by some as little short of a scandal. But it is an artistic scandal and we have learned to live with those. When the Globe was reconstructed on Bankside, acoustic experts were not considered a priority. This in itself negates the worthy attempt being made at authenticity, for example in the design of costumes. In the same way a blazing Sun dazzling one's eyes can defeat any attempt at visual spectacle. It is a help to be offered a sun-hat by the ticket office, but this is an admission that the orientation of the playhouse is debatable. If the stage were positioned in the diametrically opposite direction, the Sun would illuminate the acting area, providing natural lighting to enhance the costumes, properties and features of the actors. At present, the audience has to look behind the sun's rays to where the texture of materials is deadened and energy drained from the actors' faces. In this situation both the audience and the actors have to work a little harder. The same would apply on a cloudy day.

It may well be that most visitors will be carried away by the novelty of the 'experience', convinced that the reconstructed playhouse is a success. However, I left with an uncomfortable feeling of having witnessed a venture whose impressive combination of talents had been frustrated from achieving their goal. I speak here not just of the actors but the builders, designers, directors, musicians, artists and craftsmen. They may not be aware that there is something 'not quite right', or, if they are, they may not realise that the cause for their dissatisfaction is absolutely basic, inherent in the building itself. Admittedly we are here talking partly of intangible properties – the vibrations or resonances set up by the spaces created in a building. We recognise their presence, as for example Frances Yates did when she walked into the arena of St George's and felt its magic, just as many of us do walking into a great cathedral or mosque. We are not always aware of their absence. However, there are occasions when we do feel the opposite – a sensation of discomfort, revulsion or unease. Poets such as Keats, with their finely attuned antennae, sense and can evoke such places, where

> The sedge has wither'd from the lake,
> And no birds sing . . .[15]

Such irrational responses can be traced back to the ancient Roman belief in the genius loci, the guardian spirit of the place. But even today, we readily accept that a particular place can have its own special atmosphere. Sometimes this is due entirely to natural surroundings, but in buildings it is created by the design and orientation.

THE BEAR GARDEN

In this connection there are drawings in the Byrom Collection concerned with the Elizabethan arenas but imbued with a totally different spirit from the rest of the theatre illustrations. That spirit emanated from a pattern which I recognised and which I was reluctant for some time to address. The unease I felt in analysing them was understandable when I realised that they were directly concerned with the Bear Garden.

The Bear Garden, as its name implies, was used as a venue for animal baiting in a variety of forms, and its function introduces us directly to one of the least attractive aspects of Elizabethan life. No reasons can be put forward to justify it either as a spectacle or a sport: it was cruel, bloody and degrading. The fact that it was watched by kings and their ambassadors does nothing to lessen modern revulsion. But we judge from hindsight. The spectacle of Henslowe and Alleyn suing for the Mastership of the Game merely confirms that few, if any, ever paused to question the rightness of such a 'sport'. There were public executions of the most hideous kind, and life was cheap. It is asking too much to expect the attitude of the average Elizabethan towards animals to be any better than his attitude towards his fellow-men.

In the last act of *Hamlet*, when the Prince reminds Horatio 'There is a special providence in the fall of a sparrow', Shakespeare is not advocating a change in attitude towards animals, he is drawing on Christ's words in St Matthew for specific dramatic effect: 'Are not two sparrows sold for a farthing? and one of them shall not fall on the ground without our Father.'[16] Shakespeare was also capable of indulging the basest tastes of his audience in exhibiting the horrors of *Titus Andronicus*. This was an early play, admittedly, one of his first for Lord Strange's Men, and the distance Shakespeare travelled between that and *Hamlet*, taking his audience with him, is one measure of his genius. Even so, *Titus* remained a popular play in revival and reminds us of the darker tastes of the age. Perhaps the nearest analogy today is the popularity of boxing. Sometime in the future our descendants will shake their heads in disbelief that we were still prepared to watch two men punch each other into submission, and that women considered it a mark of progress that they should be permitted to do the same!

The actual location of the Bear Garden has been a matter of debate. But we know it was on the south bank of the Thames in Paris Garden, not far from the Clink prison and the original Globe. John Stowe in his *Survey of London* (1598) says:

> Now to returne to the West banke, there be two Beare gardens, the olde and new places, wherein be kept Beares, Buls, and other beastes to be bayted. As also Mastives in severall kenels, nourished to baite them. These Beares and other Beastes are there bayted in plottes of ground, scaffolded about for the Beholders to stand safe. Next on this banke was sometime the Bordello or stewes.[17]

In 1584, a German visitor, Lupold von Wedel, wrote a description of the arena in Southwark:

> There is a round building three stories high, in which are kept about a hundred large English dogs, with separate wooden kennels for each of them. These dogs were made to fight singly with three bears, the second bear being larger than the first, and the third larger than the second. After this a horse was brought in and chased by the dogs, and at last a bull, who defended himself bravely.[18]

In 1599, one Thomas Platter of Basle tells us a little more about the arena itself:

> The London bearbaiting usually takes place every Sunday and Wednesday, across the water. The playhouse is built in circular form; above are a number of seated galleries; the ground space under the open sky is unoccupied. In the midst of this a great bear is fastened to a stake by a long rope.[19]

In Byrom's collection there are two separate sequences of drawings for two versions of the Bear Garden, each with slightly different dimensions. Figure B is marked at the top 'Bare 18', the other version, again at the top, is marked 'Bare 16'. In an age when printing had not yet finalised orthography, 'bare' was an acceptable spelling for 'bear'. The existence of two different sequences may be explained by the fact that there was, as Stowe indicated, more than one bear-baiting ring. Or it may be that one replaced the other after the stage collapsed one Sunday in January 1583, killing eight people. The Puritan Lord Mayor wrote on 3 July to the Privy Council of this instance of God's divine wrath in the: 'late terrible example at Paris garden, in which place in great contempt of God the scaffolds are new builded, and the multitudes on the Sabbath day called together in the most excessive manner.'[20] We have already looked at the entry in Dee's diary recording this event. He was still living at Mortlake and visited London in March. He would therefore have been able

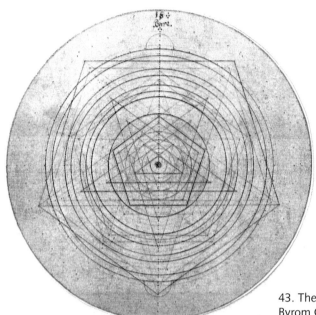

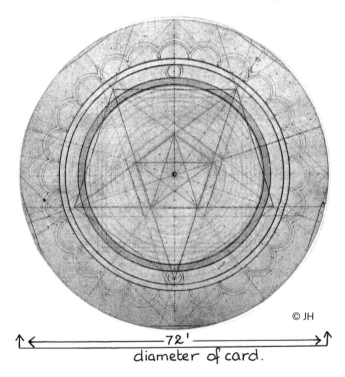

43. The Bear Garden. 'Bare 18' from the Byrom Collection; 'bare' is an early form of 'bear'. *Left:* front. *Right:* reverse. (Reproduced at 75 per cent of original size)

© JH

to advise on the rebuilding before his departure for the continent with Laski in September.

The parametric drawing for the Bear Garden is in principle the same as the others, thus showing a conformity with the overall concept. In the accompanying sequence, however, there is a geometrical design not seen in any of the other drawings connected with playhouses. It is not surprising, for the symbolism of this pattern is diametrically opposed to any we find associated with the other theatres.

The design in question is based on the pentalpha or pentagram, a five-pointed star, constructed out of interlaced triangles. The use of interlaced triangles is very ancient, and, in buildings, the six-pointed star was commonly a mason's mark. In 1949, a number were uncovered in the crypt of St Stephen's Chapel in the House of Commons (built 1135–54). The symbolism associated with the six-pointed star is invariably positive. As for the five-pointed star, B.E. Jones in *The Freemasons' Guide and Compendium* states:

> The pentalpha has been found on sarcophagi and ancient carvings, and has a long association with religions and with superstitions, including necromancy. . . . It is a 'magic' sign in astrology, alchemy, and cabalistic law; in the last of these the five points of the pentalpha signify the spirit, air, fire, water and earth. It has been regarded as a talisman against danger of fire, and the Pythagoreans thought it to be a symbol of health. . . . As a Christian symbol the pentalpha with the point uppermost is supposed to be a reminder of the five wounds of Christ, and at one time possibly symbolised a full knowledge of the Christian mysteries the 'doctrine of the Trinity plus the two natures of Christ.' But used inverted, its two points uppermost, it becomes the Witch's Foot or the Head of the Evil Goat and then signifies the devil and black magic.[21]

On the Byrom drawings the position of the word 'Bare' at the top indicates clearly which way we should look at the card. The pentalpha is inverted. It is not necessary to pursue its application to the drawings further than to say its appearance is limited to the one arena associated with blood, violence, suffering and death. It has been included in this account because the two Elizabethan amphitheatres named in John Byrom's collection of drawings are the 'Globe' and the 'Bare' (*sic*).

As the reader will now be aware, these geometric drawings are quite simply unique. I have found no others like them. My hope that some scholar reading my first book might recognise them and be able to tell me of others buried in a remote archive has proved vain. In the light of this state of affairs, it is strange to reflect that these two sequences are connected to two buildings – the Globe and the Bear – and also to other sequences of drawings which can be related to other buildings of similar design, such as the Rose and the Theatre.

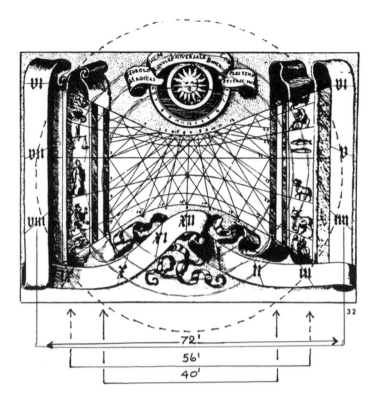

44. *The Magical Calendar* – a feature from the chart. Circles and measures have been added. Signs of the zodiac adorn the walls of what appears to be a three-tiered theatre.

THE MAGICAL CALENDAR

One curiosity exists that helps to substantiate my belief that the de Bry publishing enterprise runs through the collection like a strong current in an underground stream. That is a treatise called *The Magical Calendar*. I have seen one copy in the British Library with the signature of Theodore de Bry in the form of 'Jo. Theodre de Bry excut'. This was Johann Theodore de Bry (1563–1623), the son of Theodore. The origin of this remarkable document is a copper plate covered with complex engravings of a very high order and typical of the de Bry dynasty. It is a single, large plate measuring 48 inches × 24 inches and was produced in Frankfurt in 1620.

The calendar is a register of symbols, tables and sigils connected with white magic. It details correspondences associated with the numbers one to twelve – the twelve signs of the zodiac, the four elements, the seven planets, etc. It was, in other words, a dictionary for reference and use by hermetic scholars, first compiled, it is thought, by Abbot Trithemius of Sponheim (1462–1516). He was one of the most respected scholars of Renaissance magic and, as we saw, an influential source for John Dee. What we should note here is that central to the plate is a representation of a theatre stage, three storeys high. Moreover there are divisions discernible within the plate which are compatible with the units of my seventy-two measure. I had long regarded the de Bry family as the artists responsible for the theatre drawings. Here was proof from another source that they were indeed not only familiar with, but also employed the 72 measure in their work.

CHAPTER 7

The Cast Widens

The physical existence of a rebuilt Globe on the South Bank has confused rather than clarified the answers to many of the basic questions initially associated with its construction. For example, its shape – should it be round or polygonal and, if polygonal, how many sides to the polygon? The building now stands and is an answer, *the* answer apparently, to our uncertainties. The London tourist or the theatregoer booking for the latest production will in all probability never stop to think such questions were once asked and debated hard and long.

JAN CLAES VISSCHER

Scholars know of several pictures of the first Globe, but these tell us conflicting things. For a long time the most highly regarded was the engraving of the London panorama by Jan Claes Visscher, published in about 1616. This was the one that interested me most, since it showed the Globe as octagonal – as does the setting-out plan in the Byrom Collection. However, there is an earlier engraving by John Norden in his panoramic view drawn in 1600. Norden shows the Globe, the Rose, the Swan and the Bear Garden in their correct positions, but here the Globe and Rose appear to be hexagonal, the Swan and the Bear Garden octagonal. To make matters worse, in an inset of the Bankside to one side of the panorama all the playhouses appear round. Another small panorama by Jodocus Hondius, dated 1610, depicts the Globe as round. There is also a very handsome panorama by Wenceslas Hollar of much later date, 1647 – by which time all the public theatres had been closed by the Puritans. It shows both the second version of the Globe and the Bear Garden. Their names, however, were transposed by mistake and both were drawn as circular. Another engraving showing the Globe as polygonal was made in 1638 by Matthias Merian.

For years the Visscher engraving was regarded as the most authoritative depiction of the original playhouse. Then, in 1948, an American scholar, I.A. Shapiro, conducted a detailed examination of Visscher's panorama and came to the conclusion that he had relied heavily on Norden's earlier engraving for his depiction of London on the north bank of the River Thames. From this moment scholars discounted

45. Visscher's engraving of the Globe, 1616, clearly shows it as polygonal. This closely relates to the geometric pattern laid out in the Byrom drawings.

Visscher as unreliable. Some went even further: 'There is no reliable evidence that Visscher ever set foot in London: if his Globe, Bear Garden and Swan are polygonal it is merely because he saw them as polygonal in his source.' So wrote John Orrell in *Rebuilding Shakespeare's Globe*,[1] and for him that settled the matter once and for all.

However, I had reasons for not discounting Visscher's view of the Globe even if, as seemed correct at the time of my writing *The Byrom Collection* (in 1991), Visscher had not himself visited London. Nor was I unduly perturbed by the claim made by some critics that Merian's engraving was indebted to Visscher. Merian had married a grand-daughter of Theodore de Bry, who had given visual and geometric expression to Dee's concept of the playhouse. Moreover, Merian's daughter married a brother of Michel Le Blon whose initials are on some of the original drawings in the collection. Living in the close-knit world of a family of engravers, Merian would have known from de Bry's family that the Globe was both polygonal and eight-sided.

Confirmation of this belief came after the publication of *The Byrom Collection* in 1992. One of the people who wrote to me about the book was Professor John Gleason, by then Professor Emeritus of San Francisco University. He had been intrigued by my adherence to the octagonal shape and my belief that Visscher and Merian were right. He had for some time been working on his own ideas about the origins of the unique design of the Elizabethan playhouse. Part of his research had drawn him inevitably into an examination of the arguments against Visscher's engraving. In the process he had discovered evidence which showed unmistakably that Visscher had been in London at the time the engraving was drawn. It is not for me to rehearse that evidence in detail; Professor Gleason will publish it in due course. But he has very kindly allowed me to read his unpublished manuscript and the cogency of his argument is beyond dispute. He has demonstrated that Visscher was in London and drew the Globe as polygonal because that is what his own eyes showed it to be. The evidence Professor Gleason cites reinstates Visscher as a prime authority for the appearance of the exterior of the first Globe playhouse. The evidence also vindicates the shape of the Globe as shown in the setting-out plan in Byrom's collection. Professor Gleason's reassessment of Visscher's panorama confirmed that I was on the right track, and I remain indebted to him for his generous help at a crucial period – the months immediately following what could only be a general introduction of the Byrom drawings to the public at large.

There remained the problem of proving beyond reasonable doubt the exact purpose of the drawings. Were the sequences that I had put together reflections on the design of the playhouses, or were they patterns for their construction including the measurements in them for builders? From the beginning it seemed clear that the drawings must have been completed in the lifetime of the theatres. Who, after their closure in 1642 and the interruption of the Commonwealth, would have been able to show such detailed knowledge of their design? From where could such information have been reassembled? Who would have wanted to do that, and why? No, the theatre drawings came before 1642. The fact that there were other drawings in the collection with dates on them from the 1720s was irrelevant. What these later drawings showed was a continuation of interest in the geometrical and philosophical aspects of this particular body of material over at least two centuries.

At this stage in my investigations, the additional corroboration for the theatre drawings from the geophysical radar scans of the Globe site had not yet appeared. Accordingly it was necessary to prove that the knowledge of measurements and design which had been detected in the drawings was related to practical realities and not something plucked out of the air to suit an hypothesis. To appreciate the size of the problem, the reader needs an idea of the physical breakdown of the Byrom Collection. Altogether there are 516 pieces of card or paper; 176 of these have drawings on one side only, but 210 have drawings on both sides. In addition, there are 90 prints, many of which are repeats, making a total of 130 prints in all. Thus 596 drawings altogether added to the 90 prints make up a grand total of 686 diagrams.

THE SCIENCE MUSEUM

In the pursuit of new evidence, I returned to the Science Museum. I had originally visited the library there in search of the men and instruments capable of the precise skills demonstrated in the geometry of the drawings. In the course of one of those visits my attention was drawn to a manuscript in the library entitled Ms 471. This was a book bound in vellum made up of blank pages to a number of which had been pasted prints as well as original geometrical drawings. These were similar to some in the Byrom Collection; two of them in fact were identical.[2]

However, during my first round of visits to the Science Museum, when I had discussed Byrom and his drawings with members of staff, I had been shown a series of three-dimensional copies in brass of platonic solids and with them some engraved

46. Ms 471. These two pages show prints from the same source as the Byrom drawings.

brass plates of various shapes and sizes. The series of cones, cubes and pyramids were examples of an interest typical of the early days of the Royal Society. Consequently, I did not choose to examine the brass plates in any detail. I looked at them briefly, letting them drop from my attention with just a flicker of feeling that they were not entirely alien. Into what corner of my subconscious they fell I cannot say, but they lay like a forgotten seed, ripening slowly into a realisation that they had more than a passing relationship with the theatre drawings I had selected from Byrom's collection.

Accordingly, in the summer of 1997, I returned to the Science Museum to study the engraved brass plates more closely. In the Globe sequence of drawings there is a circular card which has written on it the words: 'Underneath is the sets of the brass patterns for the larger and lesser Starrs mall'. I had already concluded from the geometry that the 'Starrs mall' was that part of the theatre where the groundlings stood and which was open to the sky. The card fitted precisely into the centre of the Globe design and was compatible with the rest of the sequence. If a spectator looked up from the groundlings' area, he would see above him the pathway of the stars. The 'larger' and 'lesser' stars are the Sun and Moon respectively, the two chief stars that give life and light to the globe we inhabit, and of which the playhouse was, as its name indicates, a symbolic representation. This much had been clear for some time. But suddenly the reference to 'brass patterns' recalled a series of small circular brass plates I had looked at in the Science Museum.

Now, armed with exact copies of the original drawings, I was able to compare them with the brass plates. In one of the long hangar-like galleries filled with an extraordinary array of historical scientific equipment, ranging from a battery of telescopes to early weighing machines, I was presented with a pair of white gloves with which I was permitted to handle the plates. I superimposed one of the small round plates upon my copy of the Byrom card. There was a precise match. However, one match could be a coincidence. I made many other checks that morning. The results were all the same. There was an undeniable and direct connection between the museum's brass plates and John Byrom's theatre drawings.

One of the most important matches involved the parametric drawing of the Globe which we have already discussed. For a long time I had called this a 'bottle drawing' because of its shape, but eventually settled on the term parametric to indicate that it contained both the horizontal and vertical planes in one drawing. Because of its composite nature the parametric was covered with complex patterns full of information. I had brought a copy made to the exact size of the original with me together with an acetate.

Among the brass plates was one in the shape of a large equilateral triangle. On it was engraved the outline of the parametric drawing. It took only a matter of seconds to show that the card matched the outline of this 'bottle' shape. Replacing the card with the acetate revealed much more. Acetates are one of the wonders of modern reprographics: their transparent surfaces can carry the detail of a drawing which would be beyond the skill of any but the most accomplished draughtsmen to reproduce; their accuracy is self-evident. This particular acetate provided the ultimate proof of the connection between the brass plates and the drawings, for the patterns on both matched in every way. It was not just a matter of compatibility in shape and size. What became immediately clear to the eye was that the pattern of the Byrom drawing was the same as the pattern on the brass plate but in reverse. This could only mean that the Byrom Globe drawing was in fact a mirror image of the brass plate and that the drawing was a print made from the plate. However, further details had been added to the drawing. This holds true for the other parametrics as well. The conclusion was obvious: all the parametric drawings of the theatres are adaptations of this one plate. It is their common source.

Several visits were needed to establish how far the drawings were compatible with the brass plates, but by the end of the summer it was absolutely clear that the plates were indeed an integral part of a large section of the Byrom Collection, in particular the theatre drawings. This now led to new questions since, unfortunately, there was no indication on the plates of when they were made or by whom. But this is to anticipate, for it became apparent immediately that it was necessary to work on the brass plates side by side with the Byrom drawings. The Science Museum arranged for the entire collection to be photographed in manageable groups according to their shape and size. Some photographs were of just one or two large plates, others contained as many as eight. However, each frame also included a photograph of the seventy-two measure, which I had made, to provide a constant scale throughout. I was thus able to enlarge or reduce individual photos to the same scale as the drawings for close individual scrutiny with the measure.

The museum is constantly arranging special exhibitions, and at the time of my visit a small, representative number of brass plates was on display; the rest were in store but available for study. I was shown a very simple, handwritten catalogue which had come with the collection. Its rough and ready appearance was, to say the least, intriguing. There was a list of items, all numbered, but not in numerical order. Item 33 (listed between items 39 and 36) was described as: 'Forty one Brass Plates Engraved with Astronomical Astrological and Mathematical Delineations.' Moreover, at the top of the first page of this catalogue was the following heading:

A list of Some Curious Mathematical Bodys, Figures, &c: from the Collection of the Great Mr. Boyle. Supposed to be made two Centurys Agoe, as Described in a German book of that Date which was sent (with this Collection) to be placed in his Majesty's Observatory at Richmond 13th March 1770.

47. The brass plates. In the foreground are circular plates related to the starr's mall of the playhouses.

If the attribution was correct, and there was no reason to doubt it, then two things became clear immediately. Item 33, the forty-one brass plates, was older than John Byrom, for Boyle died in 1692, the year Byrom was born. Secondly, the phrase 'supposed to be made two Centurys agoe' must relate to the 'Mathematical Bodys, Figures &c' not 'the Collection of the Great Mr Boyle', for they were apparently described in a book that was dated 200 years prior to 1770. Since the plates could not be described as 'Mathematical Bodys' or 'Figure' they were lumped, presumably for convenience, under the collective '&c' of the heading together with the rest of Boyle's items. Moreover, if they appeared in the 'German book', there was no doubt about their age – they must date from about 1570. That would bring us neatly to the period when the unique design of the playhouses first appeared in Burbage's prototype, the Theatre, in 1576.

The catalogue seemed to be signalling all sorts of information. Both Boyle and Byrom were members of the Royal Society and this was in all probability the arena in which many of the items in this catalogue were discussed. Boyle was in fact a founder

A Drawing of a Scale on Vellum, in an old Velvet Case

A Large Scale with an Index on Wood

A Tryangle Box Rule

Six Ebony Sliding frames

An Old Printed German Book, describing some of the Above Instruments &c: Printed Anno 1568

Two Manuscript Books - of the Astronomical, Astrological & Mathematical Plates

A Pye with thirty-Six various Odd Peices

Inv. 1927-2065.
Boyle 41 (pt)

A List of Some Curious Mathematical Bodys, Figures &c: from the Collection of the Great Mr Boyle

Supposed to be made two Centurys Agoe, as Described in a German Book of that Date which was sent (with this Collection) to be placed in His Majestys Observatory at Richmond 13th March 1770

The five Regular Bodys, about 8 Inches Diameter, most Curiously and Transparently Constructed in Brass, so as to be taken into various peices ——— in painted wood Cases

Five promiscuous Transparent Bodys, about 3 Inches & ⅞ Diameter in Ditto ——— no Cases

Six very Large Hollow Cones, which Unscrew in Various parts weight 36 lbs

Part of a Ditto, and two Large Hollow Balls that Unscrew weight 8 lb

48. Pages from the catalogue of the George III Collection.

The five Regular Bodys in Brass - 4 Solid, the Triangle Hollow 2 Inches full Diameter

Ditto all Solid, about 1 Inch & ½ Diameter

Ditto in Ivory, in a Shaggreen Case Silver hasps & Joints

Ditto in Ditto, in an Ivory Case

Three Small Brass Spheres (delineated) in Brass Cups & Stands

Three Triangles Ditto - in Ditto

A Solid Triangle and Piramid on Ditto

Two Brass Spheres - and five Ivory Ditto Delineated - no Stands

Three Ivory Ditto and a Cube, in a Brazil Case

A Ditto, in Ditto

Five Solid Brass Cubes & an Ivory Ditto

Four promiscuous Regular Bodys, Solid in Brass

Seven Pyramids, Triangles, a Dodecahedron &c: Mounted on Rings

A Curious Brass Cube in five peices, which fitt in & fills a Cube Box of 1 Inch ½ Diameter

Four Small Silver Pyramids with Various Sides, in Brazil Cases

Sixteen Brass Cones, Pyramids &c: in Ditto

Thirty Ditto Pyramids - no Cases

Six Brass Cones, and two Ivory Ditto

Eighteen Small Brass Triangles

Seven Starr Pyramids

A Small Diagonal Cone & Cover in Brass - which Unscrews

A Shot Gage in Brass with three Divisions

A Dodecahedron & an Ificahedron - in Wood

Two Large Optical Glasses on Stands

A half Convex Ditto - no Stand

A Watch Makers Glass in Ivory

A Small Concave Double Ditto - in Black Ditto

A Large Load-Stone

Forty one Brass Plates Engraved with Astronomical, Astrological and Mathematical Delineations

One Square Copper Ditto - Ditto

A Square Brass Scale plate in a Case

49. Pages from the catalogue showing item 33.

member of that august body. He had been a leading figure in the small circle of mathematicians and philosophers which he called the Invisible College and which was the forerunner of the Royal Society. His chosen field of excellence was chemistry which had its roots in alchemy. There is evidence that, together with his dedication to the process of experimentation as the basis of the scientific method and his devout Christianity, Boyle also had an active interest in cabalistic and hermetic studies. This all lent weight to the claim in the catalogue that the items had once belonged to the 'Great Mr. Boyle'.

I also turned my attention to identifying the 'German book' from the 1570s. It was listed in the catalogue, too, as item 40. The numbering of the items was very haphazard. Item 40 appeared on the third sheet of the inventory incongruously placed between items 16 and 76! The book was entitled *Perspectiva Corporum Regularium* and had been written by a goldsmith from Nuremburg, Wenzel Jamnitzer. Published in 1568, it was almost two centuries earlier than the catalogue which I had been shown at the Museum.

The book consists of 49 leaves of illustrations and three of text. The illustrations are as follows: a title page, a page introducing each of the five regular solids, four pages depicting solids based on each of the five, and 23 other illustrations of more complex geometrical skills.[3]

The problem was puzzling. John Byrom's collection of drawings was a unique resource. No one had been able to show me similar drawings, apart from those in Ms 471. Now, here was another body of artefacts – the plates – which were linked with the drawings, although the link was not absolutely clear. Item 33 in the inventory seemed a very mixed bag. The brass representations of platonic solids in the collection spoke for themselves: they had been objects of study for centuries. They were all beautifully made, exhibiting again exquisite workmanship of the highest order. However, the plates were not so straightforward. Yet, as I studied them, one feature emerged which afforded a possible clue. This was on a plate concerned with surveying land.

On it are engraved six small squares of equal size, each numbered with Roman numerals I to VI. Square I was the face of a compass on which all four cardinal points and thirty-two sub-divisions had been engraved. As before, the numbers and letters on the plates were in reverse. It was evidently made to print from. Squares III to VI were illustrations of four readings of different angles, each constructed within a circle calibrated into degrees along the circumference. These calculations indicate various stages in surveying. We are left in no doubt by the last remaining illustration (number II). Here, the square depicts a landscape with hills rising from each side of a

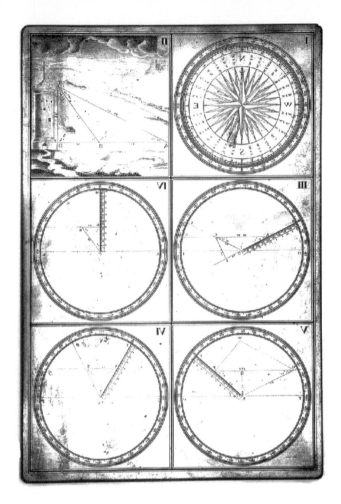

50. Surveyor's plate. The illustrations are in reverse, as can be seen from the cardinal points on the compass. The roman numerals are likewise reversed for printing.

river. On opposite sides of the bank are three tower-like structures, two of them flying a flag. Lines have been drawn from a point in the foreground of the landscape to the turret of the nearest building, with calculations for height and distance. This drawing is the key to the plate.

The brass plate is complete and all of a piece. The Byrom Collection contains a print of squares III to VI. The first two squares, the compass and the landscape, are missing. An examination of the print shows that these have been cut off from the rest of the print. Whereas the brass plate tells us quite clearly what its purpose is, the truncated piece of paper inevitably is not so helpful. A surveyor would recognise the sort of calculations being made within the circles, but the average layman might not. Since the first two squares were not to be found anywhere else in Byrom's collection, the question arises whether they had been cut off deliberately and, if so, why?

It might well have been a deliberate act, for there are in the collection two pieces of paper with some relevance to this very question. One is a drawing of what I consider to be the winch used to lower people or properties from the 'Heavens' above

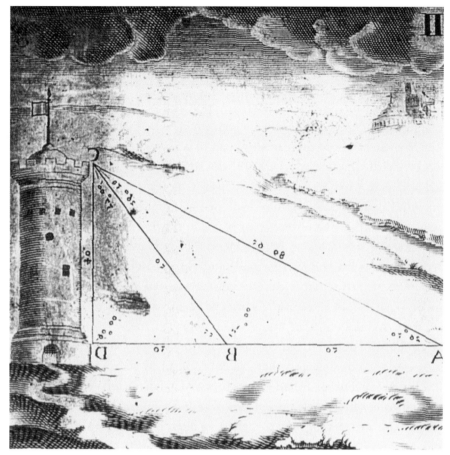

51. Enlarged section II of the surveyor's plate in figure 50.

the stage, the other a few lines written on the cabala. The two were once joined together, but have also been separated, this time by a tear. By the grace of God, both parts had been saved and can be shown to match, but for some reason they had been deliberately separated. In the case of the surveyor's print, which belonged to the brass plate, we have not been so lucky. However, the Science Museum's original plate shows us what the missing sections represent.

I studied these two squares on the plate. The face on the compass was not particularly different from that of many other compass cards which I had seen and of which there are prints in Byrom's collection. Of necessity the divisions on a compass have to be standard; it is the ornamentation which distinguishes them from one another. Some have the maker's initials on them and this has helped to date them. The one on the plate did not and the ornamentation was minimal. It was simply a depiction of a compass for functional purposes. However, the landscape engraving in square number II possessed several points of interest, particularly the three buildings. In the foreground we can see an elongated, tower-like structure whose windows clearly indicate three storeys. Across the river, on top of a hillside, blending into the horizon, are two others, rather more squat because of the perspective. They seem to be back to back, but that is no doubt the effect of foreshortening. The one slightly to the fore has a square base and a curved upper storey. Bearing in mind how many other drawings in the collection were connected with Elizabethan playhouses and that one of these had been torn in two, I had to consider whether this plate, also, was concerned with the theatres. Were the buildings with flags intended as representations of playhouses? Had they been removed from the print for the same reason as the cabalistic writing from the drawing of the winch?

The realisation that there were brass plates in the Science Museum related to the theatre drawings was a major development. The surveyor's plate, the sequence of rings concerned with the 'Starrs mall' and the triangular plate containing the Globe parametric raised rather different questions. The Byrom Collection could no longer be regarded as a completely independent corpus of material. The plates opened fresh avenues and that was a hopeful sign for the way ahead. By their very nature the brass plates were more sturdy and durable than any of Byrom's pieces of paper or card. It was amazing that his collection had survived in the first place. The fact that no one else had come forward with other examples since the publication of my first book proved how fragile they were. However, now we had the plates and other tangible pieces of evidence, including the handwritten catalogue. Perhaps these more solid artefacts would lead to the answers which until now had seemed so elusive.

During the summer of 1997 I made repeated visits to the Science Museum, where Jane Wess, Curator of Astronomy and Mathematics, together with the Associate Curator, Kevin Johnson, offered me every help. In the end my visits and the discussions they provoked led to a most profitable conclusion. One of the first matters we discussed was the seventy-two measure. The museum has an impressive collection of different types of linear measure dating from the time of ancient Egypt. It so happens that, together with her other duties, Jane Wess is responsible for these exhibits. Even so, when she saw the measure that I had devised from the intervals pricked out on the theatre drawings, she admitted that she had not seen one like it before. This seemed to emphasise once again the uniqueness of the Byrom Collection just when I was hoping to establish common ground with other artefacts.

As we discussed the plates, photographed them and compared them with the drawings, it became apparent that it was necessary to establish their age within reasonable limits. Accordingly, the museum decided to arrange to have the plates dated, and engaged the services of Dr Peter Northover of the Department of Materials, Oxford University, to conduct a metallurgical analysis on a selection of the engraved brass plates to determine their age.

Dr Northover's Analysis

Seven plates were chosen and samples taken. These samples were then prepared for electron probe microanalysis using wavelength dispersive spectrometry. This part of the procedure was carried out by Dr T. Williams of Oxford University's Department of Mineralogy. Five areas on each sample were subjected to the analysis. Each of the seven plates was found to contain thirteen elements which are duly listed in Dr Northover's report. The analysis showed that: 'All seven samples proved to be plain zinc brasses with over 30% zinc, the zinc contents ranging from 32.3% to 35.85%.'[4] Tin and lead were at trace levels in all but one plate. Most impurities were at trace level, the only significant ones being iron, 'a standard impurity in old brass', and arsenic. Dr Northover goes on to explain:

> The late 16th and early 17th centuries are a key period in the development of brass. Until that time in western Europe the method of making brass was that introduced by the Romans, the cementation process. The problem with smelting zinc to produce brass is that at the temperature at which zinc is reduced from the ore it is above its boiling point and so to accumulate zinc metal a means of condensing the vapour is required. This had been discovered in India by the 10th century AD and was in use on an industrial scale there soon afterwards, but the technology appears to have been unknown in the west. There brass was made by reducing zinc oxide or carbonate in a sealed vessel in contact with copper, the zinc diffusing directly into the copper.[5]

Dr Northover concluded that at least two of the seven plates required the use of zinc in their manufacture:

> This was being imported from China and, possibly, India by the Dutch and British East India Companies in the 17th century, while a second source of zinc was . . . Aachen . . . However, this last source was apparently regarded as expensive and may not always have been used for making high zinc alloys.[6]

An examination of a series of English monumental brasses of the late sixteenth and seventeenth centuries shows a gradual rise in the zinc content during the second half of the sixteenth century. The source for the brass plates is not known. Dr Northover concludes:

> However, it seems unlikely that they were made in Britain. The first English brass was produced at the Mineral and Battery Works established at Tintern Abbey in 1568 using calamine from the Mendips and copper supplied by the Mines Royal.

The brass, though, was of poor quality and was not very malleable, perhaps because of the quality of the copper. The initial product was an alloy with only 20% zinc, later improved to 24% zinc, but because of the difficulties production soon ceased and the works turned to manufacturing iron wire.[7]

The high level of zinc in the samples indicated that the plates must have been made on the continent. The conclusion of Dr Northover's report is as follows:

The alloys used in the engraved plates are yellow brasses with 32–36% zinc. Comparative analyses from monumental brasses and scientific instruments show that these alloys were available and used from the second half of the 16th century onwards in north-west Europe. Thus the alloy contents are consistent with the suggested date of the plates.[8]

In a letter accompanying his report Dr Northover wrote:

The ultimate bottom line is that there is no reason why the plates should not be c. 1600. There is still work to do on the source of the brass, and on determining whether what was the norm on the Continent also applied over here.[9]

Thus the scientific analysis of the composition of the plates took them back to the period when the Elizabethan theatres were being built.

INDUSTRY AT TINTERN

Before I received Dr Northover's conclusions, even before the plates had been sent for analysis, I had begun to study the history of brass-making in this country, especially its earliest years at Tintern. That beginning says much about the enterprise of Elizabethan merchant adventurers. As the story unfolded, certain facts emerged from both local and national records, which could not be ignored, despite Dr Northover's later reservations about early Tintern brass. The brass plates now seemed highly relevant to the Byrom Collection.

We do not normally think of Tintern in the Wye Valley as a centre of industrial activity but there was a time when this remote and sparsely populated village was as famous for its iron and wire works as for its abbey. The iron works has long since disappeared and there is no mention of it in Wordsworth's celebrated poem on Tintern Abbey. Each year visitors are drawn by the outstanding beauty of the landscape, but few are aware that close to the impressive ruins of the Cistercian abbey once lived and worked a small but thriving industrial community.

In 1563 a company was created to investigate and work the minerals in certain counties of England and Wales which were a rich but still undeveloped source. It was a joint venture between a wealthy German business house and English entrepreneurs. The German investors were able to offer not only money but much needed mining skills. This was the origin of what became known as the Company of the Mines Royal. At first they concentrated their activities on copper mining at Keswick in Cumberland.[10] However, while this development was taking place, other projects for the commercial exploitation of the country's natural resources were under consideration.

The government was anxious to make England less dependent on imports of wire for domestic products such as curtain rings, needles, small chains, etc. In 1565, William Humfrey, the Assay Master and Paymaster of the Royal Mint, wanted to establish a company which he hoped to develop with the help of a German expert, Christopher Schutz from Saxony, to hold sole rights of battery. (Battery meant the beating of iron under the battery hammer into iron plate for armour, the making of brass, the beating of brass and the forging of cannon, etc.)

> Schutz was an expert in working calamine stone (zinc ore) and he was to teach his skill to English workers. For the brass industry depended on zinc ore with its alloy, copper. Humfrey and Schutz were given the sole right to: search for and to smelt ores, including calamine to be compounded with copper for the making of latten (brass) in certain parts of England, Wales and Ireland outside the sphere of the Company of the Mines Royal.[11]

Humfrey's enterprise was called 'The Company of the Mineral and Battery Works'. However, from the beginning the manufacture of iron was an important part of its work. The men responsible for getting the company started were Humfrey, Schutz, Thomas Smythe, William Williams and Humphrey Cole.

During the winter of 1565–6 surveys were undertaken of various rivers to establish whether they could provide water power. In June 1566 Schutz arrived from Germany to take up his duties, 'with so many workmen as shall be thought good according to the forwardness that is already prepared'. The total number of workers brought from Germany was twenty-two. Their arrival coincided with the discovery of a rich vein of calamine ore in Somerset. According to Dr W. Rees: 'The ore, on test, was found to be superior in yield and quality to that of many German ores and the site was to prove a valuable source of zinc.'[12] This find, together with the availability of fuel and water transport, led the company to move its search for a base near to Bristol. Humfrey had hopes that the Earl of Pembroke might help his enterprise get the castle of Bristol as a site for the zinc works, but the water supply proved inadequate.

The search led eventually to Tintern where a tributary to the Wye, the Angiddy, could be dammed to provide the right level of power. As it happened, this small river formed a natural boundary between the lands of the Earl of Pembroke and William Somerset, third Earl of Worcester. Worcester's family had acquired the abbey lands after the Dissolution, and the present earl had married a Herbert, so we were truly in the territory owned by two of the noble families who had been patrons of the Elizabethan theatres.

Here, the company decided to set up its works in 1565 within the precincts of the former abbey. Humfrey wrote to Sir William Cecil about the decision:

> We have found our Lord of Pembroke our very good Lord not only in commanding the use of Bristol castle but also the water courses and otherwise to prefer a building there. But the waters not being of force as we expected we were forced to search the country by Severn side more than 40 miles. And finding all the pleasant rivers set full of grist and tucking mills, we crossed the Severn to view the rivers of Usk and Wye in Wales where the like place is not to be found in Christopher Schutz's judgement.
>
> Finding the river of Wye far above our reach to deal with at this time we have sought by the riverside to find some water descending from the mountains and we have found a convenient place upon my Lord of Worcester's land to build on. Nothwithstanding the water comes between my Lord of Pembroke's land and my Lord of Worcester's. If the platt had so served as we might have built on my Lord of Pembroke's land, we might have begun our building a month past. For we have found our Lord of Worcester hard to us and we are forced to give £4 a year for that which the country esteems at 4s a year. And for that the land rests in remainder to the Queen's Majesty my Lord cannot grant longer lease than 21 years. Notwithstanding he does promise for him and his heirs to renew the lease at any time for 21 years longer upon fine. Being desiring to have him nominate the fine, he will not as yet name less than £30.[13]

During archaeological excavations funded by the Welsh Office in 1980, a medieval smithy-type forge with furnaces, kilns and metal slag was uncovered at Tintern Abbey, next to the ruins of the guest house, giving substance to the belief that the Cistercian monks who had lived there had practised some limited ironwork and copper and lead smelting, in addition to farming, before Humfrey and his workers moved in.[14] This is probably the site where, according to a plaque on the abbey wall, 'in 1568 brass was first made by alloying copper with zinc'.[15]

After building two furnaces and two forges the new company hoped to produce up to 1 ton of metal per week either of steel, iron or brass. By July 1567 Humfrey

52. Tintern Abbey from the road (nineteenth century). Within the abbey grounds nearby was the site of the first brass-works in the kingdom.

announced the works were ready to produce latten (thin sheets of brass). But like many ambitious entrepreneurs he was a little premature, for he was still waiting for essential pieces of equipment, such as rollers and casting stones, and the completion of the hammer house. From the beginning there seem to have been production difficulties. The original furnaces for making brass, installed by a German, John Hinckens, and his sons, produced brass of the right colour, but it was not sufficiently malleable.[16] Other problems made it necessary to bring over another German, Barnes Kayser, to help sort out the production techniques. A wire-drawer by training, he changed all the wire-drawing engines and spent two and a half years teaching operators.

Schutz, an engineer and inventor, had, according to one authority,[17] discovered a revolutionary technique in the use of calamine for mixing metals, and in rendering iron more malleable for industrial purposes. However, his real expertise lay in the area of brass making and it was this aspect of the work that he was engaged to develop at Tintern. Humfrey was a goldsmith. The company hoped to manufacture two different products – iron wire and brass – and the combined talents of all four men – Schutz, Kayser, Hinckens and Humfrey – were needed to make a success of the venture.

Humfrey maintained from the outset that brass-making, if successful, would be more profitable than manufacturing iron wire. First returns were encouraging, but: 'high quality brass was not easily produced and much experimentation was called for before a marketable brass could be obtained comparable with the best Continental product.'[18] British craftsmen were better at working iron and therefore the latter offered a 'more immediate and reliable market'. Accordingly, the company capitalised on skills in making iron wire.[19] However, it is a matter of opinion how far the production of brass can be described as a failure. There is evidence to show that the 'experimentation' continued and that good brass was made by the company. As Dr Rees points out, Schutz was held in high regard by Cecil as a man of great skill. Humfrey described him as a 'jewel such as all Germany hath not the like . . . the lantern of Germany as touching mineral and metal affairs'. After arriving in England in June 1566, it was not long before he became a naturalised British subject. So, he evidently foresaw a successful future for the enterprise. Moreover, Schutz had come with a glowing reputation from a successful career in a flourishing German industry to live in a quiet valley in Wales and help to set up a new venture. What inducements could there be to make such a wilderness tolerable, apart from the determination to succeed afresh? Humfrey did his best to look after the creature comforts: he made sure that both he and Schutz had substantial houses in Tintern with three or four servants and that these were maintained by the corporation at the cost of £100 per annum. When criticised, Humfrey defended this policy by saying: 'no country could afford to treat its master miners after the manner of hirelings. With them, the realm had attained within a relatively few years to a standard of development which had taken Germany many hundreds of years.'[20] In the light of such a claim one is bound to ask who were the personalities behind this enterprise? The more so, perhaps, because Tintern has already appeared in connection with certain patrons of the theatre companies and their lineage. Is this where the brass plates had originated?

In May 1568, the Company of the Mineral and Battery Works was granted a royal charter and formed into a corporation called 'The Governors, Merchants and Society of the Mineral and Battery Works'. The list of shareholders is impressive, indicative of the hopes of the great and the good to make a fortune out of the company's activities. It includes Sir Nicholas Bacon, the Duke of Norfolk, the Earls of Pembroke and Leicester, Lord Cobham, Sir William Cecil, Sir Walter Mildmay, Sir Henry Sidney and thirty-one others including Humfrey, Schutz, Thomas Smythe, Edmund Roberts and Andrew Palmer.[21] A number of shareholders of this company also had a stake in the Mines Royal and the Muscovy Company. Among the most important of these were Sir William Cecil, the Earl of Leicester and the Earl of Pembroke. These last two names bring us back to the patrons and supporters of the

Elizabethan theatre companies. Was their presence here simply a coincidence, characteristic of the men who made up the 'Elizabethan Establishment', or did it indicate something more?

My feeling that Schutz had succeeded in manufacturing brasses seemed to be borne out by the testimony of a wire worker at Tintern speaking in 1603, some years after Schutz's death: 'Schutz was a work master of great cunning, knowledge and experience at finding calamine stone and the proper use thereof for the composition of the mixed metal (brass) in reducing it to be soft and malleable and in the working of the same into all sorts of battery wire.'[22] From the start, then, the company appears to have had some success in the development of a native brass industry. So much so that eventually the: 'brass making side of its activities with the right to mine calamine and to erect brass-works was leased by the Corporation in 1582 for a term of 15 years at an annual rent of £50 to one of its members, John Burde, goldsmith or gold finer of St Giles, London, and partners.'[23]

The name Burde recalled to mind a William Burde who also happened to be a goldsmith in London and who had shares in the Tintern company. In 1581 he transferred a quarter share to one William Smythe who in turn sold part of his share to Sir William Herbert of Saint Julian's, Newport, in 1585.

The appearance of Sir William Herbert on the scene also brought resonances, but different ones. He was a direct descendant of the first Herbert to be created Earl of Pembroke, the William we looked at earlier, who had been Chief Justice and Chamberlain of South Wales, and whose beheaded body had been buried in Tintern Abbey in 1469. I knew that this Sir William Herbert had worked closely with John Dee on the ideas expounded in the *Monas Hieroglyphica*, and that he had a house at Mortlake not far from Dee. In addition, he had a home at Tintern where he planned to found a college, and continued to maintain the family residence close by at Saint Julian's, near Newport. So, after 100 years we still find the influence of the Herberts and Pembrokes in Tintern. The past linked with the present, and the activities of Sir William Herbert seemed to narrow the distance between the Byrom drawings and the brass plates. The purchase of a part share in the company by Sir William looked like another deliberate intervention by the Herbert/Pembroke family in an enterprise which they felt was worth supporting and in which the Earl of Pembroke had been involved from the beginning in the lease of land and as a shareholder.

Evidence exists to show that not all the brass from Tintern was as poor as we have been led to believe. In 1596, John Burde was involved in a dispute with his partners which went before the Privy Council. In his deposition Burde stated that the success he had achieved in manufacturing brass was the result of fourteen years hard work by him and his workforce, and he claimed to be 'the first person in England to bring the process to perfection without external aid'. Whatever the truth of this, brass-making skills could not have been very bad or John Burde's enterprise would not have enjoyed success. Moreover, illicit manufacture of brass-ware was carried on for some time unknown to the corporation: in 1629 a brass-works was discovered near Bristol run by two men from that city with the help of workmen from Tintern.[24]

The enterprise at Tintern also attracted the acquisitive ambitions of other buccaneers. One particularly worthy of note was Richard Hanbury, a merchant and ironmaster, who first tried to corner the market in timber needed for industrial buildings and in the supply of charcoal. During the late 1570s the Society of Mineral and Battery Works sought to restrain Hanbury's ruthless felling of trees for his own gain. Moreover, in concert with Sir Richard Martin, he attempted a takeover of the wire works at Tintern through leases granted to two intermediary lessees. Humfrey was opposed to this move because at the time (1570) experiments were under way to improve the making of brass and he still had great hopes for the industry at Tintern.

It is not necessary to give a blow-by-blow account of the activities of Hanbury and Martin, but they were involved in a plot to falsify the accounts with the object of obtaining a drastic reduction of rent in their lease. The situation is made less clear by Martin suing Hanbury for double-dealing and by so doing endeavouring to free himself from any suspicion of collusion with Hanbury. In this he appears to have been successful. A minute of the Corporation dated 20 October 1581 states: 'The Corporation had always found Sir Richard Martin to have dealt for the general good of the whole Company and especially in preventing Hanbury in the wire works, and other his friends in the latten battery works, from their purpose to bring them to no worth.'[25]

Wherever the truth ultimately lay, there seems to have been a great deal of intrigue and some questionable keeping of accounts at Tintern. Hanbury's ruthlessness won him many enemies, causing further tension and conflict. On one occasion in 1577 he was met on the main road between Usk and Chepstow by a band of angry locals and threatened with physical violence. 'It were a good deed', said one of them, 'to give him a stripe or twain so that he should not have good liking or will to come to Monmouth to maintain iron works and destroy our woods.'[26] In December the same year tenants in Gwhelog woods organised a revolt and attacked the woodcutters, set fire to the timber and damaged the charcoal burners' pits. In an effort to restore law and order, Sir William Herbert sent his bailiffs who were themselves attacked and had to fight to save their own skins.

Against this background and with the interplay of old familiar figures (and all that their presence implied), the likelihood that Mr Boyle's brass plates did indeed have connections with the brass-works at Tintern grew stronger.

A SEARCH FOR SAMPLES

If the provenance of the plates was to be established further it was desirable to find examples of brass known to have come from the Tintern works. This was not likely to be easy because it has long been a practice to melt down metal artefacts to re-use the basic component, a practice not confined to the more precious metals such as gold or silver. Records of business in Welsh ports show that in 1566 old brass, or 'scruff' as it was called, was considered worth collecting and shipping to Bristol, no doubt to be used afresh.[27]

The best brass is likely to have been on the monuments of people connected with Tintern Abbey itself, memorials to its patrons or supporters when it was still a thriving religious community – this takes us back to the original founders and the very first earls of Pembroke. But, of course, when the abbey was dissolved by Henry VIII he took whatever valuables he wanted before giving the land to the Earl of Worcester. The lead disappeared from the roof and the local inhabitants took the stone to build or repair their houses. No brass could be expected to have survived from there. However, there were other Pembroke earls buried in Westminster Abbey.

In the chapel of St Edmund at Westminster lies the tomb of William de Valence, Lord of Pembroke and Wexford, half-brother to Henry III, the sovereign responsible for rebuilding and enlarging Westminster. William was born in 1225 at the Cistercian abbey of Valence near Lusignan. The abbey at Tintern was also a Cistercian foundation, and a previous earl of Pembroke, William Marshall, had founded another Cistercian house near Wexford in Ireland with a colony of monks from the Wye Valley community. He even called the Irish foundation Tintern Parva. Earls of Pembroke, whether Marshalls, de Valences or Herberts, seemed inextricably linked with this order and these two foundations.

William de Valence was the father of Aymer whom we looked at in Chapter 5. Henry III had brought William from France to serve by his side and William was fiercely loyal both to the king and his son, Edward I. Returning from campaign in the Holy Land, de Valence brought back a cross with a beautifully wrought base of gold and emeralds. He died in 1296 and was buried in Westminster Abbey; his tomb is remarkable for being the only example in England of Limoges enamel work. The effigy and the chest on which it lies were once covered with enamelled copper plates. Most of these have been lost but those which survive show workmanship of the finest quality, with the shield of Valence blazoned in silver, azure and gold. I remembered the traces of the monks' early interest in metalwork.

When Aymer succeeded his father he was styled Earl of Pembroke, though never formally created earl. He, too, served his sovereigns well, both Edward I and Edward II, his uncle and cousin respectively. Aymer's second wife, Mary, Countess of

Pembroke, the founder of Pembroke College, Cambridge, bequeathed the bejewelled cross her father-in-law had brought back from the crusades to Westminster Abbey. Here, like his father before him, Aymer was buried in 1324. Aymer's tomb is another outstanding example of medieval artistry, richly carved and again adorned with enamel. It lies in the Confessor's Chapel close to the shrine itself. This is the very heart of the abbey redesigned and rebuilt by Henry III. As a resting place, it was intended for royalty, their blood relations and subjects of the highest distinction. Close by is the Sanctuary pavement; the abbot imported craftsmen from Italy to construct it and it is another extraordinary, indeed unique, piece of ecclesiastical art. The intervention of the abbot here is not without significance. It was he who brought the materials and artists from Italy, not the king.

It was time to reflect on the significance of the Cistercian connection in the history of the plates. The Cistercian abbeys spread in a systematic way both in England and Wales until eventually there were seventy-five monasteries and eleven more in Scotland. The organisation was on an international scale. In the case of Tintern, an abbot with a colony of at least twelve monks left the 'mother' abbey at l'Aumone in France to found the new monastery. But by that time, 1131, strict regulations were already in force about the founding of new communities. Prior to the monks' arrival certain buildings, such as the refectory, dormitory, oratory and a guest chamber, all temporary structures made out of timber, would have to be ready for them so that they could carry out their religious duties immediately. The founding party would also include lay brothers who would carry out all the manual work while the 'choir monks' concentrated on their services. Although the new abbey was a separate community, it was part of a much wider order. The abbot of l'Aumone was expected to make an annual visit from France to see how his 'child' was developing. In addition, the abbots of both Tintern and l'Aumone were expected to attend the general chapter held every year at Citeaux where the first Cistercian monastery had been founded. Here there would be a review of all the abbeys throughout Europe. These meetings were of the utmost importance for maintaining discipline and to ensure a united policy on all matters affecting the Order generally. The abbot of Tintern crossed over to France to attend a general chapter even when the two countries were at war. Abbots could be removed from office: in 1188 Abbot Williams was forced to resign from Tintern after a visit of inspection sent by the general chapter. In other words, we are dealing here with a highly organised movement that not only laid down rules for the spiritual conduct of its members in great detail, but also drew up guidelines on the style of buildings and even the layout of abbeys. For example, in the second half of the twelfth century it became a Cistercian practice to build the refectory at right angles to the cloister to make better use of the space available.

During Tintern Abbey's 400 years' existence, the monks would have had builders constantly at work, enlarging and altering their buildings. With time and increasing prosperity, the original austere style of architecture began to be transformed by more decorative features, some copied from Westminster Abbey as rebuilt by Henry III, others introduced directly from the continent. Tintern is known to have had at least thirty-one different designs of tiles for its floors. Masons were home-grown but the men who decorated abbeys and cathedrals were often imported. The large religious communities with their international network and tight discipline were an ideal means of transmitting new ideas, new artists and new standards in art for their foundations and for the benefit of their sovereigns and patrons. This is what had happened at Westminster when Henry III rebuilt the Confessor's shrine: Henry took the marble he needed from Purbeck, but it was Abbot Ware who knew about the cosmati mosaics and imported the workmen and materials necessary for the design. The copper and other metals employed at Westminster would have been of the best. So too, would those fired in the small forge at Tintern.

Westminster Abbey was a Benedictine foundation. The Cistercians were an off-shoot following a more austere form of the Benedictine rule. It is instructive to reflect on the close ties of the Valence family with Cistercian abbeys in Tintern and in France, and their kinship with the reiging house of Henry III, Edward I and Edward II, clearly shown by the burial of William and Aymer in Westminster Abbey. In this context the cross set in jewels which Mary de Valence, Countess of Pembroke, gave to Westminster is a perfect symbol of the connection between the two Orders and their use of the finest art in the service of God.

In 1536 the process of destroying the kingdom's monasteries began. On 3 September Tintern Abbey was surrendered to the representatives of Henry VIII and the community was dissolved. The last abbot, Richard Wyche, was given a pension of £23 and the twelve remaining choir monks received £8 8s 0d. Two became curates in nearby churches. The remaining ten received dispensations from their vows which enabled them to take church livings elsewhere. Thirty-five lay monks or servants were granted £16 5s 1d. Since most of the lay staff were usually drawn from the locality, these men may have been absorbed back into the working life of the neighbourhood which had expanded into a busy commercial community as the abbey itself had prospered. Thirty years elapsed between the end of the monastery and the beginning of the brass-works. Did some of the lay brothers continue to make use of the abbey forge to eke out a living in the world outside? Did others find a place for themselves and their skills in the households of the new aristocratic landlords, enriched, like the Earl of Worcester, by the plunder of monastic estates?

Although I have not found a sample of brass for comparison, the pedigree of artistic endeavour revealed in the previous pages persuades me that it is only a matter of time before an example comes to light. Dr Northover is an undoubted expert in metallurgy and his conclusions are invaluable. However, a review of the history of Tintern, both at the abbey and the first brass-works, has produced sufficient indications for the brass plates to be linked with the theatre drawings. This resulted in a dilemma that could only be resolved by further enquiry. Some of the most important personalities involved in the Tintern enterprise were also supporters of the theatres: the three earls of Leicester, Pembroke and Worcester. The queen herself became a shareholder. Above all, the figure of Sir William Herbert, with his houses at Mortlake and Tintern and his friendship with John Dee, seemed to be a crucial factor. Were these disparate facts or clues to a subtext of hidden truths? It was essential to find out.

CHAPTER 8

Elizabethan Enterprise

O n 3 October 1574 Dee wrote a letter to William Cecil, now Lord Burghley, in which he made an astounding claim, even for a man with his remarkable gifts. In part it reads almost like an early draft of his *Compendious Rehearsal* for Dee begins by complaining that he has not been adequately rewarded for his years of service and boasts that:

> in zeal to the best learning and knowledge, and in incredible toil of body and mind, very many years, therefore only endured, I know most assuredly that this land never bred any man, whose account therein can evidently be proved greater than mine.

He takes care to remind the Lord High Treasurer of his worth because he had just claimed that he will discover a mine of gold or silver in the queen's dominions that will belong to her, on condition that:

> her Majesty do freely give unto me, by good warranty and assurance of her letters patents, her right and propriety to all treasure trouvé, and such things commodious, as . . . by digging or search, anywhere, in her Grace's kingdoms and dominions, I, or my assignees, shall come to, or find.[1]

So certain was he, that he offered Burghley half the proceeds. However, the licence he hoped to obtain was not forthcoming.

Burghley had been interested in mining for precious metals in England and Wales since the early 1560s. It was only with his approval and on his advice to the queen that the Company of the Mines Royal was set up in 1565. A letter showing the extent of Cecil's involvement was written in April 1566 by Daniel Hechstetter, a German partner in the enterprise. He wrote to Alderman Lionel Duckett, one of the chief investors from the City:

> It is joyful news to hear that Mr. Secretary Cecil has shown himself so friendly and forward in this our works and that his money hath been so ready with the first and

also so willing for their next payment. They had hoped the Earl of Leycester would have been the same.[2]

Duckett was a leading figure in the venture. When the Company of the Mines Royal was formally inaugurated in May 1568, the alderman was named one of the two governors in tandem with Hechstetter. Another Duckett, Anthony, was appointed a Deputy Governor. Later, when the number of shareholders was increased from twenty-four to thirty-six, a third member of the family, Jeffrey, became one of them. In 1571, Lionel Duckett wrote to Cecil because of the suspicion felt by the native labour force towards the German directors. He asked Cecil to appoint two Englishmen to supervise the interests of the English shareholders and emphasised the need for the injection of more English capital.

At some time before 1579 Dee became financially indebted to Lionel Duckett. A diary entry for 3 October 1579 records: 'Sir Lionel Duckett his unkind letter for money.' By this time Dee had become involved in Duckett's mining concerns and evidence for this can be found in a later investment by Dee. In 1583 Sir Lionel (as he now was) extended his mining interests to Cardiganshire, Cornwall and Devon, and we know Dee was a part of this enterprise. We have already looked at a diary entry for 13 May 1583; the last part of it is now much more meaningful:

I became acquainted with Albert Laski at 7½ at night, in the Earl of Leicester his chamber in the Court at Greenwich. This day was my lease of Devonshire mines sealed at Sir Lionel Docket's house.[3]

Ten days later he wrote:

23 May . . . I made prayer both in my oratory and at my desk rendering thanks for E.K. his safe return and for the benefit received of late of the governor and assistants for the Mines Royal (which I perceived was the extraordinary working of God for their inward persuasion: they being else very unwilling so to let the lease, as I obtained it. . .)[4]

Dee's choice of words in the second entry tells us that he is writing about a lease not shares. His mining interests have attracted less attention than his other activities and actual records are scarce, but his own diary is clear. Leasing a mine indicates a very different level of commitment from taking out a share. The Governor of the Mines Royal at this time was none other than Dee's respected and powerful neighbour, Sir Francis Walsingham. Within a span of fifteen years two of Dee's close associates, Lionel Duckett in 1568 and 'Good Sir Francis' in 1583, were governors of the organisation. Thus, without having an official position himself, Dee was well placed to play a role of influence at the top of the company.

One wonders where Dee, so often hard-pressed for money, got the wherewithal to purchase a lease. It looks as though he either borrowed or, more probably, was allowed to owe the purchase money in expectation of a very swift return for an 'input' in an advisory capacity, and that Walsingham vouched for his probity. As Governor of the Mines Royal, Walsingham's opinion would carry the day. (We saw Dee's confidence about the rewards from mining in his letter to Cecil of 1574.) Certainly Dee owed money to Duckett's estate for in 1590 another diary entry reads:

July 10, the executor of the Lady Duckett required the debt.[5]

Lady Duckett died that year and Sir Lionel had predeceased her. Understandably the executors of the estate called in any monies owed. Whether this particular sum was a later debt or the old one referred to in 1579 is not clear, but Dee was certainly involved in the mining enterprises of Lionel Duckett from an early stage.

The number of Ducketts mentioned in the records of the Company of Mineral and Battery Works shows the extent of the family's financial commitment. Yet another member, Richard, seems to have joined the enterprise and settled at Chapel Hill, close to Tintern Abbey and the site of the brass-works. Described as a 'yeoman', he is listed as a witness in one of the many enquiries into the sharp practices of Richard Hanbury which took place in the 1590s. One of the local dignitaries before whom Richard Duckett gave evidence at Chepstow was Henry Herbert, another of the Herbert/Pembroke dynasty. From the beginning, the contemporary records of mining at Tintern contain frequent references to friends, associates or patrons of John Dee.

ADRIAN GILBERT

One of the names linking Dee with both the mines and the Herberts was that of Adrian Gilbert. We looked at his connection with Mary, Countess of Pembroke, in Chapter Three. In addition, Dee's extensive knowledge of contemporary geography had led to him being engaged as an adviser for several voyages of discovery and in 1583 he formed a project with Adrian Gilbert and John Davis to colonise and develop North America and to convert the 'natives'.

Through the early 1580s we find frequent references to Gilbert and Davis in Dee's diaries at a time when Gilbert seems to have been based in Devon. The historian Dr W. Rees talks about 'two prospectors Gilbert and Popple' who had great success in re-opening a lead mine at Combe Martin in Devon. According to Rees,[6] the mine proved 'singularly rich and was said to have yielded a return of £10,000 to each of the partners for two years and £1,000 during the year 1590'. These two men may well be the same as the 'Mr Adrian Gilbert and Mr Pepler' who had visited Dee in May 1583 and then rode back 'into Devonshire'.[7] Moreover, four days after Dee returned from Prague in 1589, he recorded that:

> Mr Adrian Gilbert came to me to Mortlake, and offered me as much as I could require at his hands, both for my goods carried away and for the mines.[8]

The following month, Dee recorded writing two letters to Gilbert on the same day, but neglected to say what their contents were. The relationship between Dee and Gilbert was close and complex. He was one of the few people who were permitted to witness Dee's practical experiments with the cabala, so he was aware of some of Dee's most secret activities. Yet, it would appear from the diary entry above that he did not hesitate to plunder Dee's home at Mortlake for books and other items while he was on the continent. Did he feel entitled to do this precisely because Dee had chosen to try his fortune abroad and was no longer near to advise him personally either on his proposed voyage to America or on the alchemical interests that were to occupy his later years? Recently scholars have proved that John Davis, the navigator and the two men's mutual friend, had helped himself to a number of Dee's books.[9] He had been part of the plan to colonise North America. In addition, Gilbert readily associated with Dee in the mining venture and sought to buy him out at an opportune moment.

Dee's attitude to Gilbert over the years was somewhat uneasy. They had a serious quarrel and, although they were reconciled, Dee's commitment to the mining venture appears ambivalent. Did he feel that Gilbert had presumed too much upon him?

SIR PHILIP SIDNEY

Dee signed the lease for the Devonshire mines at Sir Lionel Duckett's house in May 1583. That same year, between January and July, Ambrose Dudley, Earl of Warwick, was busy petitioning Burghley for an official government post for his nephew, Philip Sidney. At the same time, Sir Henry Sidney, his personal fortune depleted in the service of the queen, was strenuously negotiating the marriage of Philip to the daughter of Francis Walsingham. All he could offer Walsingham was the promise of his son's abundant talents. Fortunately, Warwick was successful in his petitioning, and Philip started that same year in a minor post at the Ordnance Office. After two years he was appointed joint Master of the Ordnance with his uncle Warwick. Since Sidney would now be responsible for the supply of cannon and artillery to government forces, this was no doubt a welcome and useful appointment from the point of view of his father-in-law, who was now Governor of the Mines Royal and

53. Sir Philip Sidney, 1554–86. Soldier, statesman and poet, son-in-law of Sir Francis Walsingham, he was responsible with his uncle for the supply of artillery to Elizabethan armies.

therefore in the business of supplying sheet metal for 'battery' or ordnance. When one considers that Philip's sister Mary had married the Earl of Pembroke, and that her father had gone to the expense of repairing the Pembroke effigy in Dublin because of his newly acquired family connections, there seems little doubt that the metal required for ordnance would now be produced at Tintern. There is, of course, nothing new in this display of 'Elizabethan networking'. It is one more example of a phenomenon observable in every age and at almost any level of society. However, the realisation that the personalities involved in these commercial activities, namely the Bacons, Herberts, Sidneys and John Dee, were also connected with, or part of, the intellectual and literary circles of the day, encouraged me to pursue the connection between the brass plates and the theatre drawings.

In the previous chapter we saw that there were identical matches between the drawings and the plates and that some of the illustrations were prints from the plates. Furthermore, Dr Northover in his report had acknowledged that the brass could date from mid-sixteenth century. Evidence from the early history of the brass-works at Tintern pointed to it as the source of the plates themselves. If the natural ores were not good enough, the company at the Tintern brass-works had the professional expertise and incentive to obtain whatever they needed to produce good quality plates.

SIR WILLIAM HERBERT OF ST JULIAN'S

Because of his relationship with John Dee, Sir William Herbert of St Julian's plays a key role in the provenance of the brass plates. Here was a man with a splendid ancestral home at St Julian's, near Newport, a house in Mortlake not far from Dee, and another home which he had inherited, at Tintern. He was also a shareholder in the Mines Royal at Tintern. An entry in Dee's diary for 31 May 1579 reads as follows:

> Sir William Herbert of Saint Julian's at 12 o'clock. He set off at two toward London.[10]

Unexceptional on the face of it, the entry becomes noteworthy because in the original text the first sentence is written with Greek letters substituted for their English equivalents – a clear indication that Dee wished to conceal the meeting, which lasted two hours, from prying eyes. The second sentence is half in Latin, half in English. What was it that Dee wished to hide? Why record the meeting at all? The two men shared an interest in the Monad and in the Mines Royal. Perhaps it was their work together on the Monad that Dee wished to keep secret. Dee had joined the household of the Earl of Pembroke in 1552. Now twenty-seven years later he was intimately involved with another Herbert. Furthermore, Dee was still recording Herbert's visits to Mortlake in February 1581, and again in December the same year, when he brought with him 'Mr. Bromley', the son of the Lord Chancellor.

The men became such good friends that Dee simply noted the visits that were remarkable for one reason or another, such as the occasion when one of his servants, Robert Gardner, asked permission to join Sir William's household, evidently at the prompting of Herbert himself. Gardner had been employed by Dee as his alchemical assistant. His removal to the Herbert household would surely have been because of his expertise, particularly since alchemy was one of Sir William's avowed interests. Did he wish to use these skills for some reason at Tintern? It is known that Herbert hoped to set up a 'college' of some sort there. Had he already made a first tentative effort with this project?

Certainly the two families grew close enough for their children to play together. In 1582, Dee recorded a charming glimpse of Elizabethan children:

> 22, 23 Jan. Arthur Dee and Mary Herbert, they being but three year old, the eldest, did make as it were a show of childish marriage, of calling each other husband and wife.[11]

Expert astrologer as he was, Dee was so taken by the children's make-believe over these two days that he noted the propitious conjunction of Jupiter and Moon at the time, which apparently foretold 'wealthy wife, and marriage with a person of great birth'.[12] This augured well for his son's prospects. If in later years Dee looked back to this incident, he may well have considered that the omens had not been far wrong. When he moved to Manchester to be Warden of the Collegiate Church, he took his family with him and naturally became acquainted with many of the local gentry. Arthur married Isabel Prestwich, daughter of Edmund Prestwich of Hulme Hall and sister of Sir Thomas Prestwich, Bart. – not as wealthy as the stars foretold, perhaps, but still a thoroughly good match. Arthur made his own fortune as a doctor and became personal physician to Charles I. And what of Mary Herbert? She has her part to play in the story.

Her father, Sir William, was a zealous Protestant and loyal subject of the queen. In 1588, he wrote to Walsingham that he was anxious to show his affection for God and his prince by, among other things, 'a colony of my planting'. This he created in Ireland in an effort to help secure the Protestant supremacy. He was allotted lands once belonging to the earls of Desmond and set about colonising them with loyal English settlers, forbidding the Irish to practise a number of their customs and trying to persuade them to abandon Catholicism in favour of the Anglican settlement. Whatever we may think of such a policy today, there were people in authority in Ireland prepared to assure Burghley and Walsingham that Herbert treated the Irish with more consideration than many of the other Elizabethan colonisers.

EDWARD, LORD HERBERT OF CHERBURY

By the time he died, Sir William Herbert's wealth was considerable; it included his estates in Ireland, land in Anglesey and Caernarvonshire, as well as St Julian's. On her marriage his daughter Mary would certainly have been described as a 'wealthy wife' but only if she agreed to her father's wishes and married another Herbert. Sir William was able to trace his pedigree directly and legitimately back to the first Herbert earl of Pembroke and he was proud of it. His own two sons had died from rat poison he had put down on the shelves of his library and which they had mistaken for sugar candy. Despite, or because of, this he was determined that his estate should remain within the family, as the litany of clauses in his long and detailed will made clear. He died in 1593 and eventually in 1599 the conditions he had laid down were met when Mary married Edward Herbert, afterwards Lord Herbert of Cherbury. Edward was a distant cousin from the collateral line of the Herberts of Montgomery. In his autobiography he describes how the alliance was made:

Mary, after her father died, continued unmarried until she was one and twenty; none of the Herberts appearing all that time, who, either in age or fortune, was fit to match her. About this time I had attained the age of fifteen, and a match at last being proposed, yet, notwithstanding the disparity of years betwixt us, upon the eight and twentieth of February 1599 . . . I espoused her. Not long after my marriage I went again to Oxford, together with my wife and mother, who took a house and lived for a certain time there; and now, having a due remedy for that lasciviousness to which youth is naturally inclined, I followed my book more close than ever, in which course I continued until I attained about the age of eighteen.[13]

Like so many of the Herberts, Edward was cursed with a singularly handsome appearance. His looks were praised by Queen Elizabeth and many of the wives at the Court of King James were susceptible to his charms. Copies of his portrait were in great demand. After ten years of marriage, Edward abandoned fidelity to his wife to enjoy numerous conquests. He served in the forces of the Prince of Orange against the Spanish, sharing the characteristic Herbert anti-Catholic sentiments. During an interval in the campaign he travelled to Heidelberg, becoming another supporter of Frederick of the Palatinate. While in Italy he went to Florence to meet Robert Dudley, the son of the Earl of Leicester and an engineer of some note. Edward himself had a wide range of interests, including mechanical inventions.

Not surprisingly, Edward's popularity was not confined to Court circles. He could boast a number of serious writers among his friends – John Donne, Ben Jonson and Thomas Carew – and his learning and wit won genuine admiration. A volume of his own verse, collected together by his brother Henry, was published after his death in 1665, although it lacks the distinction of his brother George's poems. In short Edward's life conformed in its own way to the characteristic Herbert mix of politics, literature and science. George, a genuine if minor poetic talent, was a close friend of Francis Bacon. Since Edward had literary pretensions as well as 'scientific' interests in common with Bacon, the two men are likely to have known each other. Indeed, Herbert-and-Bacon connections are many and varied.

When Sir George Buck was removed from office as Master of Revels because of insanity it was to Edward's brother, Henry, that Buck's successor sold the position. Henry carried out the duties from 1623 to the closure of the theatres in 1642. As master, he considered he had the right to license every kind of public entertainment in the kingdom from plays to performing elephants. So, right up to the closure of the theatres and the beginning of the Commonwealth, we see one generation of Herberts after another supporting or involved with theatre companies, actors, playwrights and poets.

THE PEMBROKES, THE THEATRE AND MINING

The Herbert family link with the theatre started modestly with William, the first Herbert earl of Pembroke whose future and fortune were assured when Henry VIII married Herbert's sister-in-law, Katherine Parr. His great house at Wilton was built on the land of an abbey suppressed by the king and, on this occasion, given to him. During the reign of Elizabeth, the earl's loyalty was questioned on more than one occasion, but the queen appointed him Lord Steward, a position he held from 1567 to 1570, and as such he was responsible, among other things, for entertaining the lords of Parliament at Court whenever Parliament met. However, even before he was raised to the nobility in 1550, and when he was simply Sir William Herbert and unable to read or write, he took into his service William Hunnis, poet and playwright, later Master of the Children of the Chapel Royal and in that capacity responsible for a troupe of boy actors. Hunnis became a protégé of the Earl of Leicester and contributed verses to Leicester's lavish entertainment of Elizabeth at Kenilworth. Long before then, however, Earl William frequently entertained Elizabeth at his London home, Baynard's Castle, arranging for a masque to be performed there in her honour in 1562. He was also the patron of Jasper Heywood who in 1561 translated into English verse Seneca's tragedy *Hercules Furens*, which he prefaced with an epistle dedicated to the earl. Along with Henry Stanley, Earl of Derby, William Herbert was made a Knight of the Garter in 1574.

We looked at the company of actors kept by Henry Herbert, the second Earl of Pembroke, in Chapter 5. His third marriage to the young Mary Sidney only strengthened his literary interests, possibly widening them further. In her life of Mary, Margaret Hannay draws attention to 'the marked increase of dramatic performances at Shrewsbury' when Henry was Lord President of the Council of the Marches of Wales and Shrewsbury was one of the customary meeting places for that council.[14] In 1591 Mary herself translated a play by the French writer Robert Garnier entitled *Marc Antoine*, and commissioned the poet Samuel Daniel, at one time tutor to her sons, to write a sequel, *Cleopatra*. The actor Simon Jewell mentions Mary as a patron in his will, and Henry's interest in drama extended to attending a performance of *Meleager*, one of William Gager's Latin plays, at Christ Church, Oxford, with the Earl of Leicester and Philip Sidney. Gager dedicated this play to Henry and another, *Ulysses Redux* to Mary. Arthur Massinger, the father of the playwright Philip Massinger, was a member of Henry's household. The historian of the Elizabethan theatre E.K. Chambers describes him as a 'confidential servant'. Philip Massinger later enjoyed the patronage of Henry's son, Philip, the fourth earl.

An interest in and support for the theatre was clearly carried on from one generation to the next. Mary's interest appears to have been in promoting plays with

54. Mary Sidney (Herbert), 1561–1621, Countess of Pembroke. Patron of players, translator of plays, mother of 'the incomparable pair of brethren'.

a political content. The two plays on Antony and Cleopatra by their very subject were bound to comment on the conflict between public duty and private pleasure. When the satirist Thomas Nashe and Ben Jonson joined forces to write *The Isle of Dogs* in 1597, it was performed by a company under the second Earl of Pembroke's patronage, and the subversive content led to an outburst of anger by the city authorities as well as the Privy Council who banned the public performance of any more plays in London that summer.

The Pembroke patronage of Elizabethan drama culminated, of course, in the 'incomparable pair of brethren'. William became the patron of Ben Jonson, whose play *Sejanus* (1603) resulted in him being summoned before the Privy Council; when it was published in 1605 it carried a dedication to William. The young earl also intervened to help the players who had been imprisoned for performing Thomas Middleton's play *A Game of Chess* with its anti-Spanish sentiments. In addition, Samuel Daniel, once the brothers' tutor, caused trouble by a pointed reference to the fall of Essex when he wrote: 'The fall of such a mighty Peere/ Doth shake the state'. From the days of Philip Sidney, the Herberts had adopted a strong anti-Catholic position in politics and this was reflected in their attitude to literature. Scholars have noted Philip Herbert's tendency to scribble in the margins of books as a sign of his intemperate and irascible nature. More recently, an examination of his comments in

55. William Herbert,1580–1630, third Earl of Pembroke. Patron of Ben Jonson, protector of actors, and joint owner of the iron/brass-works at Tintern. He was one of the two dedicatees of the *First Folio*.

the margin of *The Conspiracie and Tragedy of Charles Duke of Byron* shows 'his alliance with the anti-Spanish party and his support of military intervention on behalf of continental Protestants, the Count Palatine in this case'.[15] In other words the Herberts clearly saw the usefulness of drama as a means of making political points by analogy with known historical events.

William, the third earl's interests were wide. His mother's laboratory at Wilton no doubt provided an informed background to his involvement in mining. He became Governor of the Society of London for Mineral and Battery Works in 1604 and later obtained government protection for waterworks erected at Trellech, in the hills just above Tintern, in October 1607. The Angiddy river, so vital to the mining and brass-making enterprise at Tintern, ran between the estates of the two great earls of Worcester and Pembroke. It formed a natural boundary and provided the power for the first water-driven wire works in Britain. They remained entirely water-powered. The success of the enterprise depended entirely on the waterworks at Trellech, hence the need for government protection.

As early as 1566 the first earl William had shown that he was well disposed towards these new mining ventures. More, so it would seem, than the Earl of Worcester, who was too ready to strike a hard bargain. Dr Rees goes so far as to state that 'it was unfortunate that the works were not erected on the north side, within the lordship of Trellech, which then belonged to the Earl of Pembroke, always a good friend to the company'.[16] This remained true of William's successors, for by February 1630 the Pembrokes had granted the company a seventy-year lease on woodland abutting the north bank of the river and permission to use the bank, dams and ponds on their side of the boundary. William had also agreed that the firm could build:

> all manner of workhouses, mills or houses, for the drawing or making of the wire of iron steel or latten or for any of their iron or latten battery works . . . this at the nominal rent of 40s a year.[17]

The first earl had been a patron and friend of John Dee and his interests show Dee's influence. Earl William and his two immediate successors, his son, Henry, and grandson, William, all became financially involved with the merchant adventurers in the search for new lands and new wealth which, as we saw earlier, was part of Dee's dream for a great British empire. The first Earl William was a partner in Hawkins' trade in slaves to the West Indies. Earl Henry with his wife, Mary, had shares in Frobisher's attempt to find a north-west passage to China. William, the third earl, was involved in a number of maritime adventures, including setting up the North-West Company in 1612 and the Bermudas Company in 1615. He also invested heavily in the East India Company. Philip, the fourth earl, interested himself in the colonisation of North America and had shares in the North-West and East India Companies.

All these activities were practical consequences of Dee's teaching and, of course, the influence of Adrian Gilbert who, before turning to concentrate on alchemy, had been a navigator and voyager. What tales did he tell William and Philip at Wilton of his experiences abroad and his association with John Dee? Is it surprising that members of the family probably listened to Dee himself over the years when he spoke of other schemes dear to his ever-inventive mind: the search for minerals in England and the revival of cabalistic ideas on the continent, which he believed should underpin the design of the playhouse?

Philip Herbert, the fourth earl, was a very handsome man and soon became a favourite of the new monarch James I. His main interests at the time of James's accession were hunting and field sports. Later he developed a love of the visual arts of painting and architecture, but he continued to be a generous patron to the playwright, Massinger, and his widow. Philip built up a magnificent collection of paintings. At Wilton he carried out extensive alterations with the help of the brilliant engineer and architect, Salomon de Caus, who had worked for the young Prince Henry and Elizabeth of Bohemia. Philip's personable gifts were unfortunately outweighed by a violent temper and foul tongue that earned him many enemies.

56. Philip Herbert, 1584–1650, fourth Earl of Pembroke. Patron of the playwright Philip Massinger, the second of the two dedicatees of the *First Folio*.

However, King James initially overlooked these faults and Philip cut a considerable figure at Court. Both he and his brother in turn were appointed Lord Chamberlain. Both acquired vast wealth. Both were active in different ways at the centre of politics, although later in his career Philip was driven to champion the cause of parliament against the king. Yet, despite their grand London homes, their duties at Court and the power they undoubtedly gathered to themselves, they maintained a close and positive interest in activities in Tintern, certainly until 1630.

THE EARLS OF WORCESTER

There was another family of noble landowners at Tintern whom we met earlier and must return to now. They were the earls of Worcester. We saw that at the Dissolution of the Monasteries, Henry Somerset, Earl of Worcester, was given the bulk of the lands belonging to Tintern Abbey and its outlying estates in South Wales. Henry's father was patron of the abbey at the time of its suppression and although this did not constitute a 'right' to the lands, it may have played a part in encouraging Henry VIII's gift. The earl already had two important castles at Chepstow and Raglan and therefore felt no need to convert the abbey into a splendid new mansion, but the estates increased his wealth considerably.

Henry's eldest son, William, third Earl of Worcester, was patron of a theatre company that toured the provinces. One of its members was Edward Alleyn, in 1583 still a youth of sixteen. It was this troupe of players who entertained Shakespeare's father when he was bailiff at Stratford in 1568. Later, as we saw, it amalgamated with the Earl of Pembroke's players.

Edward Somerset, the fourth Earl of Worcester, although a devout Roman Catholic was a powerful figure at the Court of Elizabeth. She appointed him Master of Horse on the downfall of Essex, who had kept him prisoner at Essex House when Somerset arrived to thwart his attempted uprising. Edward also became patron of a company of actors which, unlike his father's, played before the queen. In 1602 the Privy Council, seeking to limit the number of London companies to two, ordered the players of the earls of Oxford and Worcester to be 'ioyned by agrement togeather in one companie'[18] and to play only at the Boars Head. It would appear from Henslowe's diary that the company, now called 'my lorde of Worsters men', were on his books and performed at the Rose. In May 1603 there is a note for an advance to 'The Earle of Worcesters players at the Rose'.[19]

STUART PATRONAGE AND THE HERMETIC LEGACY

By February 1604, early in the reign of James I, the patronage of Worcester's company had passed to Queen Anne, and the 'Queenes Majesties Players', performed at Court and the Red Bull in London, as well as in the provinces. All three of the royal children were fond of theatrical entertainment. Prince Henry, Prince Charles and Princess Elizabeth each became patron of a troupe of players.

Prince Henry's company was formed in 1603 and he maintained a troupe until his untimely death in 1612. It was taken over by Frederick, the Elector Palatine, then in England and husband-to-be of the Princess Elizabeth. Charles now succeeded as Prince of Wales and heir to James I, but even before that, from 1608, he had his own company known as 'The Duke of York's Men'. After Henry's death, they were styled 'The Prince's Men' and appeared frequently at Court before Charles and his sister. We looked briefly at her players, 'The Lady Elizabeth's Men', earlier.

What we see when we examine the Jacobean and Caroline theatre is a continuation of the aristocratic patronage begun in Elizabeth's time. There was also a continuation of belief in the hermetic–cabalistic ideas that had attended the birth of the Elizabethan playhouse. Accordingly, it is necessary to look at some of the major figures of the period afresh because the convergence of interests we have witnessed at Tintern spreads out again into the country at large.

For example, after the Restoration in 1660, the head of the Worcester dynasty, Edward Somerset, returned from exile as the second Marquis of Worcester to devote his last years to the study of mechanical devices. In this he was heir to the ground-breaking work of Dee in his 'Preface' to Billingsley's translation of Euclid. Edward, Lord Herbert of Cherbury, had earlier displayed a similar interest in mechanics and 'science', which can also be traced back to Dee's influence. These men could be said to be following in the footsteps of Robert Dudley, Earl of Leicester, a prime example of an English Renaissance aristocrat, combining a keen interest in mechanical inventions and a love of the theatre. Leicester's company of actors ushered in the dawn of the great age of Elizabethan drama. A similar breadth of *active* interest was displayed by his fellow nobles, the Derbys, Pembrokes, and Worcesters.

The same legacy can be glimpsed in the young Prince Henry, who looked back nostalgically to the 'golden age' of Elizabeth, while bringing the French garden architect de Caus to England to work for him. Typically, too, Francis Bacon – who bridged the reigns of Elizabeth and James I – not only encouraged the development of scientific thinking but was also active in producing entertainments and masques.

The temporary victory of the Puritans and the establishment of the Commonwealth destroyed popular theatre. With the return of the monarchy, the interest in science or 'natural philosophy' found an outlet in the meetings of the Royal Society, but the more spiritual elements of hermeticism which had inspired the Elizabethan theatre movement remained underground, emerging at times, for example in the work of Boyle and Newton, both of whose alchemical interests were in the tradition of Dee.

In addition to support for acting companies, there are traces of the hermetic tradition in the Stuart patronage of painters and artists. Among the artists who painted Charles II and James II in their youth were Joachim von Sandrart and Michel Le Blon. Both men had known hermetic connections. They were cousins, prominent engravers and painters. Sandrart had been trained by Mathaeus Merian and Johann Theodore de Bry and both spent some time in England. Prior to 1627 Sandrart worked for Charles I painting copies of portraits of Henry VIII, Sir Thomas More and Erasmus, among others, for the art collection of the Earl of Arundel. One of Le Blon's English clients was the Duke of Buckingham, the great favourite of James I. Le Blon was appointed Swedish ambassador to the English Court, a position that undoubtedly involved him in espionage and shows how frequently he must have been in the country. Beneath one portrait he is described in French as 'Agent to the Queen of Sweden [Christina] and His Majesty the King of Britain [Charles I]'.

Le Blon is important in reconstructing the 'pedigree' of the Byrom Collection, because it includes eleven geometric drawings bearing his initials – 'MLB'; there are also in existence engravings commissioned from him in 1615 by Gerard Thibault which are directly related to other drawings in the collection.[20] There is evidence from these that Le Blon could have been in London working on plans for the rebuilding of the Globe after it had been destroyed by fire, and also on the Hope (1613/14). Moreover, as we saw earlier, he was related by marriage to Merian who engraved a panoramic view of London showing Bankside with the theatres in position.

Le Blon's role as 'agent' or spy reminds us of the widespread network of espionage prevalent through the reigns of Elizabeth and her successor. Becoming a spy was one way in which many ambitious men lacking the advantage of high birth could find advancement. Dee's friend 'Good Sir Francis Walsingham' built up and developed a network of formidable power. After his death in 1590 that network came to an end, but spies were available for work and one person who set about hiring them was Francis Bacon on behalf of Elizabeth's current favourite, the Earl of Essex. One of his most notable recruits was the notorious Thomas Phelippes, Walsingham's chief code-breaker who had entrapped Thomas Babington and, through him, Mary, Queen of Scots. Phelippes became the Earl of Essex's chief operator and was engaged in attempts to discredit Sir Walter Raleigh. Phelippes' influence with Bacon grew in consequence, so much so that when Edward Somerset wanted to meet Bacon, he sent a servant, William Sterrill (himself a spy), to Phelippes to say that he was 'desirous to be acquainted with Mr. Francis Bacon by your means'.[21]

The work of spies serving in the households of men like Worcester and Essex was a logical extension of the secret meetings about codes that went on years earlier between John Dee and Sir William Herbert at Mortlake. In this connection we should note that in August 1582 Dee recorded an intriguing visit from 'Mr. Bacon, Mr Phillips of the Custom House'. Thomas Phelippes (who chose to spell his name differently from his father) was the son of the customs inspector at Leadenhall and had entered Walsingham's service in 1578. By the time Walsingham died he had become indispensable. Espionage in the hands of men like Phelippes and Walsingham could bring about the downfall of the highest in the land.

A COLLEGE AT TINTERN

Of all the Herberts who had featured so far in my researches, the one who occupied my thoughts most was Sir William Herbert of St Julian's. His long friendship with John Dee, his interest in Dee's Monad and philosophical ideas, his own experiments in alchemy and avowed wish to establish a 'college' indicated a man with a determined agenda which he intended to complete and which, by its very nature, was linked with Tintern and the activities at the brass-works. After all, he was a shareholder. Why else keep a property in Tintern when St Julian's was not all that distant? I was reminded of Dee's desire to find a suitable setting for a college of his own where men could come and go without being noticed. Dee had his reasons for secrecy. No doubt Sir William did too. It was not by accident that he chose a spot like Tintern. The countryside was remote enough but could be reached easily and unobtrusively by water.

Reflecting on the long-established Herbert interest in the players' companies, science in general and the brass-works at Tintern in particular, it seemed logical that the advantage to Sir William Herbert of having property in Tintern was associated with those brass-works, and the brass plates which I believe were made there. The cabalistic ideas Sir William had imbibed at Mortlake in discussion with Dee appear throughout the series of theatre drawings and on the brass plates that accompany them. Indeed, the philosophical truths of the drawings were no doubt part of the programme that he wished to impart to the privileged few whom he planned to attract to his 'college'. Where exactly was Sir William's house likely to have been situated?

Cheek by jowl with the stretch along the River Wye which most people today know simply as Tintern, but which, strictly speaking, formed the parish of Abbey Tintern, is the smaller parish of Tintern Parva. It is heavily wooded on one side of the river and at one time the trees provided regular employment for the small number of inhabitants as skilled wood-cutters, hoop-shavers, etc. Although the small parish church of St Michael was radically rebuilt in 1846, parts of it date from medieval times, and the site had been a place of worship long before the foundation of the abbey. The Celtic saint, Tewdrig, retired to a hermit's cell here in 555 AD and by 765 a Celtic church had been built. A manor house and estate were established in Tintern Parva in the thirteenth century. A house was built, it is believed, by Elizabeth de Burgh and its history is not without distinction. It was here that Queen Isabella stayed in 1326 when her husband Edward II chose to make his last stand against rebel forces at Chepstow Castle. The manor of Tintern Parva, I discovered, belonged later to Sir William Herbert.

When I visited Tintern myself to establish the precise site, the area seemed ideally suited for Sir William's proposed 'college'. It included a house set on a hillside above the church of St Michael, close to which was an ancient landing stage on the banks of the Wye. Visitors could easily arrive via the river, mooring alongside the quay. Such an approach would be safe from prying eyes. It was, in the words John Dee used to describe St Cross at Winchester, 'the more commodious place for the secret arrival of special men'.[22] It may well be that one subject Sir William wished to study and teach at this house was a sophisticated code system. It was, after all, to Walsingham, director of a spy network himself, that he had expressed his wish to set up a 'college'. His old mentor Dee was an adept at codes and acquainted with Thomas Phelippes. Moreover, Sir William had discussed the Monad at length with Dee. Herbert's interest in codes may be the reason for the entry in Dee's diary in May 1579 written in Latin and pseudo-Greek.

As we saw earlier, in his will Sir William left the house to his daughter, Mary, on condition that she married a Herbert. It passed from her to her son, Richard who succeeded his father as Lord Herbert of Cherbury. Richard married Mary Egerton, the daughter of the Earl of Bridgewater, and, in February 1640, sold the house and estate to yet another Herbert kinsman.

THOMAS HERBERT OF TINTERN

This man, Thomas Herbert, had been a protégé of the head of the family, the Earl of Pembroke, and later distinguished himself in the service of King Charles I. According to a Ministry of Works guide (1956), it is thought that while Thomas lived at the Tintern Parva estate, he also 'occupied some part of the monastic buildings'. These lay at the other end of the adjoining parish of Abbey Tintern, next door to the brass-works. What was the connection?

Thomas Herbert was born in 1606 in York, where a branch of the Herberts had settled as merchants. He was descended from an illegitimate line of the family but decided early in life to establish links with his grander kinsman William, the third Earl of Pembroke. Certainly William was well placed to help him and, generously

57. Sir Thomas Herbert, 1606–81. Loyal servant to Charles I in his last days and one-time owner of the manor of Tintern Parva.

recognising the relationship, in 1626 obtained a post for Thomas on the staff of the British ambassador to Persia, Sir Dodmore Cotton. Unfortunately Cotton died and the embassy was aborted, but the journey to Persia and Thomas's travels in the East on the way home furnished him with enough material for a book which he later published. Thomas arrived back in England at the end of 1629. Shortly after, on 10 April 1630, his patron, Pembroke, died suddenly of an apoplexy after dining on a 'full and cheerful supper' and Thomas lost a valuable protector.

He appears to have turned for help to another kinsman, this time on his mother's side: Lord Fairfax of Cameron. Fairfax was the leader of the parliamentary army in the Civil War, and it is not surprising that Thomas joined the Parliamentarians, the more so since Philip Herbert, now the fourth Earl of Pembroke, was also being driven by circumstance into the same camp. It was through Philip that Thomas was appointed one of the attendants of Charles I after the king was handed over by the Scots at Newcastle in 1647.

As a result of this appointment, Charles entrusted Thomas with the safe delivery of a confidential message to Parliament which Thomas was not to reveal until Parliament itself made it public. Thomas Herbert acquitted himself so loyally that from that moment the king trusted him completely and appointed him a groom of the bedchamber. In this capacity, he stayed with Charles until the end. In fact he was the king's sole companion during the last months of his life, when the rest of his attendants had been dismissed. He slept in the same room as Charles right up to his execution on 30 January 1649. In his memoirs Herbert describes their walk together from St James's Palace to Whitehall and the execution. The king:

> bidding Mr Herbert take with him the silver Clock that hung by the Bedside, said 'Open the Door, Hacker has given us a Second Warning.' Through the Garden the King pass'd into the Park, where making a stand, he ask'd Mr. Herbert the Hour of the Day; and taking the Clock into his hand, gave it him, and bade him keep it in memory of him; which Mr. Herbert keeps accordingly.[23]

After the Restoration, Charles II created Thomas a baronet for services to his father.

Part of the Tintern Parva estate included the building known as 'the abbot's house' because it was thought to have been substantially rebuilt by the last abbot of Tintern, Richard Wyche, after the Dissolution. It stands to the east of the abbey proper, facing what was once the main road, and was evidently at one time a large Tudor mansion. It was not a palace, nor did it bring with it a large estate. Curiously indentures dated 9 February 1640 do not mention the price Thomas paid for the property.

The year 1640 was a trouble-filled one for Royalists. The king's quarrel with the Scots ended in defeat and members of the Long Parliament imposed strict limits on his powers. Thomas would have lived at Tintern with his wife and children until he was recruited to the Parliamentarian cause in 1642. During the Commonwealth, after the death of Charles I, he disappeared from public life to Tintern. Did he have a special function there?

The house stood alongside the old highway from Tintern to Llandogo which still survives as a public footpath. The site is now hidden from the main road and this seems typical of the mystery that surrounds it.

The kindness of Earl William in helping Thomas Herbert at the outset of his career was not misplaced. Thomas proved that beyond doubt in discharging his duty to the king. The day before he died, Charles took care to write a note certifying that Thomas had not been imposed upon him but had been chosen by the king himself and had served with faithfulness and loyal affection. Charles also entrusted to him his personal Bible with the king's handwritten notes in the margin. This he was asked to give to the young Prince Charles 'so soon as he returned'. Herbert was also a prime mover in suggesting that the final resting place for the king should be St George's Chapel, Windsor. In the light of this, one is forced to conclude that his personal merits must have been remarkable. Yet, after carrying out all this sad commission he took no further part on the public stage. Was there another role waiting for him elsewhere, more private but nonetheless important? On his return to Tintern, if he did occupy part of the abbey buildings, then it is most likely that he was acting in a supervisory capacity in charge of certain Herbert interests.

The death of Charles I was the end of an epoch. The return of Charles II the beginning of another. Thomas Herbert straddles both reigns. Whatever his political and religious affinities were when he entered the service of the king, his spirituality was deep and broad enough to encompass the beliefs of his monarch, and, one suspects, of the surviving members of the hermetic tradition so long guarded by John Dee, his aristocratic adherents and Dee's own son, Arthur.

We first met Arthur when he was a child playing with Mary Herbert at Mortlake. As a youth he had been well schooled in his father's beliefs. He had accompanied him on his travels to hermetic centres in Germany, Poland and Bohemia and, after studying medicine, had been recommended by James I, no less, to the Tsar of Russia. After fourteen years at the Russian court he returned home to be appointed one of the physicians-in-ordinary to Charles I. Sir Thomas Browne, a close friend, describes him as a 'persevering student in hermetical philosophy'. The recommendation of James I and Arthur's service with Charles are indicative of continued Stuart interest in the ideas Dee had espoused. Perhaps this was why, in Moscow, Arthur was employed as an agent for the English intelligence network. In addition, he wrote a text tracing the history of the *Secret Hermetick Sciences*. The Latin original, published in Paris in 1631, was translated into English by Elias Ashmole and appeared in 1650. With both

Arthur Dee and Thomas Herbert in the service of Charles I the continuity of the hermetic tradition in England was in good hands.

In this connection we should remember, too, that in addition to being given the silver watch by Charles I, Thomas Herbert had the cloak the king wore on the scaffold and a collection of books that included Charles's personal copy of the 1632 folio edition of Shakespeare. On the flyleaf of this, the king had written 'Dum spiro spero' ('While I breathe, I hope'). To this Thomas added in Latin: 'A gift from his most serene Majesty Charles to his humble servant, T. Herbert'. The cloak was eventually sold by one of Thomas's descendants to Caroline, Princess of Wales, wife of the future King George II. The folio Shakespeare is now in the library at Windsor Castle. I found the fate of this folio deeply moving. That Shakespeare's plays and poems might in some way have brought comfort to the doomed monarch is, perhaps, one measure of their greatness. But there seemed here to be a peculiarly apt and rich resolution of themes, as at the end of a great symphony, when the last royal patron of the first great period of English drama bestowed his own copy of Shakespeare on a member of the dynasty which had been so involved in that extraordinary outburst of theatrical talent. It is strangely symbolic, too, that the king's mantle should come to Princess Caroline, for, with her deep and wide-ranging intellect, she can be regarded as a true inheritor of much hermetic and cabalistic thought.

All that has gone before in this chapter made the involvement of the Herbert dynasty with the Elizabethan theatres and the brass-works at Tintern clearer. The name of Princess Caroline had resonances that called me back to the Boyle collection and the handwritten catalogue in the Science Museum. The catalogue needed to be re-examined. That re-examination brought with it other issues.

CHAPTER 9

A Scrapbook and its Pictures

I frequently studied the handwritten catalogue that accompanied the brass plates in the Science Museum. I was bemused by the seemingly haphazard numerical order of the items – 8, 13, 9, etc. I also noticed that the entry for item 33, which listed 'Forty one Brass Plates Engraved with Astronomical Astrological and Mathematical Delineations', was incorrect since the plates referred to numbered forty-six. Most of the plates were connected in one way or another with those identified as theatre drawings in the Byrom Collection.

I then began to look at other items in this catalogue, most of them held in the same storage area of the museum. I saw enough markings on a few brass solids to recognise their similarity to those on the plates. Photographs of these objects, too, helped in the study of the rest of the material. Among a group of small three-dimensional objects I recognised several brass versions of what seemed to be broached thurnels, a sharply pointed tool used in stone form by ancient masons.

I had already seen the 'German book' referred to in the inventory, filled with illustrations of the five regular solids and other geometrical drawings. It was the work of a Nuremberg goldsmith, Wenzel Jamnitzer, and had been published in 1568. I remembered that this was the year Sir Nicholas Bacon completed his splendid new house, Gorhambury. Later it became carved in my consciousness as the year the brass-works started at Tintern.

A major step in my searches came when I learned that the handwritten inventory had been replaced in 1992 by a splendidly bound, fully illustrated and thoroughly researched catalogue on the George III Collection entitled *Public and Private Science*.[1] This is a very impressive tome produced by two curators of the Science Museum, Dr Alan Morton and Jane Wess, and gives a detailed account of the scientific apparatus which forms the basis of this collection. The objects fall into four main categories: apparatus provided for King George III in 1761–2, equipment used by the scientist Stephen Demainbury in public lectures on natural philosophy, a miscellany of other items collected by the royal family and a later group of items added to the collection in the nineteenth century. Although the collection bears the name of George III, the authors of the catalogue point out that members of the Hanoverian royal family were showing a real interest in 'science' as early as 1716: 'Perhaps Caroline, then Princess of Wales, was most active in pursuing an interest in the fashionable subject of natural philosophy. Her interest arose from her close acquaintance with Leibniz whom she knew before she came to England.'[2] I found this an interesting connection because of Caroline's links with John Byrom.[3] Leibniz was a great mathematician and philosopher, equivalent in stature to Isaac Newton, with whom he became involved in a dispute as to which of them first invented calculus. Leibniz had been a tutor to Caroline who continued to correspond with him even after she came to England in 1714. Caroline of Anspach was one of Britain's most intelligent and learned queens.

I looked through the illustrations in *Public and Private Science* for those of the 'Boyle Collection' and, under the photograph of 'Ms 471', I read the following:

> The manuscript is one of the two corresponding to item 41 on the list of the Boyle Collection; the other appears to have been lost. It is bound in calfskin and contains 12 plates of geometric drawings in ink and crayon; some have been filled in with watercolour. Christ on a cross is superimposed on one drawing.[4]

The last sentence clearly referred to the drawing I had reproduced in *The Byrom Collection* as an example of the iconography of Christian cabala. The entry ended with a reference to my ongoing work on the manuscript, but the catalogue was published before my own text appeared in print. I returned to the phrase 'the other [i.e. manuscript] appears to be lost'. I had done some preliminary work on a manuscript that had been recommended to me separately by the hermetic scholar Adam McClean. It contained drawings similar to those in Byrom's possession and was in the British Library, catalogued under 'Theophilus Schweighardt' because the volume, essentially a scrapbook, contained one printed text, a Rosicrucian pamphlet written in German by a man using that name and published in 1618. The name Theophilus Schweighardt is thought to be a pseudonym and the rather unwieldy title, *Speculum Sophicum Rhodo-Stauroticum*, translates as 'A Wise Man's Mirror into the Institution of the Rose'. On the front of the German pamphlet was written in English 'An Account of the Rosicruc: Fraternity'.

This book, beautifully bound in leather, at one time belonged to the Royal Library presented to the nation by George II. It had joined Sir Hans Sloane's collection of books to become part of the library in the British Museum founded in 1753. It would have included Queen Caroline's library which she housed in a new building at St James's Palace, but never lived to enjoy. When I considered the book's contents afresh, I realised that this was most likely the missing manuscript referred to in the handwritten inventory of the 'Boyle Collection'. It must have become separated while the handwritten catalogue was still considered reliable, and probably for a time had been in the custody of Queen Caroline. Confirmation of this could be seen in the prints of fifteen geometric drawings stuck on separate pages between its covers. Clearly there were drawings and prints in the Byrom Collection and in the Schweighardt scrapbook that were not only identical with each other but also with the brass plates. I noticed that on some prints in the Schweighardt the geometrical lines of the design had been continued from the print on to the page of the book to which it had been attached and that the pattern had been extended outward. Sections of some of them had been highlighted in colour by hand to emphasise certain features. In a word, they had not been simply included but personalised by a former owner. There were drawings in both manuscript books which I considered to be connected with buildings, and in particular the Elizabethan theatres.

A COLLECTION IN THREE PARTS

Taking into account the years I had spent in the study of the drawings and the extent to which the area of my investigations had spread, I was left in no doubt that this material was in no way commonplace. Perhaps it was even unique. Moreover, the Byrom Collection could no longer be taken in isolation. It was part of a larger resource which at one time had been kept all together in one place. The other items I discovered in the Science Museum catalogue are an extension of that resource. Byrom was the catalyst who had brought the material back to life through the formation of his Cabala Club, his election to the Royal Society and his relationship with Queen Caroline. Some drawings connected with activities at his Cabala Club and clearly dated had been added to the collection at some time. Later on, he had been content simply to preserve his part of the collection for posterity – part only, for the material had unfortunately become fragmented and separated off in different directions. Two sections remain in the public domain in national collections. The remaining third, Byrom's, is in private hands and therefore less accessible. Until now each part has been thought of as a separate entity and this raises problems for anyone engaged in their study, as I had rather laboriously found out. For example, the brass plates, despite their permanence, give us few clues at all. The Byrom Collection, much more physically fragile as it is, is heavily dependent on a knowledge of number symbolism, arcane geometry and philosophy.

   With the appearance, or rather reappearance, of the Schweighardt manuscript the picture changed dramatically. My initial interest in the book had been limited to establishing its relevance in what was a general search for the provenance of the geometric drawings it contained. But once these are put alongside the brass plates and Byrom's collection of drawings, it is necessary to view the body of material as a whole. As I said in *The Byrom Collection*, the scrapbook is certainly a very odd compilation of esoteric verses, coloured diagrams, small, extravagantly – some even crudely – executed sketches, symbolic engravings and a handful of geometric drawings.

ILLUSTRATIONS AND SYMBOLS

Earlier I had considered everything in the scrapbook, apart from the geometric drawings, outside my brief in writing a general introduction to Byrom's collection. Now I had to take stock and reconsider the rest of the volume. Either it was simply a scrapbook of miscellaneous items or it had a unity of theme or subject matter which had a bearing on the brass plates and the drawings. I had to consider this as a serious possibility despite the strange appearance of a number of items. The only way to make sense of the material was to find facts on which to focus. I had already recognised the connection of the text with the Rosicrucian movement, a society with claims to knowledge of the Secrets of Nature, alchemy and elemental spirits. One day, I chose to work through a particular set of handwritten verses. In part I was attracted to that particular page by the carefully drawn illustrations in pen and ink which accompanied the words, not only in the left- and right-hand margins, but occupying much of the top half of the page. This quasi-heraldic design, heavy with royal symbolism, was done with such neatness and care that it immediately caught the eye and drew you into the poem:

> Then who first barr of argent balls a law
> Canst cite. Or why he ramps ye Red paw.
> This being penned Next to ye Publick good
> For meer acquaintance wth ye brotherhood.
> Begging this boon at Each readers hands,
> No more to censur than he understands.

Beneath these lines is a square containing the main feature of the illustration, a coat of arms. At the bottom of the square is a heraldic description (blazon) of the devices shown: the red lion rampant with the golden orb of a fire ball and the accompanying colours – red (gules), black (sable), blue (azure) and silver (argent).

A short verse follows, separated off between two straight lines:

> Reader this book to thee doth yeild
> As Judg, who sittest allone sunk into this Sheild.
> The Eagle's turnd to a Lyon first to dance
> wth Sor[t]. Jove & next his pike to advance

In coat of Steel & 3dly haveing wonn
The feild on Vulcan how unto ye sonn
he is Extoll'd, where being spy'd at Game
of Tennis with faire Venus, he for shame
doth Blush & foame wth Aphrodite art
The Heavenly Urne to joy ye Dumpish ♡

The lines contain a reference to a game of tennis. The mention of such sport in an heraldic context seemed incongruous. I was aware of the popularity among Tudor monarchs of real, or royal, tennis. I was aware, too, of the use Shakespeare had made in *Henry V* of a gift of tennis balls as a calculated insult. In this poem, however, the reference seemed to be to a particular game. Then my memory was nudged by an incident recounted by Edith Sitwell in *The Queens and the Hive*, her account of Queen Elizabeth and her conflict with Mary, Queen of Scots:

> At this time, when she was pretending to arrange his marriage with the Queen of Scots, the Scottish Ambassador Randolph had been scandalized by the report in the Scottish Court that while Leycester and the Duke of Norfolk were playing tennis in the presence of the Queen, 'Lord Robert being very hot and sweating, took the Queen's napkin out of her hand and wiped his face,' and that the outraged Norfolk had threatened to break the racket over his head.[5]

For some years I had wondered whether this was a piece of historical fiction invented by Sitwell, particularly since her book was dedicated to a famous Hollywood film director. However, in checking the *Calendar of Scottish Papers*, I discovered the incident actually took place. An account can be found in a letter from Ambassador Randolph to Sir Nicholas Throckmorton, a leading Protestant and supporter of Leicester. It was written on 31 March 1565. Unfortunately the first part of the letter has been lost:

> lately the duke's grace and my Lord of L[eicester] were playing at 'tennes, the Quene beholdinge of them, and my lord Rob[ert] beinge verie hotte and swetinge, tooke the quene's napken owte of her hande and wyped hys face, which the Duke seinge, saide that he was to sawcie and swhore that he wolde laye his racket upon his face. Here upon rose a great troble and the Quene offended sore with the Duke.' The tale is told by Atholl the same day that Fowler came here with his master's licence. We lack no news, for what is most secret among you, is sooner at this Quene's ears, that some would think it should be owte of the previe chambre door where you are! These things so please me that I would your doings were better, or

58. 'The Game of Tennis'.

your titlynge tonges shorter. Bothwell said in F[rance], both the Quenes could not make one honest woman; and for his own, if she had taken any but a cardinal it had been better borne with. Of this you shall know I have written to my lord of Leicester. Edinburgh, 'reddye to ryde to Sterlinge.' signed Tho Randulphe. P.S. See that you take heed to my letters: for if you were as innocent as our Lord Jesus Chryste, if any evle comme to me, I wyll make you partaker.[6]

Both the Duke of Norfolk and Lord Arundel spoke angrily to Leicester, rebuking him about this incident and his behaviour towards the queen, which they considered far too familiar. Later, in 1572, Leicester had the satisfaction of seeing Norfolk executed for his attempted rebellion.

The poem and the accompanying illustration in the Schweighardt scrapbook in which this incident is embedded is numbered at the top of the page 'No. (i)'. This presumably is to be taken as a sign of its place and importance in a sequence. Separated off between that number and the top of the picture are lines of verse quoted above which are addressed both to the individual reader and 'ye brotherhood'. These read like a challenge to interpret the heraldic symbolism which will reveal its meaning to those with 'the understanding'. For the rest, the writer urges the reader to 'censure no more than he understands', the implication being that, if the reader does not understand, then he should refrain from being critical. One important feature that should not be missed is the mark in heavy ink over the word 'argent' in the first line. Argent, the heraldic term for silver, is a symbol of purity. The 'ink mark' over the word is not a careless blemish by the writer of the script which, as can be seen, is neatly and thinly lettered. The mark is a letter from the Hebrew alphabet deliberately written by hand on top of the word as a meaningful addition. This is a device which occurs elsewhere in the scrapbook with other Hebraic letters. Here it is the twenty-second letter, ת, or Tav, the symbol of truth. As we saw in an earlier chapter, the cabala emphasises the mystery of language. It is a gift from God and as such every word, letter or accent in the Torah has layers of significance. According to the cabalist, 'Truth stands more firmly than falsehood'. This belief derives from the fact that: 'the letters of the Hebrew word for "falsehood" all balance precariously on one leg somewhat like an English r, whereas those of the word for "truth" all rest solidly on two feet like h.'[7] This is precisely what we see here with the letter 'Tav'. Another cabalistic device was gematria which gave a numerical value to each letter.

It is clear that in this illustration and poem we have an original piece of work created especially for this volume which expresses its meaning through a variety of complex levels. On the level of historical fact an incident occurred during a game of tennis at Court involving Robert Dudley and the queen. However, before attempting to decide why it should have been included here, I should, perhaps draw attention to another feature on the same page which surprised me. In the right-hand margin a series of dots, which are in fact pin pricks placed at regular intervals, start at the word 'censure' and travel as in a trail down by the side of the two figures to the last word 'was'. Written at the side of this word is an instruction to turn back to the previous page where more verses can be seen. The number of dots from start to finish is seventy-two. They may indicate that the word censure is being used here in a sense now obsolete meaning 'to censor'. In other words everything between the two words is to be censored or kept secret.

My reading of hermetic literature had, of course, made me familiar with the kind of emblematic illustrations which filled the pages of the scrapbook, but I was also aware of the different levels of meaning such emblems contain. In the interests of accuracy, I decided to consult someone whose expertise in iconography had been demonstrated in my first book *The Byrom Collection*: the Reverend Neville Barker Cryer.

Mr Cryer is a senior Freemason and a former secretary and editor of the leading Masonic research lodge, Quatuor Coronati. He is also the author of several books on Freemasonry. I had long since come to value his utter integrity. His association with Freemasonry for over fifty years has made him fully conversant with a mode of thinking and approach to subjects that was once part of the teaching in further education in this country, but that has increasingly been eliminated by modern forms of secular education. Freemasonry, however, has had a great ability to retain the communication of truths by symbol and allegory. It still employs this method to instruct its candidates in the reaches of moral truth and human behaviour so far as it does not infringe the boundaries of personal religious faith. On that it does not feel entitled to comment. In addition, Mr Cryer is also a clergyman and, therefore, has studied the symbolism of the Bible in order to be able to communicate the truths of the scriptures. His dual roles as Freemason and clergyman encouraged him to study related areas of symbolism, such as heraldry and the allegorical meanings of stained-glass windows, carvings and representations in religious literature. These disciplines taught him to look at architectural structures not simply in terms of geometry, although geometry itself has its own symbolic significance.

Not surprisingly Mr Cryer had no difficulty with the 'cartoon-like' impression some of the Schweighardt illustrations give to the unitiated on first encounter. Indeed, his own experience convinces him of the value of retaining symbolism as a way of communicating truths. Even today cartoons are still a potentially important means of conveying ideas on film, by television or in comics. The retention and refinement of such techniques in adult life can, when properly used, continue to help our understanding of symbolism in communication. Accordingly, I asked Mr Cryer for his comments on the illustration that accompanied the 'tennis verses'. He saw this as 'an entry picture' with four figures raised on two pillars at the entrance. He noted the planetary symbols on the robes of the four figures and felt that the fruit they were holding suggested some kind of intermingling among them. He also noted that there were two variant types of coronet. (Four 'finials' on the two left-hand crowns, five on the right.) The intermingling or sharing of the fruit of themselves produces the symbolic figure described as a 'Lyon Rampant' and seen to be holding a golden figure or circle. Alternatively, the emblems signify that the figure on the shield is one that owes its being to the fruit that lasts, for the leaves are suggestive of evergreen life. The richness of this process of receiving or giving is emphasised by the two further bunches of grapes which hang from the intermingling leaves.

As for the words 'First Chapter' that appeared *beneath* the verse about the game of tennis, separated off by a line across the page, we thought their meaning was akin to that of a group of like-minded souls, as in the original monastic sense when monks prefaced their communal meetings with a reading from a chapter in the Bible. (The term was later adopted by Freemasons.) Here the chapter implied some sort of 'brotherhood' such as the one mentioned at the top of the page. Did it mean that the information conveyed in the verses was in some way a beginning, or of basic importance, to this group? There is also another important symbol: a phoenix rising not from ashes but from another coronet, an emblem of a resurgent or resurrected person of royal birth.

We turned to the illustration on the reverse where our attention was caught by the small oblong box that seemed like a key to the drawing. It contained four rows of crosses meticulously drawn. The first row contains nineteen crosses, the second row contains seventeen, the third eighteen and the fourth eighteen. Added together these make a total of seventy-two, and, of course, this side of the page was also pierced with the seventy-two pinpricks. So, this number had a special significance for whoever drew these illustrations, just as it did for the creator of the 'seventy-two measure' used in the geometric drawings concerned with the theatres.

Mr Cryer commented on other features of the reverse page: 'Here the golden orb is once more repeated at the centre of what may be described as a diagrammatic representation of Zoroastrian knowledge.' I was not unduly surprised by the reference to Zoroaster. The beliefs of this spiritual teacher from Persia had been absorbed into the hermetic tradition by Renaissance scholars with so much else from the Middle East. As Mr Cryer pointed out, the words incorporated in these geometric patterns clearly reflected the importance placed on the usefulness of the Platonic bodies in the late sixteenth and early seventeenth century in expressing philosophical ideas. The five regular solids are: cube, tetrahedron, octahedron, icosahedron and dodecahedron. In the dialogue *Timaeus*, Plato explains his belief that the four basic elelments from which the world is made are: earth, fire, air and water. He relates each of the first four

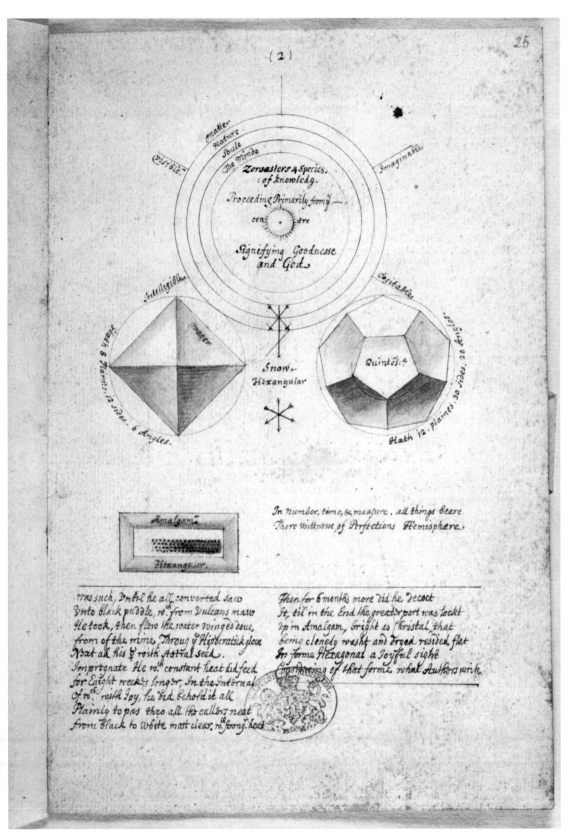

matter
nature
Soule
The minde
Zoroasters 4 Species
: of knowledg.

Proceeding Primarily from ye
cen   tre

Signifying Goodnesse
and God

Sensible

Imaginable

Intelligible

Cogitable

Quater

Quintes:a

Hath 8 Planes. 12 sides. 6 Angles.

Hath 12. Planes. 30 sides. 20 Angles.

Snow
Hexangular

Amalgam̄

Hexangular.

In number, time, & measure . all things beare
There witnesse of Perfections Hemisphære.

was such, Untill he all converted saw
Unto Black puddle, wch from Vulcans maw
He took, then flew the water winged doue
from of the mine. Throug ye Hippocratik gloue
Next all his & roith Astral seed.
Impregnate He wth constant heat did feed
for Eaight weekes longer. In the Internal
of wch with Joy, he did behold it all
Plainly to pas thro all the callours neat
from Black to White most clear: wth strong heat

Then for 6 months more did he decoct
It, til in the End the greater part was lockt
Up in Amalgam, bright as Christal, that
being clenely washt and dryed resided flat
In forme Hexagonal a Joyful sight
Confirming of that forme what Authors write.

59. Reverse of 'The Game of Tennis'.

solids to an element (cube represents earth). Many philosophical ideas developed from these associations.

At this point I paused to consider a likely date for what I was now examining. The historical game of tennis took place in 1565. The scrapbook in which it appears had to be compiled after the Schweighardt paper had been published in 1618. That the anonymous author knew of the incident connected with the game and chose to include it in these pages so many years later posed questions that needed to be answered.

The poem was addressed 'to the brethren'. Who were they? What was the nature of the code being used? I soon learned that the man considered to be the 'father of Western cryptology' was Leon Battista Alberti, one of the most distinguished graduates from Bologna University. The old Latin name for Bologna is Bononia, and in the 'tennis verses' reference is made to 'Thomas of Bononia'. In the context it is clear that this particular Thomas was a cipher man. Alberti was a leading Renaissance architect and polymath who believed ardently in the importance of the laws of proportion and whose treatise *De Re Aedificatoria* (1485) popularised the theories of Vitruvius. It was Alberti who added a new feature to the open-air theatre, an awning painted with stars, to protect the spectators from poor weather and to improve the acoustics. My search for information about ciphers had brought me resolutely back to the design of the classical theatre! Dee, I recalled, was an expert in ciphers and also the driving force behind the English version of the classical theatre with its 'Heavens' above the stage. An understanding of the complexities of the cabala had led both Dee and Alberti to an interest in ciphers. Their knowledge of architecture and mathematics brought them to advocate the same classical concept for the playhouse where the laws of proportion were supreme.

I shall not take the reader through the scrapbook page by page. But we should also look at the very first page, which gives us clues to the theme of the series of drawings and verses that follow. The anonymous author usually chooses to communicate his message in a dual form. Some of the hand-drawn illustrations are coloured, others not. This first illustration with a commentary is entitled 'Ænigma Philosophicum'. Enigma is the key word, for the text is full of paradoxes like riddles, forcing us to decipher what the writer is really saying. From the beginning things are not what they seem and we must remember this as we go through the manuscript. Here the enigma is concerned in some way with the age-old paradox of the relationship between Nature and Art.

These two opposing ideas are placed at opposite sides of the drawing. The drawing itself is an allegory, showing in five stages a transformation which is tantamount to a rebirth. The robed figure in the centre is an alchemist and by means of alchemical symbolism we see a new form of life being created. We move by a specific process

Within the illustration:

NATVRA. ... ET ARTE.

Tunc ME

Ænigma Philosophicum.

There is no Light, but what liues in y̆ sun,
There is no Sun, but which is twice begot
Nature and Art y̆ parants; first begotten
By nature twas; but nature perfects not
Art then what nature left, in hand doth take,
And out of one a Twofold worke doth make,

A Twofold worke doth make, but such a worke,
As doth admit diuision none at all,
See heere wherein y̆ secret most doth lurke,
Vnless it be a Mathamaticall,
jt must be two, yet make it one and one,
And you doe take the way to make it none,

Loe heere the Primar Secret of this Art,
Contemne it not, but vnderstand it right,
Who faileth to Attame this formost part:
Shal neither knowe art's force, nor̃ Nature might,
Ne yet haue power of one, & one soe mixed,
To make of one Fixt, One vnfixed, Fixed,
Vide Theä Chym: Ashmoles 4ᵗᵒ Page 423 W:R:
Est in &c̃ quicquid quærunt Sapientes

1. Whilst I keepe my self shut vp I auaile no body any thing.
2. I suffer my self to be set free. I am the same tho' charged from my
3. I perrish of my one accord by my self, and in my self, & also my self,
4. Then I purefie my self, and rise againe brighter and cleaner,
5. ... and at last I glorefie my self, & triumph in great virtues.

(the alchemist's art) from stage 1, where the man is confined by chain and lock, through to the glorious freedom of stage 5. This being is 'natural' in origin because he comes from Nature, but knowledge and wisdom (Art) transmute him or her into something higher. Art improves Nature. We shall see this stated in different forms in other pages of the scrapbook, and, as it is elaborated, we shall be expected to unravel other emblematic drawings that encode additional, for us even startling, ideas. For example, it is now clear in this picture that alchemy no longer means simply the transmutation of metals. It is clearly concerned with a spiritual change and even hints at a physical one.

Man sees an apparent opposition between Nature and Art, but this is false because what Nature creates, Art can improve and change into a higher form. In this reconciliation of apparent opposites I recognised the presence of an on-going debate of the day which finds clear expression in one of Shakespeare's late plays, *The Winter's Tale* (1610). In Act IV, scene iv, Perdita, a shepherdess (but in reality a Princess, although she does not know it) greets Polixenes, King of Bohemia, father of her suitor, Florizel, with flowers, but has to confess that her garden does not contain the 'fairest flowers of the season' which at that time of year happen to be 'carnations and streak'd gillyvors.' Polixenes asks her why, and Perdita replies:

> *Perdita*
> For I have heard it said,
> There is an Art, which in their piedness shares
> With great creating Nature.

> *Polixenes*
> Say there be:
> Yet Nature is made better by no mean,
> But Nature makes that mean; so over that Art,
> (Which you say adds to Nature) is an Art
> That Nature makes: you see, sweet maid, we marry
> A gentler scion, to the wildest stock,
> And make conceive a bark of baser kind
> By bud of nobler race. This is an Art
> Which does mend Nature; change it rather, but
> The Art itself is Nature.[8]

The two passages present different aspects of the same theme. But both Shakespeare and the anonymous author of the 'Ænigma Philosophicum' scrapbook believe there is an 'Art' that can change Nature for the better. It is no accident that at the end of

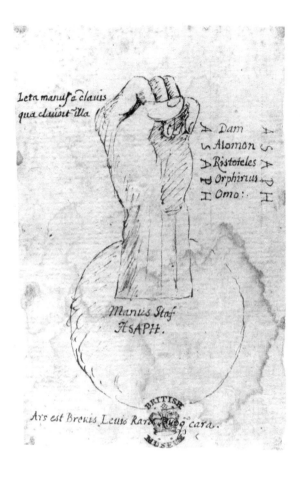

Leta manuf a clauis
qua clauiut illa

Dam
Alomon
Ristoteles
Orphirius
Omo:

Manus Staf
ÆsAPH.

Ars est Breuis Leuis Rara Labor cara.

61. The Symbolic Hand.

The Winter's Tale there is a 'Resurrection', with Hermione, long thought to be dead, 'magically' restored to life by the apparent Art of Paulina.

On the page facing the 'Ænigma' illustration, almost as a companion to it, there appears a fascinating symbol with a double significance. A clenched fist suggests that something is being held tightly or grasped. One is compelled to ask what it could be that is being held in such a tight grasp. Is it some truth that gives the possessor great strength, the strength of such a fist as shown here? I had asked myself this question many times until my attention was drawn by Mr Cryer to the fact that the clenched fist is resting on a base that is not a wrist but a representation of a medieval clamp used for inserting into great stones in order to raise them into the complete and finished building. Once one knows this, then the symbol as a whole suggests that, if truth is to be properly understood, it has not only to be grasped but used to bring the fullness of that knowledge to completion and into its rightful place.

If, then, we were being urged to grasp the truth, I asked myself what particular truths were contained within these pages? I was ready to take on board the spiritual dimension of the alchemical allegory – I had already encountered that in my work on Dee and others. But were there other elements that demanded consideration? Perhaps I should be turning my attention once more to the first discernible fact which I had found – the reference to a game of tennis and its application to Queen Elizabeth and Robert Leicester. Accordingly when I noticed another page with the words 'Dedicated to Q. Elizabeth' on it, it seemed reasonable to think this might be a link and, therefore, this page should be considered next.

The heading at the top of the page is 'The Key of Alchymie Dedicated to Q. Elizabeth'. Again, I include the verse that appears with the illustration for the reader to study at leisure:

> These wch yor Highnes heere doth see
> Are leaves of Hermes secret Tree:
> Through Wisdomes lore warilie bro^t to pass
> By Sowing Seeds in Wombs of Glass.
> And given they are to let you know
> The garden where such fruit doth grow.
> Elixers thre so called of Old.
> For Health of Man. Sun. Moon. Silver. Gold
> This Soile is dew'd by Impe of Saturnes race
> Whose Sire Dame Maija did Imbrace
> The crooked God, whome Loveing Dame did wed
> With heat doth cause our tree to Spread.

Of the picture Mr Cryer said:

The illustration has, it would seem, a double purpose and allusion. On one level the glorious figure, whose face appears at the centre of the picture surrounded by a circle of glory, and from which emerge leaves of growth which indicate the stages of ancient alchemical preparation, would seem to have produced a creature that in one sense could be interpreted as the offspring of Aphrodite, symbolised by the crescent and an infant Hermes with a caduceus and winged helmet as well as winged feet. But while that interpretation might appear to be valid, it is in, some respects faulty. For the apparent figure of the antique or classical Hermes has no caduceus prominently in his arm, but is rather apparently hiding it behind the tree trunk, and the wings of the feet are both incomplete and also falsely attached. In addition the figure begins to reveal some elements of a later characteristic, to wit the nailed feet to the tree and the nailed right hand which suggest a Christian interpretation. In this case, the child or young figure, which is naked and

The Key of Alchymie   Dedicated to Qr Elizabeth

These wch yor Highnes heere doth see
Are leaues of Hermes secret Tree;
Through Wisdomes lore warilie brotopass
By sowing Seeds, in Wombs of Glass.
And giuen they are to let you know
The garden where such fruit doth grow.

Elixers thre so called of Old.
For Health of Man. Sun. Moon. Siluer. Gold
This Soile is dew'd by Impe of Saturnes race.
Whose sire Dame Maija did Imbrace.
The crooked God, whome Ioueing Dame did Wed
with heat doth cause our tree to Spread

The Tree of   Alchyme

62. 'The Key of Alchymie'. Although symbolic, the face in the tree is full of life, particularly the eyes.

unashamed for all the truth to be seen, stands on the crescent Moon that was sometimes interpreted as representing the Virgin Mary.

This could take the whole imagery into a Christian cabalistic area rather than a classical or medieval, alchemical interpretation. And if, as seems very likely, the face at the centre of the glory or aureole of the tree is of a contemporary, noble character, then the alchemical leaves could refer not to a metallurgical process but to the process of creating a new kind of human being. Presumably, the child is intended to be an example. What more might be interpreted in the light of the words written above the tree is for others to comment on. But I would suggest that the picture is capable of this double interpretation.

The title 'The Key of Alchymie' (*sic*) tells us that this illustration, like much else in the book, is presented at a surface level as instruction in the mysteries of alchemy. Each of the leafy branches sprouting in a circle from the tree bears the name of a stage in the alchemical process. In the centre of the tree can be seen the face of a man. But it appears to me to be that of a particular man rather than of Man in general. I conclude this from the small but important addition of a moustache to the features. I am not suggesting that we are immediately expected to hunt down some moustachioed male as the origin of the sketch – that would be naïve – but I take the detail of the moustache as an addition to these features which is not true of all male faces, and is therefore saying to the observant viewer: 'Take note. We are not dealing in generalities.'

Similarly, like Mr Cryer, I had noticed the ambivalence of the symbolism connected with the naked figure standing against the tree. It is unquestionably youthful, boylike in appearance – a representation of Hermes holding before him the planetary sign for Mercury. In Roman mythology, Mercury is the equivalent of Hermes. But his planetary sign is also the symbol for transmutation in alchemy and in keeping here with the alchemical meaning of the drawing. However, the reader is reminded that this symbol is also very similar to Dee's symbol for his Monad. Pictures of Hermes usually show him carrying the caduceus, or staff entwined with two serpents, in the crook of his arm. Here, however, he appears to be in the process of hiding the staff behind the tree trunk. This may be intended to indicate that the ancient beginnings of alchemical truth associated with Hermes had now been or were now being replaced by a modern form of alchemy. In more general terms a new order of things was replacing the old. This seems to be confirmed by other unusual features, such as the single wing attached to the boy's left foot. Normally Hermes has two wings, one on each. The size of the wing is so out of proportion to the rest of the figure we are evidently expected to notice it. And, of course, as Mr Cryer noticed, the feet appear to be nailed to the tree trunk, below which is the shape of a crescent moon. In Greek mythology, the goddess of the Moon was Artemis. One of her attributes was the ability to cure or alleviate the suffering of mortals. This characteristic is congruent with the overall alchemical allegory, but we have to account for the nailed feet and hand, and these are strongly suggestive of Christian associations which must link the alchemical tradition with the later cabalistic use of alchemy as a spiritual, not metallurgical, process. This reinforces and develops the allegory of the substitution of the Mercury/transmutation sign for the caduceus. The leaves of the tree can then be seen as representing different stages in a man's life.

If we now turn to the verses that accompany the drawing we learn that the queen is being shown the 'leaves of Hermes secret tree'. But there is a suggestion that this is not only a spiritual but also a physical process. The writer continues to use mythological figures to disguise the truth, but this also serves a secondary purpose of giving divine sanction or approval to what is happening or what has happened. The gods themselves are involved. Hermes, the grandson or 'impe of Saturn', waters the soil. His father was the supreme god, Zeus, who married Maia, and she is the 'impe's' mother. The 'crooked God' is Vulcan (crooked because of his limp) who married Aphrodite, the goddess of love. Vulcan was the god of fire, whose heat is indispensable for working metals. (Again the alchemical and mythological levels are intertwined.) He, therefore, became regarded as the supreme artist and all the palaces of Olympus were his workmanship. Here it is his heat, not the heat of the Sun, that combines with water to make the tree of alchemy spread.

The classical mythology is used to emphasise that this process of change or coming into being has a divine origin and therefore the queen can be reassured the process is also a holy one. But we still have another very strong image to examine. It is used to describe the start of the process: 'By Sowing Seeds in Wombs of Glass'. This, like so much in these few lines, can be read in more than one way. On a purely alchemical level it refers to the alchemist's laboratory. On a physical one it is an image of fertilisation. This would appear to have a direct human application when taken in conjunction with other symbols such as Aphrodite, goddess of love, and the idea of the heat of love's fire making things spread, not just grow but spread. The reader is forced to look again at the heat and confusion surrounding Leicester in the incident of the game of tennis played before the queen which we examined earlier. At this level Leicester is the 'crooked God' whom, we are told, the 'loving dame' (Queen Elizabeth) married, and the 'impe of Saturn's race' is a metaphor for a child with the noblest pedigree. The poet is not saying that the imp is Elizabeth's offspring, but, by a careful, analogous use of classical and alchemical imagery, that her marriage with Leicester has produced or will produce a child of noblest pedigree who will constitute, like the impe, like the figure under the tree, a new order of human being.

This multi-layered richness of meaning may come as a surprise to readers unaccustomed to the allusive tradition of alchemical texts. It is worth noting that in this very poem the poet tells us that 'Wisdomes lore' acts warily to bring things to pass. Such complexity is certainly present in other examples and this was an age when cipher and allegory went hand in hand both to convey and conceal important truths.

My next choice is a page which is noticeably different from the rest of the Schweighardt scrapbook in that it consists of eight separate symbols neatly arranged but without any written commentary at all. It is a document demanding further investigation. Six of the symbols are contained within circles. I took this to mean that in one sense each is complete in itself, even if all six are also intended to complement each other as a group. The remaining two are both arranged symmetrically opposite each other on the page in such a way that the absence of a border must be deliberate, although the reason for it is not immediately clear. I think we can assume that the page as a whole is intended as a story in pictures. Working down the page from the top and reading left to right, the first three symbols have been coloured, and so has the last. The remainder are line drawings in ink. The first symbol is the largest and stands on its own above a line separating it from the rest. After studying the sequence Mr Cryer observed:

> The overall implication of the first of the figures, coloured in red and grey, is that here we are looking at the flowering of the fruit of the ground, and, therefore, what appears below the line separating it from the rest has to do with the origin and flowering of whoever is referred to in the remaining symbols.
>
> Of these, the first shows a regal figure reclining on a slab or tomb and with a child resting upon its breast. The child, however, has a strangely adult face and hairstyle and would therefore seem to suggest that the child is emblematic of the man.

Alongside this is the emblem of the peacock. Its symbolic use derives ultimately from the *Physiologus*. This is a very early text dating from *c.* 370, and was probably written by a Syrian monk. It is a valuable source of animal symbolism in the Middle Ages throughout Europe. In England, both Langland in *Piers the Plowman* and Chaucer in *The Parlement of Fowles* are indebted to it for their allegorical use of birds and beasts. Langland refers to the peacock 'with here proud federes' [feathers] that 'Bytokenth ryght riche men that regned here on erthe'. The peacock's voice is ugly, and so he is praised for his feathers and the rich man for his wealth.[9] In this sequence, then, we are dealing with the rich and the powerful.

Having spoken with Mr Cryer about these symbols, I came to the conclusion that the order of them was significant in itself. For example, the image of the peacock is placed

63. A narrative in picture form.

between two others. On the left is the crowned nude with the child. This is suggestive of new life and succession. If the child had been wearing a crown as well it could have been an alchemical symbol, but in both instances on this page the child is not crowned and must therefore be taken to mean a child. On the right is a sketch of an altar with sacred bones beneath. Mr Cryer reminded me that it was a medieval and Catholic practice, which continued up to and through the Tudor age, to place sacred relics of a saint within or below the altar stone when building a church or sanctified place. At this period in history the image of saintly bones is suggestive of the miraculous and of life after death. Increasingly, as I examined separate illustrations throughout the scrapbook, I encountered the same ideas: royalty, the creation of life, change, transmutation either with rebirth or resurrection. A consistency of theme was emerging.

On this particular page, below the three symbols we have just discussed, is a pair of animals: the unicorn and the hart. Both animals are male, although the unicorn, because of its purity, was often used to represent the female principle and seen here with the hart may be intended to suggest the pairing of female and male in life. According to legend, the way to capture a unicorn was to place a virgin in a field where the fierce and fleet-footed animal would quietly approach her and lie down in her lap. Not surprisingly the unicorn became a strong symbol of sublimated sex or courtly love. In Christian symbolism it was associated with the Virgin Mary and her immaculate conception. Thus the figure of the unicorn is heavily imbued with both spiritual and erotic associations. Placed, as it is here, beneath the picture of the regal nude and child, and with its horn pointing in their direction, the symbol suggests a virgin queen is involved in this conception.

The hart or stag is often linked with the Tree of Life because of the resemblance of its antlers to branches. The Tree of Life is a central feature of cabalistic belief and there are numerous examples of it among the drawings in Byrom's collection. Because of the way its antlers are renewed, the hart is also a symbol of regeneration and renewal. The range of allusion here is rich and wide. As an animal the hart was endowed with wisdom and subtlety, choosing its moment to attack with care when it was most likely to succeed. On another level, because of the strict game laws introduced by the Normans, the hunting of the stag or hart became a royal prerogative. The symbol here, therefore, may hint at some royal prey hunted down by the Virgin Queen.

We now come to the last two emblems on the page, I will let Mr Cryer comment first.

And finally we have two symbols linked with a ring which no doubt signifies their union, if nothing else. And this strangely shows a phoenix about to rise in flight, but attached to a naked revealed child holding a dagger and mounted on a small porcus or pig, from which we get bacon.

THE ILLUSTRATIONS AND SIR FRANCIS BACON

Bacon? The word had many associations. Most immediately it was the name of the family of Sir Nicholas Bacon, Lord Keeper of the Great Seal of England in the reign of Queen Elizabeth and his more famous son, Sir Francis, who held the same office under James I. Both men had already appeared in my researches, Francis in particular because of his interest in the theatre, his acquaintance with Dee and his involvement with the cipher expert, Thomas Phelippes, and Walsingham's spy network. More recently he had featured among those with interests in the brass-works at Tintern.

It was common practice for animals to feature as heraldic devices in coats of arms: the Byrom family had adopted the hedgehog. Both the Earl of Leicester and his brother, Ambrose, Earl of Warwick, employed the figure of a bear; the Earl of Arundel, a white horse. I knew, too, that the coat of arms of Francis Bacon, as Viscount St Alban's, was surmounted with the crest of 'a boar passant'. I therefore noted Mr Cryer's last remark, and placed it alongside other facts that had begun to emerge independently from my own investigations.

I had noted several features that amplify Mr Cryer's observations. For example, the figure of the bird in the penultimate circle. Was it a phoenix, some other species or even a combination of two creatures? The other symbols show clearly that the artist had sufficient skill to draw an accurate representation when he chose. For example, in the illustration of the unicorn trouble had been taken to sketch in his mane lightly and neatly. So I did not feel I could attribute the incongruities I saw in the 'bird' symbol to clumsiness. They were deliberate. While I also felt the bird was intended to represent the phoenix, there were two disconcerting variations. First the crop under the neck, which I associated with the cockerel and other domestic fowls. There was also a crest, which reinforced the cockerel idea, but I had seen that feature elsewhere on pictures of the phoenix. The second puzzling difference was the dragon-like tail and wings. These seemed to hint at associations other than the phoenix, but what were they?

As a symbol the phoenix reinforces the earlier suggestions of rebirth and regeneration. Moreover, since the phoenix is supposed to remain dead for three days and then rise again as a new bird, it provides an apt metaphor for the death and resurrection of Christ. There is one other association which we should not ignore. The phoenix dies by self-immolation. It can therefore allude to someone choosing to 'die to the world' in order to live a new or different life. On this page the creature is evidently linked with the last symbol of all, the child. Perhaps the dagger raised aloft is the weapon with which it is to be killed.

I considered the coupling of these two symbols in the hope of wresting some meaning from them. A child upon the back of a pig – in this age some emblems were very literal in their symbolism. Was this figure of the child saying that he was supported by the Bacon family? Was the fact that the artist had painted him with the same flesh-coloured tint as the child shown earlier with the nude queen significant? Was it meant to be the same child – a royal offspring? I also recalled that Bacon's death had gathered around it a certain mystery. A considerable number of people question whether Bacon did in fact die in 1626 on, of all days, Easter Sunday, the day of resurrection. They believe that having lost his office and his reputation, he withdrew from society, staged his own death, and went abroad to live.

The supposed date of Bacon's death was the day Thomas Herbert, already embarked for the Middle East, reached Land's End. He was sailing in a ship belonging to the East India Company, named *The Rose*. William Herbert, Earl of Pembroke, was Governor and his brother, Philip, a shareholder of the company, and it can be no coincidence that another of its ships was called *The Globe*. The names were intended to commemorate two of the playhouses. Could there possibly be another coincidence in the 'death' of Bacon and the departure of *The Rose*?

According to his editor and chaplain William Rawley, Bacon died on 9 April 1626:

in the early morning of the day then celebrated for our Saviour's resurrection . . . at the earl of Arundel's house in Highgate, near London to which place he casually repaired about a week before; God so ordaining that he should die there of a gentle fever, accidentally accompanied with a great cold, where by the defluxion of rheum fell so plentifully upon his chest, that he died by suffocation.[10]

Later this version of events was elaborated by John Aubrey, who claimed to have his facts from Thomas Hobbes, Bacon's former secretary:

As he was taking the air in a coach with Dr Witherborne (a Scotchman, physician to the King) towards Highgate, snow lay on the ground, and it came into my lord's thoughts, why flesh might not be preserved in snow as in salt. They were resolved they would try the experiment at once. They alighted out of the coach, and went into a poor woman's house at the bottom of Highgate Hill and bought a hen, and made the woman gut it, and then stuffed the body with snow, and my lord did help to do it himself. The snow so chilled him that he immediately fell so extremely ill, that he could not return to his lodgings (I suppose at Gray's Inn) but went to the earl of Arundel's house at Highgate.[11]

POST MORTEM

There is plenty of evidence in Bacon's own writing of his interest in experiments to preserve flesh, not only in *Sylva sylvarum* and *Historia vitae et mortis* but elsewhere. The fact that Bacon had been unwell since the end of 1625 does not disprove Aubrey. The evidence that Bacon had been experimenting with opiates in an attempt to improve his poor health does not preclude him from also experimenting with freezing snow, particularly if a sudden and unexpected snowfall offered him the opportunity. There is also a series of puzzling facts surrounding the orthodox account of Bacon's demise. We have no records of his funeral. The burial registers of St Michael's Church, Gorhambury, St Alban's, where he was supposed to have been buried, do not include him. No funeral expenses were claimed by the administrators of his estate. According to different accounts, he died in four different houses: at Lord Arundel's; at the house of a friend, Dr Perry; at his cousin's, Sir Julius Caesar; and at his physician's Dr Witherborne.[12] Finally, no sign of his remains was ever found in his supposed tomb. According to Aubrey, in 1681 Sir Harbottle Grimston, Master of the Rolls, the last owner of Gorhambury, removed the coffin to make room for his own in the vault at St Michael's Church.

I had to consider Aubrey's version of Bacon's death because it seemed to offer an explanation to the symbolism of the last two emblems on this page. According to this interpretation we are shown an infant supported by the Bacon family (carried along on the back of a pig) who is responsible for his own death (he is brandishing a dagger in the air, not at anyone else). The cockerel aspect of the bird symbol, while reinforcing the idea of resurrection in the phoenix, suggests that the death was bound up with the killing of a chicken.

Moreover, I had to bear in mind another feature of the phoenix symbol: it had the wings and tail of a dragon. These could not be overlooked. The hybrid creature we are examining belongs to that category of fabulous beasts which combines characteristics of different animals, such as the centaur, half horse and half man, or the minotaur, a man with a bull's head. These products of the imagination have their own symbolic function. They suggest other forms of creation, acknowledge the endless potential of Nature, even, as one authority states 'freedom from the conventional principles of the phenomenal world'.[13] With this in mind, the combination of phoenix, cockerel and dragon may imply that this resurrection, regeneration or rebirth is not to the same existence, nor necessarily to a higher one, but to a different mode of living. Was this extraordinary set of cameos the conjectural story of Bacon's birth and death according to rumour and speculation in picture form? Or is it a coded record of what happened?

64. 'The Sun Speakes'.

BACON'S KNIGHTS OF THE HELMET

It is perhaps apt at this point to turn to another illustration, which is startling, even comic at first sight, but which repays study by revealing yet again more than one level of meaning. We see the body of the winged god Hermes disappearing head first into a helmet. The helmet is surmounted on a shield emblazoned with the face of the Sun surrounded by an aureole. On the basic level of alchemy, the Sun represents gold, the ultimate goal of alchemical experimentation. Another name for Hermes is Mercury and here in fact he is addressed as 'proude Mercury'. Mercury is the symbol of transmutation itself as well as the element mercury or quicksilver used in the alchemical process. Its fluidity was associated with an unlimited capacity for transformation and penetration, hence its importance to the alchemist. So, on this level, quicksilver is being poured into a receptacle to make gold.

However, we have seen enough by now not to take these drawings on one level only. This particular image of Mercury is a symbol for a man involved in a process of change represented by his disappearing into a helmet. Since we are dealing with Greek mythology, we have to remind ourselves that the most famous helmet which enabled the wearer to disappear, by rendering him invisible, was the helmet of Pallas Athene, goddess of wisdom. In another of her roles, as a goddess of war, she is portrayed with a breastplate, helmet and golden staff. Sometimes the staff is shown as a spear which has earned the goddess the title, the 'spear-shaker'. Be that as it may, here a figure which begins as Mercury 'disappears' and becomes the Sun god. This would seem to be an allegory concerning a real person. Who is intended?

I remembered that the helmet had associations with Francis Bacon, dating from the time when he was studing law at Gray's Inn. It is believed he formed a society there which he called 'The Knights of the Helmet'. He took the lead in organising the traditional Christmas Revels for the students in 1594–5. These celebrations lasted the customary twelve days of Christmas, were revived for Candlemas (2 February) and ended with Shrovetide (the three days before Lent). For the duration of the festivities Gray's Inn was turned into a 'royal court' ruled over by a 'Prince of Purpool', purple being the colour of royalty and one of which Bacon became extremely fond. When he eventually married he dressed in purple from head to foot. As part of the Revels, Shakespeare's play *The Comedy of Errors* was performed on 28 December. Then, on 3 January, Bacon presented an entertainment he had devised entitled 'The Honourable Order of the Knights of The Helmet'.[14]

During this particular entertainment various law students came forward to be invested with a Collar of the Knighthood of the Helmet. They kissed the collar and all made solemn vows in the manner of chivalric knights or of some more modern 'brotherhood' such as the Freemasons.

The account of these revels recalls the Christmas celebrations thirty years earlier at another of the Inns of Court, this time the Inner Temple, when Robert Dudley, Earl of Leicester, was chosen as the Christmas Prince by the students for the Revels of 1561–2. The title given to Leicester for the occasion was 'Pallaphilos', the lover of wisdom or the lover of Pallas Athene, the goddess of wisdom, a name then used for the queen in the growing cult of Elizabeth. As her most devoted friend and defender, Leicester could be seen as the 'Shield of Pallas'. Readers of *The Byrom Collection* will remember that among the Globe drawings there is one that refers specifically to the shield of Pallas. Set against this context the symbol of the helmet is rich in associations. The same can be said for the symbol of the Monad. The drawing of it in Byrom's collection is colour coded with the Globe sequence. This may have been to indicate that the relationship between Elizabeth's 'shield', the Earl of Leicester, and the queen herself was known to the artist who created that sequence of theatre drawings. In this connection, it is worth noting that later Francis Bacon chose to decorate the title pages of two of his books with emblems of Pallas Athene: *Nova Atlantis* (1643) and *Scripta in Naturali and Universali Philosophia* (1653).

In fact the next illustration we need to look at from the scrapbook is a variant of the Monad. Here, the symbol occupies almost the entire page. The images it contains we have met in previous pages but the crescent Moon now has a face in it, as does the circle of the Sun. The two signs are linked by a cross. The Moon and the Sun also represent the male and female principles. These three signs can all be found in the planetary symbol for Mercury, but in a different order, where the sequence reading downwards is crescent, circle, cross. Here, with the cross between crescent and circle, the emphasis appears to be on the union of Moon and Sun, silver and gold, male and female. Therefore, on a simple level the cross is a sign of addition or union and also an indication, as elsewhere in the sequence, of a Christian element which has been grafted on to an older tradition. In Dee's Monad, as we saw, the cross represents the four Elements: Air, Fire, Water and Earth.

In the top right-hand corner of the page are written two phrases: 'a purplish ground' and 'Sun all philamort'. These I take to be a note for the colouring of the picture. The background is a faint mauve or purplish colour. In addition to being the colour of royalty, purple is associated in the vestments of the Church with Christ's passion, and hence becomes a symbol of power and spirituality. But it is also now a colour one can associate with Bacon. 'Philamort' is an obsolete form of the word 'filemot' and derives from 'feuillemort' the tawny colour of autumn leaves. Here it suggests a tawny-orange tint for the sun.

For some reason the drawing has been left unfinished. The face in the Sun is adequately rounded off, but the light streams from only the right side. This indicates its incomplete state, as does the inner line which the artist started to draw inside the sun's circumference. However the intention is plain. This was to be a pictorial summary of some of the chief symbols contained in the book.

At this point I need to remind the reader that my original purpose in looking at the Schweighardt scrapbook was to investigate further the geometric drawings I knew it contained. In 1992 I had reproduced in *The Byrom Collection* two hermetic engravings by Michel Le Blon which I had found among the illustrations in the scrapbook. Now I was also able to link a theatre print from the Schweighardt with a brass plate at the Science Museum and a drawing in Byrom's collection. In fact, the collection contains several drawings closely related to it. Moreover, there is among the Byrom drawings one that I had associated years ago with the Rose theatre. It is closely related to a print in Ms 471. My investigations had shown that while each of these sources is an entity in itself, the contents of each overlap, binding all the separate pieces together.

We need to remember also that on the inside cover of the Schweighardt scrapbook is written:

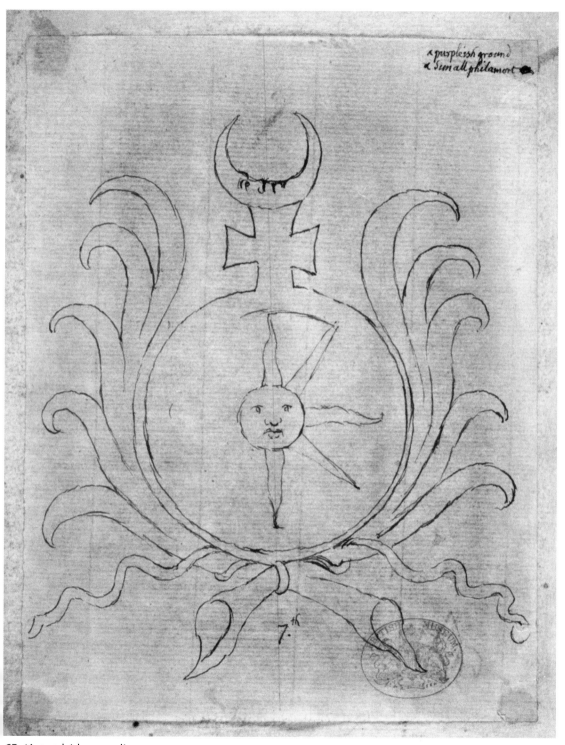

65. 'A purpleish ground'.

66. Geometric figure from the Schweighardt scrapbook, identical with the prints from Byrom's theatre drawings and one of the brass plates in the Science Museum. (Reproduced at 75 per cent of original size)

An account of the Rosicruc Fraternity by Theophilus Schweighardt with the addition of several prints and miniature paintings by Mr. Rose.

The name 'Mr. Rose' at the front of a book containing a Rosicrucian pamphlet is more than a coincidence. It is a convenient *nom de plume*, just like Theophilus Schweighardt. The paper appeared in an age when pamphlets frequently bore such token names. Allowing for variables in early German spelling, Schweighardt could be translated as 'one who is good at keeping quiet'.

67. 'Mercury Speakes out of the Ashes'.

68. Francis Bacon, by Van Somer.

SOME IMPLICATIONS

I have endeavoured to ensure that the selection of illustrations discussed in this chapter is truly representative of the whole Schweighardt scrapbook. They all show originals from the scrapbook, which are drawn in pen and ink, some with colour. The iconography is based on an established and widespread tradition. Each of the illustrations is concerned with a part of the same story. I do not believe that the scrapbook was either a hoax or a joke, but source material for a privileged circle. I have learned enough from it to be able to retell that story, but do so with some trepidation.

We appear to have been presented with a pictorial allegory for certain stages in the life of Francis Bacon. I must say at once that this was totally unexpected. I was aware of Bacon's place in history, the general outline of his achievements and of a long list of writers who had researched his role in the Shakespeare legacy. Until now his name has cropped up in this narrative as and when it was relevant. The reader will recall that, in my search to make sense of the Schweighardt inclusions, I discovered the historical tennis game in which Leicester betrayed his familiarity with Queen Elizabeth. Surviving contemporary documents show that the queen and Leicester were deeply devoted and at one time were thought to have been married. Burghley was opposed to such a match. Leicester came under suspicion when his wife,

Amy Robsart, suffered an unfortunate and fatal fall down a staircase. What we have in these pages, under the guise of an alchemical treatise, is a suggestion that Elizabeth had a child fathered by Leicester (images such as the 'Wombs of Glass' and the 'heat' of Vulcan causing the tree of alchemy to 'spread'). There is also the weight of the imagery in 'The Whole Worke's Emblem', where the fruit of royal figures brings forth a new being, symbolised by the crowned phoenix. The eight symbols beginning with the fruit of the Earth and ending with the child on the back of a pig, with dagger raised aloft, are even more specific and carry the analogy from birth to a suggestion of self-inflicted death and rebirth. The symbol of Hermes disappearing into the helmet and reappearing as a Sun figure had underneath it the words 'The Sun Speaks'. Was this a play on the words Sun and son? Were the words addressed to 'proude Mercury' – 'I'll fetter thee' – a reminder of a real threat which Bacon, alias Mercury, had lived under? Finally, did the summary of the marriage of Sun and Moon reiterate the idea of change not just of base metals into gold but of a human being from one life to another – a life with its own distinction?

After his downfall in the reign of James I Bacon was believed by some to have arranged his own 'death' and to have disappeared to live a different life at the age of sixty-six. The alchemical process provided ideal analogies for his life and the illustrations emphasise repeatedly birth, death and regeneration. Admittedly this is what we would expect of them, but in this sequence the symbols possess variations or convey undertones which hint that here they are not being used simply to tell the familiar alchemist's tale all over again.

I did not come to this conclusion lightly and I found it very disturbing. For a while I did not wish to pursue the implications it entailed, but the tendency of the Schweighardt illustrations was to support the thesis that Bacon had not died in 1626 but had 'escaped' into a new life. I was also forced to face another uncomfortable fact. The figure that the hand-written inventory at the Science Museum, with its haphazard numbering, had given to the brass plates of the Elizabethan playhouses was thirty-three. Borrowing the ancient system of gematria, cabalists allotted a numerical equivalent to each of the twenty-four letters of the Elizabethan alphabet. Thus $A=1$, $B=2$ etc. Accordingly, the name 'Bacon' had a numerical equivalent of 33 ($2+1+3+14+13$). Whether this fact was merely a coincidence or had some bearing on the number of the inventory will, I hope, become clear in the final chapter.

CHAPTER 10

Out of the Shadows

R eaders of *The Byrom Collection* will know that I prefaced it with a quotation from Francis Bacon:

Whatever deserves to exist, deserves also to be known, for knowledge is the image of existence.

At the time, I chose those words for the sentiments they expressed; they summed up the philosophy of a man whose writings were dedicated to the advancement of learning. Ironically I did not think then that Bacon would feature in this story. But the words did seem to be an apt tribute to the 516 pieces of paper and card that had survived for so long unknown and unappreciated in the Byrom archives. Moreover, while I was aware that some people doubted whether Shakespeare wrote the plays which bore his name, that was a separate issue from my own research. Over the years, as I worked on the Byrom drawings, it was inevitable that the question of authorship should be mentioned, but it was always by others and in an incidental manner – an afterthought to a conversation. I was far too busy with issues more immediately concerned with the theatre drawings – their context and the information I thought they contained. When I did pause to consider briefly the number of people credited with Shakespeare's work, that seemed a good enough reason not to concern my head further with such questions.

As we saw at the end of the last chapter, the name of Bacon could be written in numbers. It is well known that Bacon used this system himself. However, when it came to considering the inventory in the Boyle Collection, I did not know whether the fact that item 33 was concerned with the brass plates was a coincidence, an indication of haste and carelessness, or a hint that Bacon had owned them. I would not even have thought it a possibility if the numbering had not been so irregular. In making an inventory one usually numbers items consecutively to ensure order and avoid mistakes. So, it was in the context of trying to account for the odd cataloguing that I considered the likelihood of a connection with Bacon and discussed his possible ownership of the plates with Leon Crickmore among others. Mr Crickmore had for some years been head of the department of applied philosophy at a London polytechnic and I respected his knowledge of philosophy, religion and psychology. He had agreed that the numbering was curious, and had even suggested that it held a cabalistic key. During one of our exchanges he suggested I should read *Who Wrote Shakespeare?* by John Michell, a book which investigates the claims made for various candidates, including Bacon. I knew Michell's work on mathematics and had read some of it with interest, but I did not follow up this suggestion immediately. Even later, when I was given a copy to read, it lay unopened for some weeks.

Inevitably a day arrived when, I found time to flick through the pages of Michell's book. They fell open at the section dealing with Bacon to reveal an illustration that mentioned Chepstow. The name of that small Welsh town was not new to me. Chepstow is barely 5 miles from Tintern and the River Wye links the two, winding its way through a tree-lined valley until the landscape opens up into a broader expanse where the Cistercians built their abbey. The proximity is enhanced by the unspoiled countryside between. Now, on the open page before me, I read the following caption to a photograph: 'From his Wheel of Fortune Owen learnt that Bacon's manuscripts were hidden beneath the River Wye at Chepstow, and spent several seasons in search of them, hiring workmen for underwater excavations.'[1] I read the account that accompanied this and discovered that a physician from Detroit, Dr Orville Owen, was a cipher expert who had studied the works of Bacon, Shakespeare and several of his contemporaries, and concluded that Bacon was the author of Shakespeare's plays and that the original manuscripts had been buried along the banks of the River Wye, near Chepstow. The story seemed so bizarre that it lent itself readily to satire. In his book, Michell writes about all the candidates with equal levity.

When I read Michell's account of Dr Owen, it was in a moment of distraction, a break from looking for evidence that might link Bacon with the brass plates in the Science Museum. The authorship controversy was a different issue. However, the recollection of the brass-works near by at Tintern made me feel I should look closer at Dr Owen's activities, however extravagant they might appear. They could just contain some reference to Bacon relevant to my own enquiries. Apparently Dr Owen visited Chepstow every summer for fifteen years from 1909 in pursuit of the manuscripts. I had never heard of them before. Michell's account carried a picture taken from the *Illustrated London News*. I decided to go back to the first source and find the original newspaper reports of Dr Owen's visits to the Wye.

Three full-page drawings of Dr Owen's investigations, undertaken with the help and support of the Duke of Beaufort, appeared in the *Illustrated London News* for 11 March 1911. During the last week of February the same year, the *Daily Express*, then a broadsheet, carried columns of reports from its 'special correspondent' assigned

69. *Illustrated London News*, 11 March 1911, showing Dr Owen's investigations.

to the story. I read these communiqués with increasing amazement, but their author was no sensationalist. He did not have to be; the story spoke for itself. The issue for 27 February listed six 'facts' which, regardless of Dr Owen's theories, had a bearing on my own interest in Bacon if they were true.

1. A picture of Bacon hangs in Chepstow Castle.
2. Bacon was the owner of the wireworks at Tintern Abbey a few miles away.
3. He lived at Mount St Alban's, near Newport.
4. There is a petition extant in which Bacon begs from Robert Cecil the right to take wood from the Forest of Dean.
5. Bacon's father-in-law lived at Beachly, near at hand, and Bacon often visited him on the way to the wireworks.
6. He was a great friend of the Earl of Worcester, who was Lord of Chepstow.

The 'wireworks' at Tintern had included the first brassworks in this country. The two main authorities on its history are Dr William Rees and M.B. Donald. I had studied both their accounts as the reader will have gathered from Chapter Seven. I knew that in 1568 Bacon's father, Sir Nicholas, had been a shareholder in the Corporation of the Mineral and Battery Works, but neither writer had suggested that Francis Bacon had ever been the 'owner of the wireworks'.

Dr Orville Owen was not a name completely unknown to me. In January 1993, Ian Taylor, a Canadian scientist, writer and publisher, had written to me after the publication of *The Byrom Collection*. In a detailed letter he included some very interesting annotations on a number of issues I had raised. The following month, in a second letter, he drew my attention to Masonic symbolism in the title pages of three of Bacon's books and to certain books concerned with the Bacon cipher, including one by Orville Owen. He concluded by urging me to 'continue digging: Tuck these notes away in a Bacon file. . . .'

Six years later, early in 1999, I happened to reread Mr Taylor's letter, curious and intrigued that he should have thought that one day I might be interested in Bacon. We had corresponded several times since on other aspects of my work and his invariable helpfulness encouraged me now to telephone him in Canada. I explained the importance of the brass plates in the Science Museum for the Byrom collection, that I was investigating the possibility of a connection between Bacon and the brassworks at Tintern, and my surprise to learn of the visits of Dr Owen to Chepstow. Since Mr Taylor was a publisher himself, I asked him if he knew where I might find copies of the work Dr Owen had written. Owen's work had included an examination of the ninth edition of Sidney's *Arcadia*. It transpired that Mr Taylor was due to fly to Europe to give a series of talks in the Ukraine. When I mentioned Chepstow and the River Wye, he suggested that he could interrupt his flight back to Canada with a small diversion to Manchester and we could talk things over together.

SECRETS OF THE CYPHER.

NEW DISCOVERIES IN THE BACON MYSTERY.

SAMPLE SENTENCES

" Express" Special Correspondent.

Chepstow, Friday Night.

Each day adds interesting points to the story of the search for the diaries and manuscripts of Bacon which Dr. Owen believes were buried nearly three centuries ago in the bed of the Wye. Each day seems to its originators to lift the theory that Bacon was the greatest genius in the world, the author of the plays of Shakespeare, and many of the glorious works of the Elizabethan authors, out of fantasy of romance, into the realms of possibility.

The long screed which Dr. Orville Owen claims to have deciphered from Sir Philip Sidney's "Arcadia," where it was hidden by Bacon, is full of references to the past, and teems with intimate topographical knowledge of the neighbourhood such as it must have been in the days of Queen Elizabeth.

There have been, I understand, developments since the doctor first came to England with his long rolls that hold Bacon's message which he considers to be positively startling in their significance.

One of these is the fact that an old box has come to light containing the " Wise Sayings of the Earl of Worcester " and Bacon's "Apophthegms " bound together.

The importance of this in its relation to the Chepstow search is thought to be very great.

The Earl of Worcester was one of Bacon's greatest friends, and for some time he lived in Chepstow Castle. In fact, the Pembrokes and the Worcesters seemed both to have been living in the castle at this period.

The connection between Bacon and Chepstow—quite apart from the positive statement in Dr. Owen's cyphers—is very strong as circumstantial evidence alone.

BACON AT CHEPSTOW.

These are the facts that I have learned to-day :—

1. A picture of Bacon hangs in Chepstow Castle.

2. Bacon was the owner of the wireworks at Tintern Abbey a few miles away.

3. He lived at Mount St. Albans, near Newport.

4. There is a petition extant in which Bacon begs from Robert Cecil the right to take wood from the Forest of Dean.

5. Bacon's father-in-law lived at Beachly, near at hand, and Bacon often visited him on the way to the wireworks.

6. He was a great friend of the Earl of Worcester, who was Lord of Chepstow.

It is small wonder, therefore, that the hopes of the search party are at their highest, and from henceforth the angle in the bend of the River Wye will be probed with scientifically equipped apparatus.

70. *Daily Express*, 25 February 1911.

'RIVERBANK' AND FRANCIS BACON

The first thing Mr Taylor did when he arrived in May 1999 was to present me with a copy of a book: *The Sabines of Riverbank* by John W. Kopec. Published in New York in 1997 by the Acoustical Society of America, it was the story of members of the Sabine family and their contribution to the science of architectural acoustics. My first thoughts were that within its pages I might find a possible solution to the unsatisfactory acoustics at the new Globe playhouse on Bankside. However, while I was still taking an initial look at the book Mr Taylor suggested that I should read pages 180 and 181 before our meeting got under way. On page 180 John Kopec, former director of Riverbank Acoustical Laboratories, writes:

> In January 1991 I received correspondence from Ian Taylor, a writer affiliated with TFE Publishing in Toronto, Canada. Taylor had written an article, 'Francis Bacon and the Scientific Method' . . . Taylor referenced historian James Spedding's 1861 seven volume work on the life of Francis Bacon as the orthodox account. Taylor went on to say, 'However, other researchers since that date have unearthed more material and the mystery surrounding Bacon's life and silent years has slowly been revealed. It is a remarkable story.'

On the facing page of John Kopec's book was a heading:

A Colonel Fabyan Story Regarding Bacon Documents

This is a story that may never be published: In 1994 Mr. Frederic R. (Robin) Sherwood of Victoria, British Columbia visited Riverbank and told a fascinating story about Colonel Fabyan and Dr. Orville Owen of Detroit that he was still researching and planned to publish in the very near future. The story involved some unusual events that resulted from the Baconian ciphers, including a trip to England, where a river was diverted in search of some of Sir Francis Bacon's documents. As promised, I did not include the story in this book but I am referencing it here because on September 3, 1995, Mr. Sherwood passed away and someone else may want to follow up on it.

This was a most perplexing beginning to our encounter. A trip to England and a river diverted in a search for some of Bacon's papers – this must be a reference to the Chepstow investigations. All the way from Canada, via the Ukraine, came this unexpected reply from the pages of a book with which Mr Taylor himself seemed to be involved. However, we had a full agenda ahead of us and time was short. I had to acquaint him with the state of my own researches which had led to my request. I was very grateful for his swift response and sensible of the trouble he had taken to come personally in a spirit of scholarship.

After he left Manchester, I was free to read *The Sabines at Riverbank* from cover to cover. The contents, though complex and diffuse, were highly significant. The origins of the laboratory of acoustics at Riverbank, Illinois, go back to 1913 when the very wealthy American, Colonel George Fabyan, needed an acoustics consultant to help him with: 'the building and testing of an acoustical levitating machine constructed from a seventeenth-century description of a similar machine written in code by Sir Francis Bacon.'[2] This was a vertically mounted cylinder containing two sets of musical strings tuned to precise intervals. When the cylinder was rotated the strings were intended to vibrate in sympathy with each other and produce sufficient energy from their vibration to make the cylinder levitate. The expert employed to supervise this experiment was Wallace Clement Sabine of the Physics Department at Harvard University. On his advice the project came to an end, but it resulted in a long-term friendship between Sabine and Fabyan. The acoustical levitation machine demonstrated partial success and might have been more successful if it had been possible to manufacture it to finer tolerances. This raises an interesting question: if it was not possible to achieve these tolerances in the twentieth century, how did Bacon and others of the seventeenth century know of the principles in the first place?

By 1915 Sabine, still on the staff at Harvard, was becoming increasingly frustrated by the problems caused to his research into architectural acoustics by noise and vibrations from the street outside his laboratory, and Colonel Fabyan offered him the solitude and silence of purpose-built facilities at Riverbank. During the First World War, Professor Sabine was a scientific adviser to the United States Navy Department of Information and the French Bureau of Inventions on submarines and airplanes. He also provided services for the British Munitions Inventions Bureau. One of his projects, which involved Riverbank, was the use of cameras in airplanes for aerial reconnaissance. After a very distinguished contribution to the war effort, he finally resumed his work on architectural acoustics in November 1918 at Riverbank. On 5 January the following year he died at the early age of fifty.

Sabine's death was a tremendous loss to Fabyan and the laboratory he had built. The professor's achievements had made him something of a legend. Both in America and England he had been consulted on creating the right acoustics in new buildings and on improving faulty acoustics in existing ones. Searching for a replacement, the colonel was fortunate to obtain the services of Paul Earls Sabine, a cousin of the dead professor and himself a PhD on spectroscopy from Harvard.

Colonel Fabyan's immense wealth came from textiles. This enabled him to buy 600 acres of land in Geneva, Illinois, where he had founded Riverbank in the early 1900s. Through his work as aide-de-camp to the governor of Illinois, Riverbank became involved in a number of military projects. These ranged from investigations into trench warfare to the study of explosives, the deciphering of military codes and the analysis of air reconnaissance photos. In 1905 he had been chosen by President Theodore Roosevelt to serve on the peace team negotiating the treaty which ended the Russo-Japanese War. More relevant perhaps to our concerns is the fact that at Riverbank the first US military code school was established and many of the officers trained there became involved in army intelligence. In 1993 Colonel Fabyan's pioneering work was officially recognised. A plaque was erected at Riverbank 'To the Memory of George Fabyan From A Grateful Government.' The citation reads:

> In recognition of the voluntary and confidential service rendered by Colonel Fabyan and his Riverbank Laboratories in the sensitive areas of cryptanalysis and cryptologic training during a critical time of national need on the eve of America's entry into World War I. Presented to mark the seventy-fifth anniversary by the National Security Agency, United States Department of Defense, 1917–1922.

In total it is reckoned that Riverbank trained eighty army intelligence officers. The instructor for this course was a man called William Friedmann. However, the person whose work had led Fabyan to set up the school was Elizabeth Gallup. She was now advanced in years, but well known as the 'expert' on the Baconian ciphers, to which she had been introduced originally by Dr Orville Owen, the Chepstow investigator. Fabyan invited her to Riverbank, where she was employed in the background to monitor proceedings at the cipher school.

Colonel Fabyan was an ideas man and his wealth enabled him to hire the people he required for any particular project that took his fancy. He could also indulge his eccentric pleasures and give generously to those in need who came to his notice. However, when the stock market crash came in 1929 he was compelled to reduce his activities at Riverbank and to encourage Paul Sabine to find a way of making the Acoustical Laboratory pay. This Sabine was able to do, thus assuring Riverbank a key role in establishing standardised tests and their execution. Then in May 1936 Colonel Fabyan was suddenly taken ill. He died on the 17th, aged sixty-nine.

Paul Sabine was a worthy successor to his cousin. His work on acoustics naturally led to studies of the human ear and he was one of the first people to study the effects of noise damage on it. While his initial research dealt with hearing trumpets, he was later instrumental in the development of the electronic hearing aid. Paul Sabine's son Hale, who had exceptionally keen hearing, was used by his father in his experiments on hearing and later joined the staff of Riverbank. But Paul Sabine also continued research into the acoustics of the auditorium and by the 1930s the foundations for standard acoustical testing in the laboratory had been established. His work in this area became increasingly important and led to competing manufacturers setting up the Acoustical Materials Association. Between its foundation in 1933 and its dissolution in 1977 this body played an important part in the development of acoustics as a science.

All this made fascinating reading. It did not, however, help me with the acoustics of the rebuilt Globe, but as I read on I found one section that did interest me for totally different reasons. A considerable amount of work had been done at Riverbank under the direction of Elizabeth Gallup into the Baconian codes she claimed to have discovered. A journalist writing in August 1939 stated that:

> Col. George Fabyan, multi-millionaire cotton broker, spent fifty years of his life and a fortune endeavouring to solve this question [Who wrote Shakspeare?]. He collected an unequalled library of first and only editions of Elizabethan authors. His agents scoured the world buying rare code books which he used to decipher the works of Shakespeare. Just as the colonel was on the verge of solving this controversial issue, death put an end to his work. Shakespearian authorities in Chicago yesterday voiced a demand that the work to which Col. Fabyan gave his life should not stop with his death. His famous library was left in the will of his widow, Mrs Nellie Fabyan, to the Congressional Library in Washington. Thus Shakespearian scholars feel the government is in a position to fulfil Fabyan's ambition and settle once and for all the question of who wrote the plays of Shakespeare.[3]

It was an expensive interest, costing Colonel Fabyan over half a million dollars. He died believing the plays were not the work of Shakespeare but that they were by members of a society of Rosicrucians. William Friedmann, the cryptanalyst Fabyan employed and who had broken the Japanese 'Purple Code' in the Second World War, disagreed with Mrs Gallup's theories. Yet this did not stop the colonel from continuing to pour money into the project. Had he found some new evidence in the vast number of books he had bought for his library? (I was intrigued to learn that the library at Riverbank contained a copy of Byrom's shorthand manual.)

The question of new evidence was posed by John Kopec, former director, and that might explain why Ian Taylor had given me a copy of the book in the summer of 1999. The author had signed my copy, writing on the first page: 'Welcome to Riverbank World of Architectural Acoustics. Enjoy. Best Regards.' My attention was caught by the abrupt 'enjoy'. Was that all I was supposed to do?

I looked again at the reference to Ian Taylor. He had written to John Kopec in 1991 – six years before the book was published. Frederic Sherwood had visited Riverbank with his story about Colonel Fabyan and Dr Owen in 1994, three years before the book was published and twenty-eight years after Fabyan's death and the end of his investigations into Baconian ciphers. Fabyan's library had been willed to Congress by his widow. Why then did Taylor and Sherwood contact Riverbank in the first place? The institute was evidently still attracting people seeking expertise to help with their own interest in the Shakespeare/Bacon question. Did Riverbank still have something to offer such enquirers?

The institute still functions as a leading centre of research into architectural acoustics. The test chamber used today is based on the original one designed by Wallace Sabine but with additional refinements. The engineer and inventor brought in to work on the Baconian acoustical levitation machine in the early 1900s later turned his attention to developing and refining the tuning fork. That operation continues on the site today as an independent off-shoot. In the light of the solid achievements of Riverbank in acoustics and cryptanalysis, as recorded by John Kopec, John Michell's description of Colonel Fabyan as a 'showman' is inadequate and misleading.[4]

I turned back to Kopec's reference to Dr Orville Owen of Detroit. His name was coupled with that of Colonel Fabyan but nothing was said about his activities on the River Wye. I learned that Frederic R. Sherwood, who had been planning to publish his own researches into the doctor's investigations, had at one time been a solicitor for the publishers of the *Encyclopaedia Britannica*, so he was evidently a man of some standing in his chosen profession. I would have liked to know what conclusions he came to about Dr Owen, but his death had made that impossible.

Whatever method of decipherment Dr Owen had used, whatever guide he had found, had led him from Detroit to Chepstow. Now, eighty-eight years later, my own researches into the brass-works at Tintern had brought me to the same place. Dr Owen's confident assertions in the newspapers of the day were a challenge. I had to look into their accuracy, regardless of the story of buried manuscripts. If, as Owen stated, Bacon did have a house near Tintern, what could be the reason? To all intents and purposes, his career was centred on London, the royal palaces and the law courts.

THE SEARCH FOR MOUNT ST ALBAN'S

In none of the books I had read about Bacon was there any mention of a house near Tintern, but I was able to piece together anecdotal evidence from local libraries of an old Elizabethan property once belonging to Francis Bacon 'up in the hills', 'off the beaten track'. Everyone agreed that it was called Mount St Alban's, a name full of Baconian resonances. Some said that many years ago it had been a night club. All believed it had been burned down. In less permissive times perhaps the best place to site a nightclub would have been 'off the beaten track'.

Had the house been reduced to ashes because of some riotous orgy? Was there anything left? All I could do was go hunting myself in the gathering gloom of a winter's day, hoping to clothe at least one of Owen's claims with a modest vestige of fact. I had tracked the house down to a road between Caerleon and Usk, near a hamlet called Cat's Ash. A local fire station confirmed the fire, which is still remembered by older residents, but no one knew whether anything remained. As I approached the site my heart sank. A lavish golf course had tamed the tops of the hills and I feared that Bacon's Welsh mansion had made way for a bunker or fairway. Happily this was not so. Before the dusk merged the sky with the hills, I found Mount St Alban's. All that remains is the name on a sign to a private road leading to a group of handsome houses built within the former mansion's grounds. But it had existed!

The 1920 Ordnance Survey map for the parish of Christchurch in what was then Monmouthshire shows the mansion of Mount St Alban's still standing. Close by is marked the site of St Alban's Chapel, which had long since disappeared. Both were near to an old Roman road. The 1881 Ordnance Survey map for Christchurch shows the position of Sir William Herbert's house at St Julian's. Nearby is marked the site of St Julian's Chapel. But that, too, was no longer standing. However, the remains of a Roman road are shown not far away. At the time of Elizabeth I, this road would have been the main link between the two houses.

When I looked further into the history of St Julian's, I learned that in the 1580s Sir William Herbert had mortgaged two manors in the same parish of Christchurch to Sir Henry Billingsley, the man responsible for the first English translation of Euclid, for which John Dee had written his famous 'Preface'. Here, then, was another connection between John Dee and William Herbert. Herbert, as we have seen, was a friend and disciple of Dee. His rent rolls show that he was a man with a substantial income, so it seems unlikely that he was in need of the money from these transactions. Why was Billingsley so eager to obtain property in the locality? Both mortgages were later reconveyed to Sir William's widow and the St Julian's estate remained with his heirs until the Commonwealth, when it was confiscated by Parliament. After the restoration of Charles II the estate was returned to the family. However, by 1911 the once imposing house had been divided into separate blocks of tenements.

The chapels at St Alban's and St Julian's dated from about 303 and were dedicated to two of the first British-born Christian martyrs. A third native martyr was Aaron. All three were friends and had churches dedicated to them in this area because both Julian and Aaron were originally Roman citizens of Caerleon. This was once the site of a large Roman settlement and still has the remains of a magnificent Roman amphitheatre, 2 miles from Newport. It is, perhaps, the best example in Britain.

71. Roman amphitheatre, Caerleon. It was built *c*. AD 70 for gladiatorial combat and military training at the garrison town of Isca, home to the second Augustan legion.

So, there are two places in England and Wales known as St Alban's and while clearly Bacon's title of Baron Verulam of Verulam is taken from Hertfordshire and his family estate at Gorhambury, we cannot ignore the fact that he was also associated with a mansion at the other St Alban's, near Newport. Moreover, both Bacon houses were close to Roman settlements with Roman amphitheatres. Bacon would have been fully aware of this. His association with the wireworks at Tintern gave him a very good reason to spend time at the Welsh St Alban's. It is important to bear this uncanny duplication in mind at times when Bacon refers to 'St Alban's' in order to avoid misunderstanding.

After the Norman conquest, the church at St Alban's, along with other churches and manors, was given by a Norman lord, Robert de Chandos, to the Priory of Goldcliff, a Cistercian community which he had recently founded. The priory ceased to function before the Dissolution and its lands were conferred on Eton College. Records show that the church of St Alban's continued to function until 1495. Its subsequent history is incomplete. As for the house, it would appear from a will dated 1624, that it had been occupied by one Walter Powell. It remained with his heirs until 1735, when it was sold to John Williams of Christchurch and from him passed to a succession of different families.

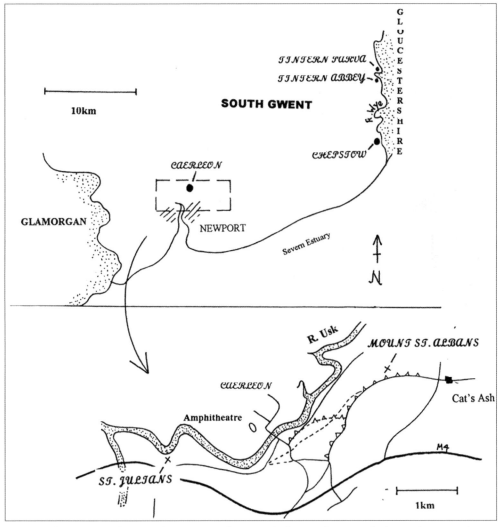

72. Map showing St Julian's and Mount St Alban's with the Caerleon amphitheatre between them.

ST JULIAN'S

St Julian's had also been part of the Priory of Goldcliff. Like St Alban's it passed from the priory into secular hands, no doubt at the time the priory closed. In the fifteenth century it belonged to Sir William Herbert, first Earl of Pembroke. (He was executed in 1469 and was buried in Tintern Abbey.) His third son, Sir George Herbert, settled there in a mansion which he built on the site of the priory. From him the property passed to his son, Sir Walter, who in 1550 left it to his son, another George, together with 'lands and tenements lying at Tynterne also my ship called the James and all cables and anchors etc.'

Ruins of the Abbatical Mansion at Tinterne Parva.

Echoes of medieval Tintern. *Top left*: 73. Ruins of an abbatical mansion. *Top right*: 74. Tintern Manor House. *Above*: 75. Nurton's, Tintern Parva.

It looks as if the property 'at Tynterne' passed to the Herberts when the Abbey was given to the Earl of Worcester by Henry VIII. Earl William Herbert had been Steward of the Abbey and left money for further building work. Abbot Wyche, the last one at Tintern, was given a pension of £23 a year and is said to have lived within the boundaries of Tintern Parva manor and to have employed his expertise in altering his house. Nurtons, which still exists today, was part of the same manor. Sketches exist of two different buildings thought to have been Abbot Wyche's house. What is certain is that Nurton's, though altered, is one of the few surviving properties in what was once Sir William Herbert's Tintern estate. Documents dating from 1647 describe its location.

> of half of one granary, one orchard and 2 parcels of land called Nortons hill in TYNTARNE bounded by lands of Henry, Marquis of Worcester, lands of Thomas Herbert esq., lands of Henry Probert esq., lands of John Thorn and the highway from Landogoe to Tyntarne.[5]

Eventually St Julian's and the Tintern lands passed to the Sir William Herbert, whom we know as the friend and disciple of John Dee. Thus the Herbert and Bacon families were linked not only by a common interest in the theatre and the brassworks but also, in the late 1500s, by properties in the Tintern area within easy riding distance of each other.

HENRY BILLINGSLEY

I returned to the question of Sir Henry Billingsley and his mortgaging of property in the same area from William Herbert. He hailed from Canterbury, so this was no nostalgic return to family roots. As a youth he had studied first at St John's College in Cambridge and then at Oxford, but without taking a degree at either university. At Oxford he developed the interest in mathematics for which he is still remembered. His tutor was an eminent mathematician called 'Whytehead', who according to the antiquarian scholar Anthony Wood had once been an Augustinian friar. Later Billingsley went to London where he became a wealthy merchant, prominent in civic affairs as sheriff (1584), alderman (1585) and finally lord mayor (1596).

Wood states that Whytehead, Billingsley's old Oxford tutor, lived during his old age in Billingsley's house and bequeathed him a valuable collection of manuscripts which he used in his translation of Euclid's *Elements of Geometrie* (1570). In his own preface to the reader, Billingsley expressed a wish to translate 'other good authors . . . pertaining to Mathematicall Artes'. So, a life-long interest in mathematics stemming from his Oxford days is clearly attested. His interest in property near Tintern followed the publication of his translation but preceded his civic role in London. It may well be that Billingsley joined Sir William Herbert in his venture to erect a college and played his own part in teaching the 'mathematicall artes' to Sir William's chosen band of scholars. That would be sufficient reason for him to seek property nearby for himself, his wife and large family. Even as Lord Mayor he kept in touch with the area, serving on an Exchequer Commission at Chepstow into complaints brought by Richard Hanbury against local farmers. Such sustained interest from Billingsley gives added significance to one of the original geometrical drawings included in the Schweighardt scrapbook. It carries written instructions on the division of a circle and the mathematical properties of certain numbers, and gives its source as 'Whithead's (sic) direction'.

Sir William Herbert had chosen an ideal place for his college in the manor of Tintern Parva. His own house was close to the wharf, and to the ancient hospice of the former abbey where visitors could still be accommodated. But he was also close to the brass and wire works which could provide the brass and expertise to make plates for prints. It is worth noting that when Herbert returned from his expedition to Kerry in 1589, he spent his time at Tintern rather than St Julian's.

BACON AND THE WIREWORKS

I was still engaged in trying to establish the credibility of the assertions Dr Owen had made to the press. He had claimed that Francis Bacon had lived at 'Mount St Alban's near Newport'. I had found the site where the house had stood. Another claim was that Bacon had been 'the owner of the wireworks at Tintern'. Could that be correct, too, when the recognised authorities on the wireworks and Elizabethan monopolies made no mention of it? Hidden away in the *Calendar of State Papers Domestic* (and not indexed under Francis Bacon) is the following entry for 7 May 1611:

> Robert Lord Lisle, Sir Francis Bacon and others of the Company of Wireworkers (to Salisbury). Ask for preference as purchasers of the King's wood to be sold in the Forest of Dean for the use of their works†at Tintern and Whitbrook.[6]

This nugget of gold settled two more of Owen's six assertions that Bacon was 'owner' of the wireworks with 'others', and that there existed a petition from him to Robert Cecil for wood from the Forest of Dean close by. As a result, I searched for more entries in the state papers.

In the records of the *Acts of the Privy Council of England* I came across a warrant 'to the Constable of the Forrest of Dean and George Marshall, his Majestie's servant'

76. Francis Bacon, by Hollar. Bacon is shown with his hand resting on the royal emblem of Elizabeth I.

dated 22 November 1613. Already, within two years, the licence for wood granted to Bacon and his partners had led to problems:

Whereas upon informacion of much abuse and disorder in the felling and cutting of wood and tymber trees within the Forrest of Dean, as well by reason of a contracte lately made on his Majestie's behalfe with the Earle of Pembrooke, touching the delivery of certen cordes of wood, at a rate, for his Lordship's iron workes, as otherwise by the borderers and near dwellers to the Forrest for their private benefitt and advantage, George Marshall, esquire, his Majestie's servant, was by his Highnes expresse commaundement and direccion sent downe with instruccions to take true informacion of the state of that complaint; forasmuch as upon viewe and enquirie thereof it appeareth that the abuses and disorders are such that, unlesse some course be taken to stay & hinder the proceedinges therein, it will tende to the utter devastacion and spoile of the saide Forrest, to the great inconvenience of the publique, in such store and provision of tymber as is requisite & necessary for the use of his Majestie's Navie. These are, therefore, to will & require you to make your present repaire unto the said Forrest, & to give order for the stay of any further cutting or felling of any kinde of wood or tree whatsoever within that Forrest untill his Majestie's pleasure be further knowne . . .[7]

Among the members of the Privy Council who signed this warrant was the Earl of Worcester, whose lands bordered on Pembroke's at Tintern and who saw himself in some ways as a rival landlord. It was clear from the warrant that, in addition to Lord Lisle and Sir Francis Bacon, one of the 'others' who owned the wireworks was William Herbert, third Earl of Pembroke.

This is an interesting triumvirate. By 1611 Bacon had at last gained the long-sought office of Solicitor General and was being constantly called on by the Privy Council to prosecute infringements of the law. Moreover he was already beginning to sue for the post of Attorney General. Lisle had been appointed Chamberlain of the new queen's household in 1605 and, among other duties, had jurisdiction over her company of actors, the Queen Anne's Players. James I had appointed Pembroke Warden of the Forest of Dean in 1608, a post Elizabeth had refused him. Accordingly the criticism of excessive wood felling affected him in more ways than one. He was also one of the two dedicatees of the Shakespeare First Folio. All three men shared a business interest in the Virginia Company, and Lisle and Herbert in the East India Company. Here we find all three linked together in another commercial venture at Tintern and faced with the problem of providing fuel for the wireworks.

Viscount Lisle was born in 1563 as plain Robert Sidney, the younger brother of Sir Philip Sidney and godfather to Philip, the fourth Earl of Pembroke. He fought at the battle of Zutphen in which his brother received his fatal wound, and for his conduct in the campaign he was knighted. The two earls of Leicester and Warwick were his uncles and each made him heir. Sidney was the chief mourner at his brother's funeral in 1587 and in that capacity would have supervised the series of magnificent engravings of the occasion prepared by Thomas Lant and Theodore de Bry. Later he saw further service in the Netherlands with distinction but had to wait until the accession of James I to achieve recognition. He was immediately created Baron Sidney of Penshurst (1603), raised to Viscount Lisle (1605) and finally Earl of Leicester (1618). According to one authority this was the year that the third Earl of Pembroke became 'Grandmaster of Freemasonry'.[8]

THE BIRTH OF A BROTHERHOOD

Reflecting on all this, I feel able to attempt some conclusions about the material under review. I had always believed that it had existed as an entity over a considerable period of time with additions made at significant moments. Taken together, Byrom's collection of drawings, the brass plates, the companion drawings in Ms 471 and the Schweighardt scrapbook form a resource that had a significant part to play in the origin and development of some kind of 'brotherhood'. It began with the Dissolution of the Monasteries (c. 1536) and the first 'Chapter' had been centred at Tintern. The subjects that concerned this group were, I believe, ideas taken from the cabala and the hermetic tradition of the Renaissance which resulted, among other things, in the design of the Elizabethan playhouse. These studies led to early forms of speculative Freemasonry and alchemical pursuits, which matured into the beginnings of modern science and, ultimately, the Royal Society.

It was the handwritten inventory from the Science Museum that had helped me to draw the different strands together. The contents of the inventory reflected both the book by Jamnitzer and the *Elements of Geometrie*. The heading at the top of the first page suggests a date of 1570, the year Sir Henry Billingsley published his translation of Euclid with Dee's 'Preface'. That Billingsley mortgaged property close to Tintern from Sir William Herbert of St Julian's, as already mentioned, was not, I felt, a mere coincidence. A centre of learning connected with the resource material, and related topics such as cryptography, existed at the Herbert manor of Tintern Parva. The Herbert connections here and at the abbey represent long and solemn obligations. As we have already noted, the first Earl William had been the abbey's steward and left money to 'build new cloisters'. Together with St Julian's, the Tintern properties remained firmly with the Herbert family when Sir Thomas Herbert purchased the manor at Tintern in 1640.

The handwritten inventory describes the glorious representations of geometrical forms which I believe were made at Tintern with the expertise of the German engineers and craftsmen at the wireworks. Sir Thomas Herbert was the guardian of this and other source material which he transmitted to members of the Invisible College who later gathered together at Gresham's College. Sir Francis Bacon was the founder of a brotherhood which I believe preceded that group.

The isolation and sense of peace at Tintern drew the Cistercians to it as a site for one of their foundations. Other seekers after truth followed in their wake. Tintern Parva still holds its own mysteries which centre round a house, an ancient church and a disused wharf. Visible evidence of additional early buildings still survives in the manor. Documents dating from the early seventeenth century show the field name of Norton, an earlier version of Nurton. This carries echoes of Thomas Norton an alchemist and master-mason who flourished around 1477 and was master mason of St Mary Redcliffe, the most important church in nearby Bristol. His great-grandson, Samuel Norton, was also an alchemist and author of several alchemical treatises; he is mentioned in the Schweighardt scrapbook.

The brotherhood to whom instruction was offered was a small exclusive group, men not simply of intelligence and learning but of vision and imagination. The wisdom it imparted was in turn shared by John Dee, Sir William Herbert, Sir Francis Bacon, Sir Thomas Herbert and William, third Earl of Pembroke. All were, for want of a better word, 'adepts'. This brotherhood was foreshadowed in an embryonic form by Bacon's group, 'The Knights of the Helmet' – a group that took its name from the helmet of the goddess of wisdom.

It was at Tintern, I believe, that the brass patterns were made for the theatre designs following the instructions of Theodore de Bry. Working drawings for the playhouses survive in the Byrom collection. It is possible still to run prints off the brass plates. They could be used repeatedly and some, it is clear, were more heavily used than others. These were the prototypes for the geometry of the playhouses. They were made available to a handful of people only. To interpret them a basic understanding of geometry and the implications of a Pythagorean right-angled triangle were required. In addition to working drawings, the collection includes ideal concepts for individual playhouses. These are coloured and, it would seem, were being prepared for publication, but the projected book never materialised. It is unfortunate that the poor state of book-keeping at the wireworks has left us no accounts for the enterprise. But records do survive which show that the wireworks did trade at Southwark. From beginning to end the management of the venture was kept within the control of certain families whom we have reviewed in this book.

Postscript

In the process of my investigations into the relationship between Byrom's collection of theatre drawings and the design concept of the Elizabethan theatre, I stumbled upon a totally unexpected avenue of enquiry. I had begun firmly convinced of John Dee's role in the original design of the playhouses and of the importance of the aristocratic patrons of the acting companies. The revelation of Dee's close, personal connection with those patrons has reinforced that conviction. The discovery of the brass plates and their relevance to the theatre drawings, together with the additional drawings in Ms 471 and the Schweighardt scrapbook, have enlarged the body of archive material concerned with the Elizabethan theatre considerably. Taken together, these three elements give us a fresh insight into the philosophical ideas behind the design of the playhouses. Recent scientific developments in the techniques of archaeology have verified my interpretation of the dimensions for three of them.

Alongside this tripartite corpus of material, we have to assess the parts played in the evolution of the playhouses, either directly or indirectly, by leading members of the Herbert dynasty, particularly William, the third Earl, Sir William Herbert of St Julian's and Sir Thomas Herbert of Tintern. Above all, the relevance of Francis Bacon to the history of the Elizabethan theatre must be considered. His known interest in playmaking at Gray's Inn has to be reassessed in the light of the unexpected discovery that he was a joint owner of the Tintern wireworks which, I believe, were responsible for the brass plates. This link extends the scope of Bacon's theatrical involvement significantly.

However, what I have found most disturbing of all is that, after prolonged study of the illustrations in the Schweighardt scrapbook, I was forced to the conclusion that the alchemical allegory depicted within its pages was being used to encode a narrative concerned with the relationship between Queen Elizabeth and the Earl of Leicester. References to a tennis game, verses celebrating the wedding of the 'crooked God' and 'loving dame', recurring emblems of a child, heraldic symbols of new life and succession – this sequence of images appears to hint that Queen Elizabeth went through a form of marriage with the Earl of Leicester and from that union a child was born. Astonishing as this may seem, the strength of Elizabeth's attachment to Leicester is attested historically by a number of contemporary accounts, and not just those of a suspicious Spanish ambassador.

In my reading, I have tried to steer an impartial course between opposite schools of Baconian biographers, although some of them may find material in the Schweighardt illustrations more pertinent to their agendas than others. However, while I have consulted some openly unorthodox authorities on his life, I have not addressed the controversy over the authorship of Shakespeare.

Bacon was a man who considered every step in his career carefully, and his involvement with the wireworks links him with the brass plates and, thus, with the Byrom theatre drawings. This involvement seems to me totally consistent with the kind of knowledge and wisdom that lay at the heart of the 'college' at Tintern and that owed so much to Dee while pointing the way forward to new forms of knowledge. Bacon was himself an advocate of the growing importance of science. The legacy of his philosophical works speaks for itself. Even so, there are a number of questions about his life that remain unanswered. The ideas concealed in the Schweighardt illustrations, together with other facts which have emerged in the process, raise important issues. Addressing these has now become something of a personal odyssey.

APPENDIX 1

Additional Illustrations

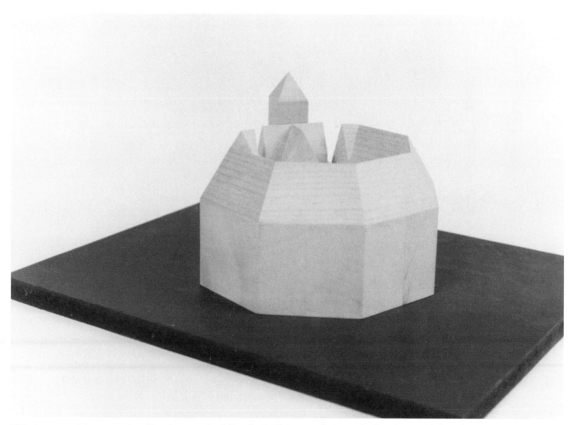

77. A geometric reconstruction in wood of the first Globe made in 1991 by the model-maker at Manchester University to the scale of the 'setting out' drawings in the Byrom Collection.

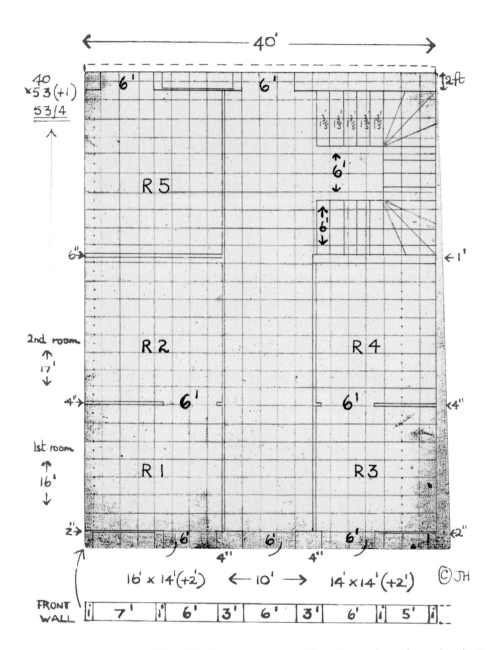

78. Tiring house drawing. The original drawing occupies the entire surface of a card in the Byrom Collection. The size is double that of the other theatre drawings and, reduced by half, fits the 'setting out' plan of the theatres. For example, the geometry of the eight-sided Globe (Figure 37) embraces the area shown by the first four rooms. Room 5 and the staircase are shown outside the main load-bearing frame of 72. For consistency, the card has been reproduced at 75 per cent of its original size, to the same scale as the other theatre drawings.

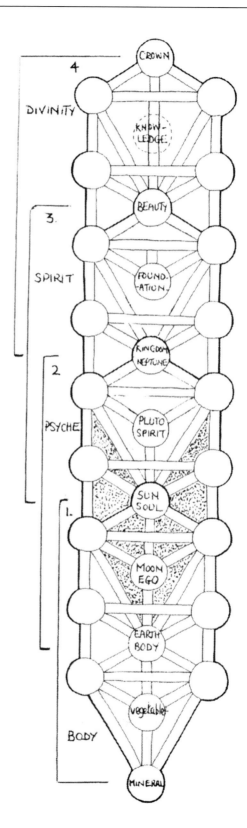

79. The Tree of Life is a fundamental element in all the parametric drawings. The extended Tree of Life shows the four worlds through which Man may pass in meditation: from the natural world of the body to the world of the psyche, then to the world of the spirit and finally to the highest world where he becomes one with the Divine Presence. A series of interdependent stages or states is indicated by the small circles. For cabalists these are the stages by which Man rises through each of the four worlds to his union with God. The scheme can be interpreted in a number of ways, for example, as a programme for psychological integration as well as of spiritual development. (Based on figures in *Kabbalah* by Z'ev ben Shimon Halevi)

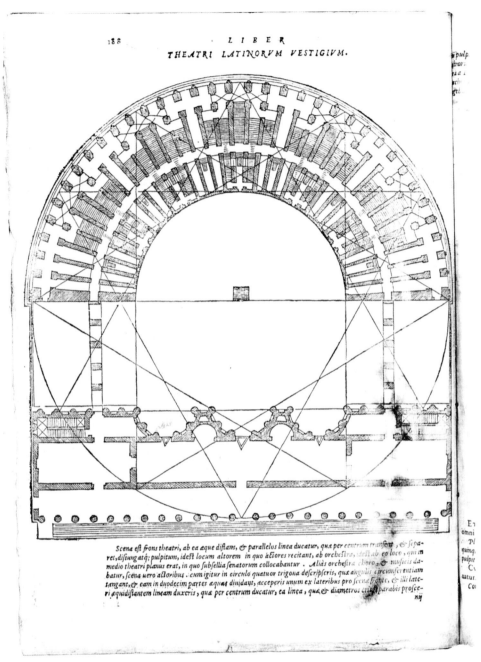

· *LIBER*
THEATRI LATINORVM VESTIGIVM.

Scena est frons theatri, ab ea æque distans, & parallelos linea ducatur, quæ per centrum transeat, & separet, disiungatq; pulpitum, idest locum altorem in quo actores recitant, ab orchestra, idest ab eo loco, qui in medio theatri planus erat, in quo subsellia senatorum collocabantur . Alias orchestra choro, & musicis dabatur, scena uero actoribus . cum igitur in circulo quatuor trigona descripseris, quæ angulis circumferentiam tangant, & eam in duodecim partes æquas diuidat, acceperis unum ex lateribus pro scena fronte, & illi lateri æquidistantem lineam duxeris, quæ per centrum ducatur, ea linea , quæ & diametros erit, separabis proscenij

80. Plan of a Roman theatre by Andrea Palladio from Daniele Barbaro's commentary on Vitruvius's architectural treatise, 1567.

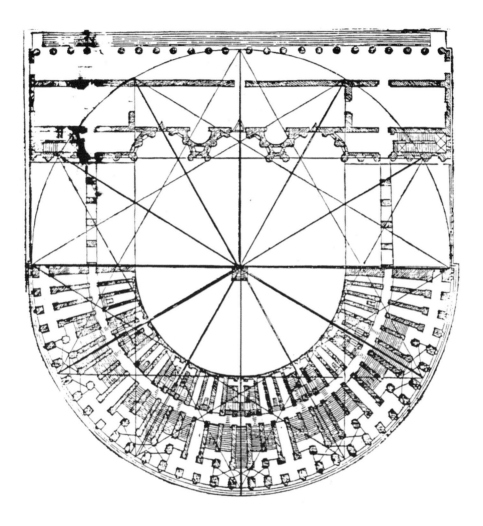

80a. To make it easier to compare the Palladio plan with that of the Elizabethan playhouses shown earlier, it has been turned round so that the stage area is at the top. Additional lines bisecting the triangle show the close correspondence between Palladio's plan and the geometric drawings. An acetate copy of this diagram, at this size, superimposed on any of the playhouse drawings in the text will demonstrate the compatability.

81. Emblem 17 from *Atalanta Fugiens* by Michael Maier. The illustration shows the four worlds of the Tree of Life outlined on page 233. This is one of a series of the emblematic pictures engraved by Theodore de Bry for Maier's book in 1617.

82. This sketch of Tintern is a reminder of its isolation – a feature that influenced both the Cistercians and Sir William Herbert in their search for a suitable spiritual/philosophical centre. Maier's four worlds, depicted against a watery landscape, strongly echo the theme of the ideal setting for the pursuit of enlightenment.

The Geometry of Human Life: An Analysis and Commentary

The ancients distinguished philosophically between the practical and speculative modes of knowledge. This distinction also applied to geometry. In the appendix which follows, Leon Crickmore explores some of the speculative and symbolic aspects of the geometry of the Elizabethan theatres in a manner that is compatible with their practical geometry discussed elsewhere in this book.

The *Theatre of Human Life* (*Theatrum Vitae Humanae*, Metz, 1596) is an engraving by Theodore de Bry from a book of the same title by Jean Jacques Boissard. It depicts the world as a theatre or circus in which mankind witnesses the miseries of the seven ages of man. In her book *Theatre of the World*, Frances Yates reproduces the engraving (Plate 23) and likens it (pp. 66–7) to the speech of the melancholy Jaques in Shakespeare's *As You Like It* (Act II, scene vii):

> All the world's a stage
> And all the men and women merely players:
> They have their exits and their entrances;
> And one man in his time plays many parts,
> His acts being seven ages . . .

Jaques goes on to characterise these seven ages as (1) infant, (2) schoolboy, (3) lover, (4) soldier, (5) justice, (6) pantaloon, (7) second childhood.

   Among a collection of 516 geometrical drawings, of which the Jacobite John Byrom (1691–1763) was custodian, Joy Hancox has discovered a representation of the detailed geometry that underlies de Bry's engraving. She reproduced this in *The Byrom Collection*. My purpose here is to offer a more comprehensive analysis and commentary, since I believe this will foster a better understanding both of other de Bry engravings and of the geometry of the Elizabethan theatre drawings.

MEASUREMENTS AND NUMBERS

All the measurements I cite relate to the '72 rule': a ruler (with units approximately, but not exactly, 1/16 inch, grouped in eights) which Joy Hancox derived from pinpricks in a setting out plan of the Globe theatre. This 'rule' represents a standard measure in Byrom's collection. The 72 measure can also be seen on the vertical spine of the Theatre of Human Life drawing. From the centre, 42 units have been marked upwards, continuing in two-unit gaps to the top.

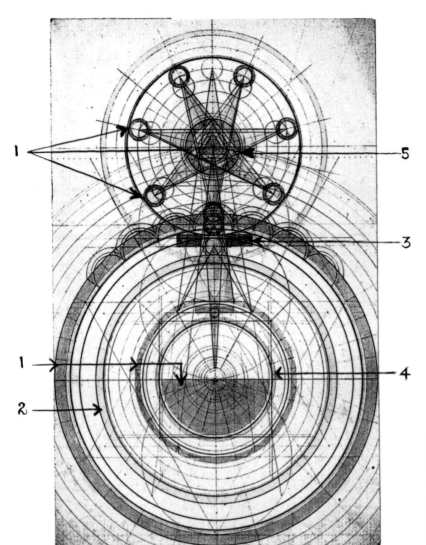

83. A geometrical
representation of the
Theatre of Human Life
engraved by Theodore
de Bry, 1596. Key to
Colours: 1. Green;
2. Gold; 3. Blue;
4. Brown; 5. Rose.

Certain key measurements recur in the *Theatre of Human Life* and other drawings in the collection. First among these are 20, 30 and 60. (Measurements, one assumes, reflecting those of the Temple of Solomon as described in The Book of Kings I:6 – 'sixty cubits long, twenty wide, thirty high'. Next, a number from the lunar and female cycles: 28. 28 is a triangular number (1+2+3+4+5+6+7); it is also a perfect number (i.e. the sum of its factors (1+2+14+4+7). A third number, relevant because it appears as the size of the frame of the Globe theatre, is 72. 72 is divisible by all the numbers from 1 to 9 except 5 and 7. 5 has already been incorporated into the *Theatre of Human Life* through the 'temple' numbers (e.g. 5×4=20). 7 is there, too, through 28 (7×4=28). In the geometry of the *Theatre of Human Life*, however, it is manifested with virtuosity in the form of a seven-pointed star. A six-pointed star (the Star of David or Seal of Solomon) is easy to construct by dividing the circumference of a circle by its radius, and joining the appropriate points. In fact, such a hexagram has been lightly drawn within the lower circle of the *Theatre of Human Life*. There is no known method, however, for accurately constructing a heptagram. The approximation displayed in the *Theatre of Human Life* has a complexity and sophistication which call to mind the subtlety of a Bach fugue.

GEOMETRICAL SHAPES

Circles

The drawing is dominated by circles. Some have coloured rims. Some are scored heavily in brown; others are sketched more lightly. Many seem to have been drawn entirely for constructional reasons. I shall focus my attention on those which appear to carry a particular symbolic significance.

In essence, the geometry of the *Theatre of Human Life* comprises two interlocking circles: below, a large, green one with a diameter (d) of 120 units; and above, a smaller, gold one whose diameter (d) is 85 units. (Its centre is set 85 units above that of the green circle.) These symbolise human life and the heavens respectively.

From the centre of the earthly circle, radials 15° apart divide the lower semicircle into 12 segments; the upper semicircle is divided into 24 (7½°). These divisions may be associated, for example, with the hours of the day, the hours of both day and night, the signs of the zodiac or solar cycles, according to the particular perspective adopted by anyone using the drawing as a mandala for meditation. Functionally, the closer radials of the upper semicircle also determine the width (14 units) and the central points of the seven scallops at the top of the earthly circle, which represent the seven ages of man. Again for constructional reasons, some of these radials are extended into the circle above. The heavenly circle itself has been divided into 14 segments, offset from its horizontal diameter. Such divisions suggest aspects of the lunar cycle.

Within the large green circle, working outwards from the centre, one finds: a brown-rimmed circle (d=45); a green circle (d=60: 120×½); and a gold circle (d=90: 45×2). The two green-rimmed circles may represent the division of human life into its material and spiritual aspects.

Theodore de Bry was a Huguenot. He has placed a blue cross-bar of a Tau cross (length 28 units) in the vesica where the circles of heaven and earth overlap, witnessing to his faith in the saving power of Jesus Christ. (Appreciation of this point will be enhanced by a comparison with the Christian cabala drawing in Ms 471 shown on p. 235 of *The Byrom Collection*.) The smaller green circle also has a Tau cross of proportionate length (14 units). In addition, the lower semicircle of one of the central circles (d=40) has been coloured green. This could represent the hours of darkness and the dark forces of temptation, sin and death which beset mankind.

Among the lightly drawn circles, three are of particular interest: each has a diameter of 56 units. The first two are contingent and fit inside the inner rim of the earthly circle. The circumference of the third touches the centre of the heavenly circle, as well as forming a vesica with the upper of the other two circles.

Looking now inside the heavenly circle, one sees a green-rimmed circle of 20 units diameter. (Kings I:6 describes the Holy of Holies as a cube 20 cubits in length, width and height.) The Hebrew Tetragrammaton, the unspeakable name of God, has been inscribed towards the top of the de Bry engraving.) Moving outwards, a series of concentric circles, 4 units apart, have been drawn. The seven-pointed star sits within a circle with a diameter of 56 units. On its circumference (at points crossed by the radials of the gold circle) hang seven gold, green-rimmed spheres, each centred on one of the points of the heptagram. These represent the seven planets known to the Ptolemaic astronomical system.

Squares

There are only two squares in this drawing. The main square has sides of 40 units; it surrounds the lightly drawn circle (d=40) which has its lower semicircle coloured green. A frame of one unit drawn around it creates a second square with sides of 42 units. The sides of both squares are extended by 15 units in four directions to produce lines of 70 and 72 units, respectively. These could have been developed into squares, but this has not been done. The whole structure seems to serve as a device for creating various series of expanding circles. Interestingly, similar structures can be identified at the centres of drawings of the Globe and Fortune theatres, and are expanded further in other drawings in the collection.

As the seven spheres in the heavenly circle represent the seven planets of the Ptolemaic system, so the proportions which the ancients believed generated 'the music of the spheres' are present in dimensions within the earthly circle. The Pythagorean musical tetractys (see Boethius's *De Institutione Musica*, I 10) which, projected into the heavens provided a theoretical foundation for Greek astronomy, as well as serving as the source of the entire practical tuning system for music in ancient Greece, (as above so below) is embodied in the key measurements of this drawing. The Tetractys comprised the following proportions: $1:\frac{3}{4}:\frac{2}{3}:2$; or in whole numbers ($\times 6$): 6:8:9:12; or, multiplied again by 5:30:40:45:60. In this drawing, these proportions are made manifest, for example, in the following measurements: 30, radius of the smaller green circle (d=60); 40, side of inner square: 45, radius of lower gold circle: 60, radius of the larger green circle (d=120).

Triangles

The lightly drawn Star of David, with its two frames of 4 units, touches the inner rim of the earthly circle. It is formed by two equilateral triangles, the lower one inverted, and overlapping the upper. The six points of the inner hexagram are each 72 units from the base of their respective triangles. The lines forming the highest point, on the spine of the drawing, are scored more heavily to highlight an equilateral triangle of sides 28 units and what looks like a pair of compasses. One is reminded of 'The Creator' (*Bible Moralisée, c.* 1250, Bodleian Library), an image of Christ using compasses to re-enact the creation of the universe.

Within a green circle at the centre of the heavenly circle, there is another equilateral triangle, half the size, and coloured rose. From its base a curious line of dots, 1 unit followed by intervals of 2 units, extends in each direction parallel to the horizontal diameter of the circle. Its function seems to be to determine the starting points for two tangents to the heavenly circle. A parallel pair of tangents, touching the circle (d=56) begin at the ends of the diameter of the more heavily scored brown circle (d=64). Considered symbolically, the rose triangle at the centre of the Godhead represents the Christian Trinity: Father, Son and Holy Spirit. One wonders, therefore, whether the seven additional uncoloured circles, six overlapping six of the spheres, and one at the top, in pride of place, where the circle (d=56) is crossed by the spine of the drawing, might symbolise the 'seven spirits of God' (Revelations 5:6).

The trinity triangle also corresponds to the tiring house triangle of the Globe theatre. If the tiring house triangle on the parametric card of the Globe is placed over the rose triangle of de Bry's *Theatre of Human Life*, the remainder of the card covers the lower gold circle (d=90). The diameter of the Starrs Mall of the Globe is 51 which is equivalent in gematria to 'de Bry' (4+5+2+17+23=51).

Keith Critchlow has shown that if the West Rose Window of Chartres Cathedral, portraying the Last Judgement, were to be tilted down, as if hinged at the floor, it would cover the maze in the nave. Similarly, if the upper gold circle of the *Theatre of Human Life* is folded down over the large green circle (at approximately 42 units above the green circle's centre), it fits exactly inside the rim of the lower gold circle (d=90). The resulting diagram (seen by placing a light behind the drawing) forms a splendid symbolic representation of the New Jerusalem.

It is puzzling that an eighth green-rimmed sphere has been included in the drawing. This sphere creates a vesica (7 units) with the lowest of the seven planets inside the central scallop. According to Hermes Trismegistus (Poimandres, 26), the soul in a trance or after death, ascending through the planetary spheres, is stripped of the qualities it had received at birth and which, during life, had been energised by the 'music of the spheres'. It then enters the Eighth Sphere. In Jonson's 'Sad Shepherd', Aeglamour tells us that his love Earine, presumed drowned, is to become an eighth sphere and that her apotheosis will harmonise all discord. In the context of *As You Like It*, the eighth sphere may symbolise the sanctity of marriage. During the wedding masque at the close of the play, Hymen says:

> Here's eight that must take hands
> To join in Hymen's bands . . .

The song that follows proclaims:

> 'Tis Hymen peoples every town
> High wedlock then be honoured.

The classical allusion is consistent with the syncretic style of Rosicrucian Christianity to be found in many of de Bry's publications. Moreover, the interlocking marriage rings lie within long narrow triangles, reminiscent of the form and matter pyramids in books by Robert Fludd (see Joscelyn Godwin, *Robert Fludd*, p. 44ff). Joy Hancox has suggested that Jaques's earlier speech about the world being a stage might be Shakespeare's tribute to de Bry for the part he had played in designing the Globe theatre. My interpretation of the masque would be compatible with such an idea.

COLOURS

The earthly circle is green. The heavenly colour is gold. The simplest interpretation of such colouring is to relate green to nature and gold to grace. The Jesuit polymath Athanasius Kircher (1602–80) associated green with Venus and gold with the Sun. He also linked the intervals of musical tuning with colours: 3rd, blue; 4th, green; 5th, gold; 7th, rose; octave, dark (brown?). *A Magical Calendar*, published by Johann Theodore de Bry (1563–1623), Theodore's son, contains a host of celestial and magical correspondences. To consider these, however, is beyond the scope of this note. Nevertheless, the richness of symbolism and imagery so far uncovered by this analysis of the geometry of de Bry's Theatre of Human Life adds new resonances of meaning to the words of another character in *As You Like It*: Duke Senior's reference to 'this wide and universal theatre' just before Jaques delivers his famous speech about the many parts played by each of us in our lifetime.

L.C.

APPENDIX 3

Genealogies

The information contained in the genealogies that follow has been taken from several sources, viz:

Bagley, J.J., *The Earls of Derby (1485–1995)* (1985)
Burke's Extinct Peerage
Dawkins, Peter, 'Dedication to the Light' (1984)
Duncan-Jones, Katherine, *Sir Philip Sidney, Courtier, Poet* (1991)
The autobiography of Edward, Lord Herbert, ed. Sidney Lee (1886)
Herbertorium Prosapia (*c.* 1681)
'The Key of Alchymie' in Theophilus Schweighardt, *Speculum Sophicum Rhodo-Stauroticum* (1618)

ROBERT DUDLEY
EARL OF LEICESTER

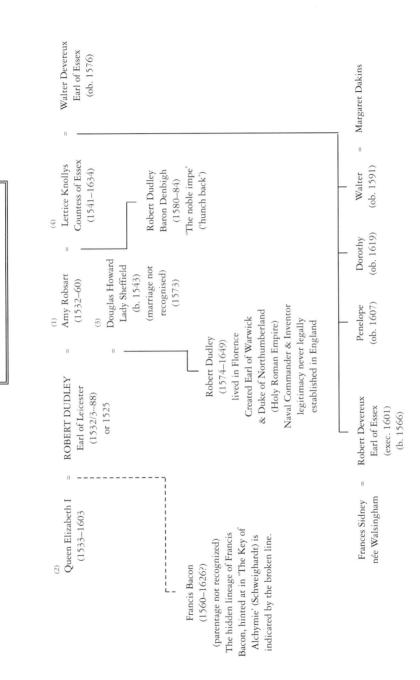

(2)
Queen Elizabeth I
(1533–1603)

Francis Bacon
(1560–1626?)
(parentage not recognized)
The hidden lineage of Francis
Bacon, hinted at in 'The Key of
Alchymie' (Schweighardt) is
indicated by the broken line.

=

ROBERT DUDLEY
Earl of Leicester
(1532/3–88)
or 1525

(1)
Amy Robsart
(1532–60)

=

(3)
Douglas Howard
Lady Sheffield
(b. 1543)
(marriage not
recognised)
(1573)

=

(4)
Lettice Knollys
Countess of Essex
(1541–1634)

=

Walter Devereux
Earl of Essex
(ob. 1576)

Robert Dudley
(1574–1649)
lived in Florence
Created Earl of Warwick
& Duke of Northumberland
(Holy Roman Empire)
Naval Commander & Inventor
legitimacy never legally
established in England

Robert Dudley
Baron Denbigh
(1580–84)
'The noble impe'
('hunch back')

Robert Devereux
Earl of Essex
(exec. 1601)
(b. 1566)

Penelope
(ob. 1607)

Dorothy
(ob. 1619)

Walter
(ob. 1591)

=

Margaret Dakins

Frances Sidney
née Walsingham

=

Note: Francis Bacon was brought up as the son of Anne and Nicholas Bacon.

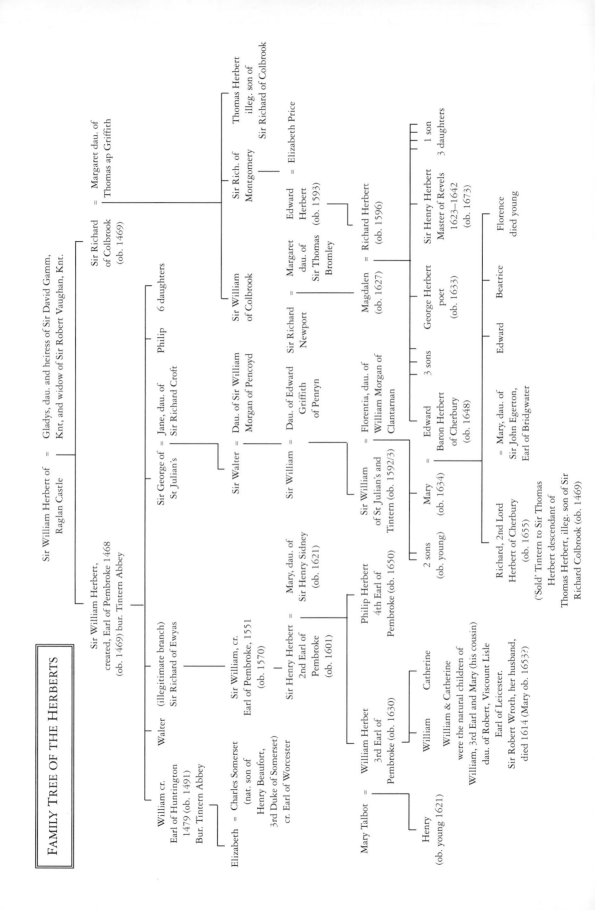

FAMILY TREE OF THE HERBERTS

FAMILY TREE OF THE DUDLEYS

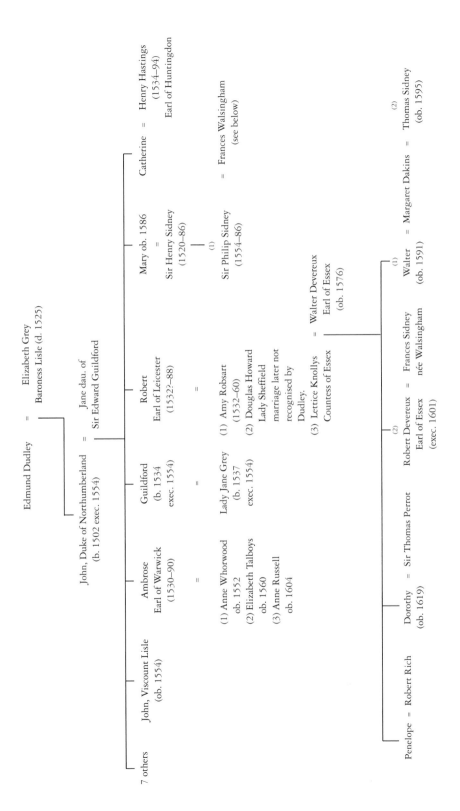

Edmund Dudley = Elizabeth Grey
Baroness Lisle (d. 1525)

John, Duke of Northumberland = Jane dau. of
(b. 1502 exec. 1554)   Sir Edward Guildford

7 others

John, Viscount Lisle
(ob. 1554)

Ambrose
Earl of Warwick
(1530–90)
=
(1) Anne Whorwood
ob. 1552
(2) Elizabeth Talboys
ob. 1560
(3) Anne Russell
ob. 1604

Guildford
(b. 1534
exec. 1554)
=
Lady Jane Grey
(b. 1537
exec. 1554)

Robert
Earl of Leicester
(1532–88)
=
(1) Amy Robsart
(1532–60)
(2) Douglas Howard
Lady Sheffield
marriage later not
recognised by
Dudley.
(3) Lettice Knollys
Countess of Essex
=
Walter Devereux
Earl of Essex
(ob. 1576)

Mary ob. 1586
=
Sir Henry Sidney
(1520–86)
(1)
Sir Philip Sidney
(1554–86)

Catherine = Henry Hastings
(1534–94)
Earl of Huntingdon

= Frances Walsingham
(see below)

Penelope = Robert Rich

Dorothy = Sir Thomas Perrot
(ob. 1619)

Robert Devereux = Frances Sidney
Earl of Essex   née Walsingham
(exec. 1601)

(1)
Walter = Margaret Dakins = Thomas Sidney
(ob. 1591)   (ob. 1595)
(2)

FAMILY TREE OF THE SIDNEYS

Sir William Sidney = Anne Pagenham
1482–1554 (ob. 1554)

Mary Dudley = Sir Henry Sidney (1529–86) | Mary (ob. 1542) = Sir William Dormer | Lucy | Mabel | Elizabeth | Ann = Sir William Fitzwilliam (1526–99) | Frances = Thomas Radcliffe Earl of Sussex (ob. 1583)
(ob. 1586)

Jane

Sir Philip Sidney = Frances Walsingham (1567–1632)
(1554–86)

2 daughters (ob. young) | Mary = Henry Herbert (1534–1601) 2nd Earl of Pembroke | Robert (1563–1626) Viscount Lisle, Earl of Leicester = Barbara Gammage (1562–1621) 2. Sarah Smythe | Ambrosia (b. 1564) | Thomas (1569–95) = Margaret Dakins

Elizabeth (1585–1612) = Roger Manners (1576–1612) Earl of Rutland

*William (1580–1630) 3rd Earl of Pembroke = Mary Talbot (b. 1580) | Katherine | Anne | Philip (1584–1650) 4th Earl of Pembroke = (1) Susan de Vere (1587–1629) (2) Anne Clifford (1590–1676) | Mary (1587–1653) = Sir Robert Wroth (1576–1614)

Henry ob. young–1621

James (1613–16)

William | Catherine | 10 others

*The natural children of William, 3rd Earl of Pembroke and Mary

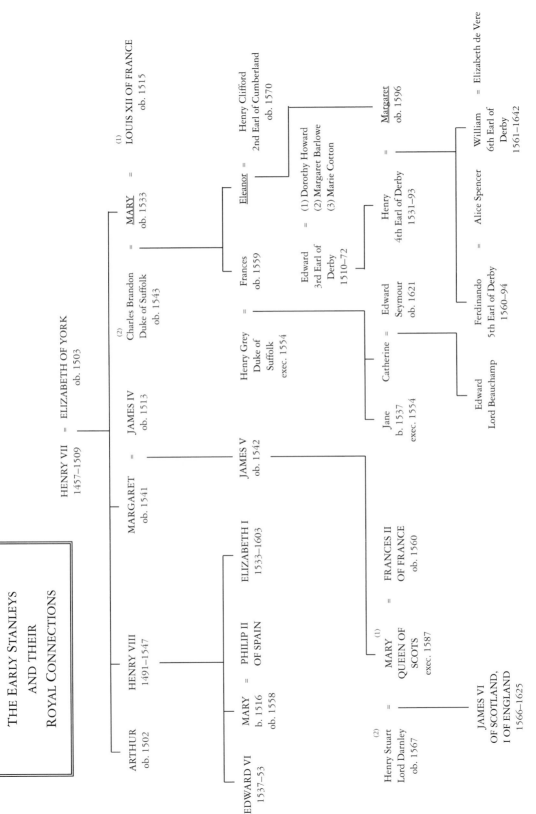

THE EARLY STANLEYS
AND THEIR
ROYAL CONNECTIONS

HENRY VII = ELIZABETH OF YORK
1457–1509   ob. 1503

ARTHUR
ob. 1502

HENRY VIII
1491–1547

MARGARET
ob. 1541

JAMES IV
ob. 1513

(2)
Charles Brandon
Duke of Suffolk
ob. 1543
=
(1)
MARY
ob. 1533
=
LOUIS XII OF FRANCE
ob. 1515

EDWARD VI
1537–53

MARY = PHILIP II
b. 1516   OF SPAIN
ob. 1558

ELIZABETH I
1533–1603

JAMES V
ob. 1542

Frances
ob. 1559
=
Henry Grey
Duke of
Suffolk
exec. 1554

Eleanor = Henry Clifford
2nd Earl of Cumberland
ob. 1570

Edward
3rd Earl of
Derby
1510–72
=
(1) Dorothy Howard
(2) Margaret Barlowe
(3) Marie Cotton

FRANCES II
OF FRANCE
ob. 1560
=
(1)
MARY
QUEEN OF
SCOTS
exec. 1587

Jane
b. 1537
exec. 1554

Catherine = Edward
Seymour
ob. 1621

Henry
4th Earl of Derby
1531–93
=
Margaret
ob. 1596

(2)
Henry Stuart
Lord Darnley
ob. 1567

Edward
Lord Beauchamp

Ferdinando
5th Earl of Derby
1560–94
=
Alice Spencer

William
6th Earl of
Derby
1561–1642
= Elizabeth de Vere

JAMES VI
OF SCOTLAND,
I OF ENGLAND
1566–1625

Note: Names underlined – Mary, Eleanor and Margaret – indicate the connections between the royal Tudors and the Stanleys.

Glossary

acetate	A piece of transparent film on which diagrams may be copied for display by overhead projector.
acoustics	The modern science of sound. The acoustic qualities of buildings, which in ancient times were the result of certain proportions in the architectural design.
alchemy	Alchemy is the idea of transmuting base metals into gold. For the simple, a chance for riches; for the unscrupulous, a cover, perhaps, for the production of counterfeit coins; but for the high-minded a quest for the gold of psychological integration. Both Boyle and Newton practised alchemy, but in secret, since at the time to do so constituted a capital offence. Probably the most beneficial outcome of practical alchemy has been the equipment of a modern chemistry laboratory.
ambience	The atmosphere or ethos of a place. Though ultimately subjective, ambience is influenced by factors such as size, shape and colour.
atom	The basic unit of matter. A monad. In his *Sceptical Chymist* (1661), Robert Boyle paved the way for modern science by introducing the concept of chemical elements. Previously, matter had been considered to be composed of four elements (earth, air, fire, water) or of three principles (salt, mercury, sulphur).
cabala	(Variously spelt, including cabbala, kabbalah, quabalah, etc.). An esoteric tradition among Jewish rabbis concerned with knowledge and meditation about the principles governing the universe (macrocosm) and human life (microcosm). From time to time, at the Renaissance in particular, certain cabalistic ideas and practices were adopted by Christian writers, both Catholic and Protestant. *See also* **gematria** and **Tree of Life**.
Cistercian	The Cistercians are an order of monks, a reformed offshoot of the Benedictines, founded at Citeaux in 1098. St Bernard, to whom the composition of the Rule of the Knights Templar is also attributed, was with co-founder of the Cistercian Order Stephen Harding, the English Abbot of Citeaux.
diapason	Consonance or concord of sound (cf. Milton's 'in perfect diapason', 'At a Solemn Musick'). More specifically, a musical octave, the consonance produced by two sounds vibrating in the ratio 2:1.
diapente	The musical interval of the perfect fifth, the consonance produced when two sound sources vibrate in the ratio 3:2.

Enochian	Supposedly the language of the angels. This language was revealed for the uninitiated by John Dee, after reading *Steganographia*, three books on angel-magic by Trithemius, Abbot of Sponheim. It is now generally agreed that the first two of these were actually about codes, while the third seems to have anticipated what we would call spiritualism.
Euclid	(*c.* 300BC) Greek mathematician who lived in Alexandria. His nine treatises on geometry have remained a standard textbook for over 2000 years.
fugue	A style of musical composition in which each voice enters, following the theme of the first. Michael Maier's book *Atalanta Fugiens* (1618) comprises fifty enigmatic engravings, verses and 'fugues', intended as a course in spiritual alchemy.
gematria	The Hebrew and Greek alphabets were used to signify both letters and numbers. Key names and words could therefore be abbreviated as symbolic numbers: for example, the Greek word for 'Truth' becomes 72. Such a letter–number code was known as **gematria**. Islamic sufis used a similar system. Gnostic Christians adopted and adapted **gematria** for their own use. For its practitioners, it quickly acquired an addictive power comparable to that of the modern crossword puzzle.
Giorgio	A Franciscan friar of the Renaissance. To explain how musical instruments should be tuned to mirror the music of the planets, Pythagoras had used four numbers: 6, 8, 9, 12 (*see* **tetractys**). In his *De Harmonia Mundi* (1525), Francesco Giorgio extended this series to generate a harmonic system capable of serving as a model for architecture and painting: 6, 8, 9, 12, 16, 18, 24, 27, 32, 36, 48, 54, 81, 108, 162.
gnosticism	A mode of religious thought, with its own dualistic myth and scriptures, which, from time to time, permeated other religions. Gnostics held that matter was evil. Each soul must look for its own salvation (the absorption of the individual's spirit into the divine whole) through intuitive mystical knowledge. From the second to the fourth centuries AD, gnosticism threatened what subsequently survived as orthodox Christianity.
hermetic	Hermetic refers to the 'Corpus Hermeticum', a collection of Greek texts composed between AD100 and 300, though sometimes attributed to an ancient Egyptian priest, Hermes Trismegistus. Their rediscovery and translation into Latin in the fifteenth century was formative in the development of Renaissance culture. Subsequently, the hermetic tradition became a humanist philosophy, drawing eclectically on Plato, Jewish mysticism, astrology, magic and oriental religions.
holistic	Pertaining to the whole. An approach to problem solving which assumes that the whole is more than the sum of its parts, or that complex problems call for multi-disciplinary solutions.

iconography	The study of the subjects and symbols used in painting and patterns.
latten	A variable alloy, used of both brass and other alloys. In *The Merry Wives of Windsor* (Act IV, scene i) Mistress Quickly says 'Hang hog is latten for Bacon, I warrant you.' In this context 'latten' is usually taken as an alternative spelling of 'latin', and the remark a reference to a family joke of the Bacons. As a judge, Sir Nicholas Bacon had once condemned to death a prisoner by the name of Hog. The prisoner had then asked for mercy, on the grounds that he and the judge were related, since hog and bacon are kindred. To this Sir Nicholas had retorted: 'I cannot be kindred, except you be hanged; for Hog is not Bacon until it is well hanged.' The spelling 'latten' highlights a pun and may also serve (in Sir Francis Bacon's phrase) as an 'instance of the fingerpost', pointing towards Francis Bacon's involvement in a brass- and wireworks at Tintern.
Limoges enamel	Enamel is a vitrified coating fired on to metal or pottery. Limoges was one of the most important European enamelling centres during the fifteenth and sixteenth centuries.
magic	Magic is the art of causing things to happen through the mediation of spirits and the secret powers of nature. Magic was believed to work on the basis of 'correspondences': doing things in the right place at the right time to correspond best with the energy patterns of the universal life-force.
magus	The three wise men who followed the star to find the infant Jesus were magi. A magus was a member of a priestly class, learned and wise in the hidden powers of nature, and thereby believed to be capable of bringing light and balance into all things.
parametric	A term coined by Nigel Pennick to describe drawings which display the ground-plan and the elevation of a building simultaneously. This is only possible when the overall design of the building has been conceived proportionately.
philosopher's stone	A legendary stone that could transform base metal into gold. A solid variant of the elixir of life. The alchemists' pursuit of it helped to lay the foundation of chemistry as a science. For the high-minded it served as an image of the quest for the 'gold' of psychological integration.
phoenix	A mythical bird that rises from its own ashes. A symbol of new life or revival, despite disintegration.
Plato	Greek philosopher (*c.* 428–347BC). Almost all Plato's philosophical output is in the form of dialogues. Among these, the *Timaeus*, which is concerned with the creation of the world and the importance of mathematics for the understanding of nature, has been seminal in the history of European thought. Although formally superseded by the ideas of Aristotle in thirteenth-century Europe, Plato's ideas re-emerged at the Renaissance and have continued ever since to inspire thinkers who have a healthy contempt for the visible world and are attracted to the contemplation of the mathematical, aesthetic and religious aspects of the universe.

Pythagoras	(fl. 530BC) Greek philosopher and founder of a religious brotherhood. His teachings about the scientific and mystical aspects of number influenced both **Plato** and **Euclid**.
Rosicrucian	The name 'Rosicrucian' or 'Rosy Cross' may have originally referred to those who used the red cross of the Knights Templar as a symbol after the Order's abolition in 1312. There may have been Rosicrucians as early as the fourteenth century, including fugitive Knights Templar.
sacred geometry	The sacred buildings of ancient cultures and the medieval cathedrals were designed and constructed by means of sacred geometry in order to be an image of heaven on earth. Thus the circle, a line without beginning or end, was a symbol of eternity. The square represented the four basic elements of the universe (fire, air earth, water). Geometrical progressions of triangles (*ad triangulum*, e.g. King's College Chapel, Cambridge), or of squares (*ad quadratum*, e.g. Chartres Cathedral) were the unifying principles of design. This ensured aesthetic proportion visually and acoustical richness aurally. The ancient geometers' attempts to construct a square of equal perimeter or area to a given circle ('squaring the circle') acquired the seriousness of a quest for the secret of the universe, for a 'Theory of Everything', to borrow a modern phrase. Symbolic geometry is also the unifying element throughout the Byrom Collection.
scruff	Literally, scurf; a term used by metal workers to describe objects due for melting down and re-use.
scryer	A crystal-gazer; a seer; a co-worker in some occult practice such as alchemy; possibly, in the terminology of modern spiritualism, a medium. John Dee employed Edward Kelly as his 'skryer', but he proved to be disastrously unreliable.
sephiroth	(singular: **sephira**). In cabala, the tenfold emanations of God (see also **cabala** and **Tree of Life**).
sigil	A magical sign or occult symbol, succinctly summarising several key ideas, e.g. the Seal of the Templars, John Dee's Monad.
St Benedict	St Benedict of Nursia (480–547) founded the Benedictine order of monks. His Rule influenced many subsequent monastic developments. Westminster Abbey was a Benedictine foundation.
St Michael	Archangel, leader of the angel hosts in the Jewish, Christian and Islamic traditions. Michael is to the angels as the Sun is to the planets and gold to other metals. The most important modern shrine to his cult is Mont-Saint-Michel in Normandy. The Knights of St Michael are the highest order of French chivalry.
tau	The letter of the Greek alphabet which corresponds to our T, hence a T-shaped cross.
tetractys	The numbers 1, 2, 3, 4; usually expressed as a triangle of ten dots; a Pythagorean symbol of the space-time world developed in three dimensions.

The musical tetractys uses the same numbers to create proportions: 1; ⅔; ½; 2, or as whole numbers (x6): 6: 8: 9: 12. These proportions formed the basis of the entire Greek tuning system.

Tree of Life   The 'Tree of Life' (*see* Genesis 3:9 and Apocalypse 22:2) is one of the central images of the cabala for exploring the archetypal patterns of the universe. Geometrically, this tree is drawn as a design of ten points, representing emanations of God, with twenty-two inter-connections, corresponding to the letters of the Hebrew alphabet. Since the cabalists rated creative imagination above intellect, the number of possible interpretations and practical applications of the Tree of Life is virtually limitless. The revival of cabalistic thought and practice in the thirteenth and fourteenth centuries highlighted how deeply the concept of the Tree of Life is rooted in a philosophical heritage common to Jews, Christians and Muslims.

tuning fork   A two-pronged fork tuned to a particular pitch or vibration for the use of performing musicians.

vesica   In geometry, two circular arcs, each (strictly speaking) passing through the other's centre.

Vitruvius   Marcus Vitruvius Pollio, Roman architect (first century BC). His *De Architectura*, dedicated to Emperor Augustus, comprises ten volumes on proportions in architecture. It was revered by Renaissance architects and greatly influenced the thinking of John Dee. Vitruvius's description of a Roman theatre is based upon the proportions of the world.

Zoroaster   The founder of an ancient dualistic religion in Persia. It still has adherents in Iran and India.

Notes

All works published in London unless otherwise stated.

Chapter 1

1. These were: the Swan, the Globe, the Rose, the Hope, the Bear Garden and Newington Butts.
2. Michael Howard, *The Occult Conspiracy* (Vermont, USA, Destiny Books, 1989), p. 54.
3. The Acte for the Punishment of Vagabondes, 1572, attempted to redefine vagabondage and increase the sentences against it. By including in the definition of vagabonds 'comon players in enterludes and minstrels, not belonging to any baron of this realme . . .' it emphasised the necessity for players to be genuinely attached to the households of the nobility as servants, entitled to wear the household livery. On the passing of the act, Leicester obtained from the queen a license for his company to perform in London and elsewhere, thus avoiding for Burbage and his men the trouble of seeking a fresh licence from every county they hoped to visit.
4. Edith Sitwell, *The Queens & The Hive* (Penguin, 1966), p. 66.
5. *John Dee's Manchester* (Manchester Education Department, 1988), p. 19.
6. F.R. Raines, *Wardens of Manchester* (Manchester, Chetham Society, 1885), p. 94.
7. F.R. Raines, *The Stanley Papers Part 2* (Manchester, Chetham Society, 1853), p. 56.
8. J.J. Bagley, *The Earls of Derby 1485–1985* (Sidgwick & Jackson, 1985), p. 56.
9. T.W. King and F.R. Raines, *Lancashire Funeral Certificates* (Manchester, Chetham Society, 1869), pp. 63–4.
10. *Ibid.*, p. 27.
11. Sir John Harrington quoted in *Dictionary of National Biography* (Oxford, 1917), p. 1342.
12. Bagley, *op. cit.*, p. 72.
13. Park Honan, *Shakespeare, A Life* (Oxford, Oxford University Press, 1998), pp. 66–7.
14. King and Raines, *op. cit.*, p. 64.
15. E.A.J. Honigman, *Shakespeare's Lost Years* (Manchester, Manchester University Press, 1985), p. 34.
16. Honan, *op. cit.*, p. 61.
17. E.K. Chambers, *The Elizabethan Stage*, vol. II (Oxford, Oxford University Press, 1951 edn), p. 102.
18. King and Raines, *op. cit.*, p. 67.
19. Barry Coward, *The Stanleys* (Manchester, Chetham Society, 1983), p. 31.
20. H.T. Crofton, *The Broughton Topography & Manor* (Manchester, Chetham Society, 1909), p. 2.
21. King and Raines, *op. cit.*, p. 69.
22. W. Shakespeare, *Richard III*, Act V, Sc. 5, lines 4–7.
23. *Ibid.*, Act IV, Sc. 4., lines 496–8.
24. *Ibid.*, Act V, Sc. 5, lines 8–9.
25. William Camden, quoted by J.J. Bagley, *op. cit.*, p. 55.
26. Harleian Ms. 1927 Folio 10.
27. Thomas Heywood, *The Stanley Papers Part 1* (Manchester, Chetham Society, 1853), extract from pp. 21–4.
28. Frances Yates, *Theatre of the World* (Routledge & Kegan Paul, paperback edn, 1987), p.128.
29. Eugenio Garin, *Astrology in the Renaissance* (Routledge & Kegan Paul, paperback edn, 1983), p. 32.

Chapter 2

1. Thomas Blundeville, *M. Blundeville his Exercises, containing Six Treatises* (1594), folio 134. Quoted in S.K. Heninger jnr, *The Cosmographical Glasse*

(San Marino, California, The Huntington
Library, 1977).

2. J.A. Gotch FSA, *The Homes of the Cecils*,
Historical Monograph Series, William Cecil,
Lord Burghley (T.C. & E.C. Jack, 1904), p. 64.

3. Peter Dawkins, 'Dedication to the Light', *The
Francis Bacon Research Trust Journal*, series 1, vol.
3, 1984, p. 72.

4. *Ibid.*, p. 70.

5. Queen Elizabeth travelled around the country
with the chief members of her household and
nobility to show herself to all classes of people in
a deliberate effort to cultivate their loyalty. These
'progresses' were ostentatious displays of majesty
often with good humoured demonstrations of
interest from the queen concerning the welfare of
even her humblest subjects.

6. Alan Haynes, *The White Bear* (Peter Owen,
1987), p. 115.

7. *Ibid.*, p. 116.

8. M. Axton, *The Queen's Two Bodies; Drama and the
Elizabethan Succession* (Royal Historical Society,
1977), p. 65.

9. *Ibid.*, p. 66.

10. L. Jardine and A. Stewart, *Hostage to Fortune. The
Troubled Life of Francis Bacon* (Gollancz, 1998), p. 80.

11. *Ibid.*, p. 167.

12. *Ibid.*, p. 167–8.

13. Frances Yates, *The Rosicrucian Enlightenment* (Routledge
& Kegan Paul, paperback edn, 1986), p. 6.

14. Jardine and Stewart, *op. cit.*, p. 336.

15. *Ibid.*, p. 343.

16. Honan, *op. cit.*, p. 225.

17. Chambers, *op. cit.*, vol I, p. 102.

18. *Ibid.*, p. 86.

19. *Ibid.*, p. 101.

20. *Ibid.*, p. 87.

21. Sir Edwin King and Sir Harry Luke, *The Knights
of St John in the British Realm* (St John's Gate,
1967), p. 5.

22. Chambers, *op. cit.*, p. 101.

23. Quoted by H.W. Furcham, *The Order of the Hospital
of St John of Jerusalem* (London, 1915), p. 43.

24. Edward Fenton (ed.), *The Diaries of John Dee*
(Charlebury, Day Books, 1998), p. 166.

25. *John Dee's Manchester*, p. 19.

Chapter 3

1. Fenton, *op. cit.*, p. ix.

2. *Ibid.*, p. 5.

3. *Ibid.*, p. 11

4. *Ibid.*, p. 18, note 11.

5. *Ibid.*, p. 10.

6. John Dee, *Compendious Rehearsal*, p. 27, quoted
by Peter French in *John Dee, The World of an
Elizabethan Magus* (Routledge & Kegan Paul,
1984 paperback edn), p. 43.

7. French, *op. cit.*, p. 45

8. *Ibid.*, pp. 57–8.

9. *The Travels of the Three English Brothers* (1607).
Christopher Edwards, *The London Theatre Guide
1576–1642* (Bear Gardens Museum, 1979), p. 18.

10. Chambers, *op. cit.*, vol. II, p. 358.

11. Fenton, *op. cit.*, p. 52.

12. Lupold Wedel, quoted in Chambers, *op. cit.*, vol.
II, p. 455.

13. *John Dee's Diary*, ed. J.O. Halliwell (Camden
Society, 1842), p. 18.

14. Margaret P. Hannay, *Philip's Phoenix. Mary
Sidney, Countess of Pembroke* (Oxford, Oxford
University Press, 1990), p. 132.

15. Fenton, *op. cit.*, p. 2. There are no exact modern
equivalents to Estotiland and Friseland. Estotiland
'might' be Newfoundland. Mercator's map of 1569
shows Estotiland as part of the North American
mainland. Ortelius, in another map, shows it as an
island between Greenland and Canada. Similarly,
Friseland seems to have been an imaginary island
in the North Atlantic. Geographers debated its
whereabouts for centuries. Dee also used the word
to mean the Netherlands.

16. *Ibid.*, p. 11.

17. French, *op. cit.*, p. 127.

18. Fenton, *op. cit.*, p. 100.

19. *Ibid.*, p. 252.

20. *Ibid.*, p. 247.

21. Hannay, *op. cit.*, p. 130.

22. *Ibid.*, p. 131.

23. Howard, *op. cit.*, p. 54.

24. Fenton, *op. cit.*, p. 231.

25. *Ibid.*, p. 247.

26. *Ibid.*, p. 247.

27. Chambers, *op. cit.*, vol. IV, p. 164.
28. Fenton, *op. cit.*, p. 248.
29. *Ibid.*, p. 275.
30. *Ibid.*, p. 53.
31. Katherine Duncan-Jones, *Sir Philip Sidney, Courtier Poet* (Hamish Hamilton, 1991), p. 248.
32. Sitwell, *op. cit.*, p. 405.
33. Ian Wilson, *Shakespeare, The Evidence* (Headline, 1993), p. 201.
34. Fenton, *op. cit.*, p. 169.
35. Thistellworth, Isleworth, Greater London. Queen Elizabeth often stayed here at Syon House, home of Henry Percy, the 'Wizard Earl', who gathered around him some of the greatest intellects of England – scientists, mathematicians and poets – including Dee.
36. Fenton, *op. cit.*, p. 173.
37. My thanks for this particular information are due to the Reverend Neville Barker Cryer.
38. Glynne Wickham, *Early English Stages*, vol. II, part 1 (Routledge & Kegan Paul, 1963), 106–7.
39. *Ibid.*, p. 105.
40. *Ibid.*, p. 114.
41. Chambers, *op. cit.*, vol. II, p. 478.
42. *Ibid.*, p. 508.
43. Fenton, *op. cit.*, p. 253.
44. *Ibid.*, p. 253.
45. *Ibid.*, p. 255–6.
46. *Ibid.*, p. 270–1.
47. *Ibid.*, p. 256.
48. John Dee, *Compendious Rehearsal*; Fenton, *op. cit.*, p. 271, note 23.
49. Fenton, *op. cit.*, p. 273.
50. *Ibid.*, p. 274.
51. *Ibid.*, p. 274.
52. *Ibid.*, p. 275.
53. *Ibid.*, p. 277.
54. Chambers, *op. cit.*, vol. II, p. 127.
55. John Michell, *Who Wrote Shakespeare?* (Thames & Hudson, 1996), pp. 190 and 192. In June 1599 a Jesuit spy reported that the Earl of Derby was 'busyed only in penning commodyes for the commoun players'.

Chapter 4

1. P.C. Mackie, W.A. McCann and A. Brown, *The Site of the Globe Theatre, A Geophysical Survey. Interim Report* (MoLAS, October 1996), p. 2.
2. Barry Day, *This Wooden O* (Oberon Books, 1996), p. 207.
3. *Ibid.*, pp. 207–8.
4. Mackie, McCann and Brown, *op. cit.*, pp. 2–3.
5. Day, *op. cit.*, p. 212.
6. Professor A. Gurr in *The Economist*, 18 December 1999, p. 84.
7. The ordinances of the Company of Carpenters were drawn up in the reign of Henry VI (d. 1471) and account and order books were kept from that time. It would be necessary for the wardens to be able to read and write to ensure that the bye-laws were enforced. See E. Jupp, *An Historical Account of the Worshipful Company of Carpenters* (London, 1887).
8. See John Peters, 'Drama in Conflict', *The Sunday Times*, 10 October 1995.
9. Mark Lewis Jones quoted by Robert McCrum in 'The Smell of The Crowd', *Observer Review*, 1 June 1997.
10. Mackie, McCann and Brown, *op. cit.*, p. 3.
11. *Ibid.*, p. 4.
12. *Ibid.*, p. 15.
13. *Ibid.*, p. 16.
14. *Ibid.*, p. 16.
15. W.A. McCann, *Site of the Globe Theatre, A Geophysical Survey. Final Report* (MoLAS, May 1998), p. 26.
16. W.A. McCann, *Site of The Theatre, A Geophysical Survey* (MoLAS, February 1999), p. 15.
17. Julian Bowsher, *The Rose Theatre, an archaeological discovery* (Museum of London, 1998), p. 33.
18. Joy Hancox, *The Byrom Collection* (Jonathan Cape, 1992), pp. 111–16.

Chapter 5

1. Rabbi Michael L. Munk, *The Wisdom in the Hebrew Alphabet* (New York, Mesorah Publications Ltd, 1995), p. 19.
2. John Michell, *The Dimensions of Paradise* (San Francisco, Harper & Row, 1988), p. 56.
3. Second Book of the Chronicles 9:23.
4. French, *op. cit.*, p. 85.
5. Robert Hillenbrand, *Islamic Architecture* (Edinburgh, Edinburgh University Press, 1994), p. 19.

6. The attack on the Order was launched on Friday 13 October 1307. In France alone 15,000 Knights Templar were arrested, an event serious enough to make any date in the calendar appear inauspicious. Christopher Knight and Robert Lomas, *The Second Messiah* (Century, 1997), p. 163.

7. Tim Wallace-Murphy, *Rosslyn Chapel, An Illustrated Guide Book* (Rosslyn, The Friends of Rosslyn, 1993), p. 34.

8. *Richard II*, Arden Edition, ed. Peter Ure (Methuen, 1966), p. xxxiv.

9. Shakespeare, *Richard II*, II i 40–3.

10. *The Taming of The Shrew* (1594); *The True Tragedy of Richard, Duke of York* (1595).

11. Chambers, *op. cit.*, vol. II, p. 133

12. *Ibid.*, vol. IV, p. 168.

13. *The Complete Peerage*, G.E.C., vol. X (St Catherine's Press, 1945), p. 413.

14. Ian Wilson, *Shakespeare, The Evidence* (Headline, 1994), p. 400.

15. Honan, *op. cit.*, p. 404.

16. Wilson, *op. cit.*, p. 401.

17. Fenton, *op. cit.*, p. 92.

18. Frances Yates, *The Occult Philosophy* (Routledge & Kegan Paul paperback edn, 1983), p. 104.

19. Frances Yates, *The Art of Memory* (Routledge & Kegan Paul paperback edn, 1984), pp. 312–13.

20. Wickham, *op. cit.*, p. 96.

21. *The Third University in England*, 24 August 1612. Chambers, *op. cit.*, vol. 1, p. 104.

22. Letter from John Chamberlain to Dudley Carleton, 30 March 1622: 'Old Sir George Buck, master of the revels, has gone mad.' Quoted in Chambers, *op. cit.*, vol. 1, p. 104.

Chapter 6

1. Keith Thomas, *Religion and The Decline of Magic* (Penguin edn, 1971), p. 519.

2. John Aubrey, *Brief Lives* (Penguin edn, 1987), p. 124.

3. Titus Burckhardt, *Alchemy*, translated by W. Stoddart (Stuart & Watkins, 1967), p. 33.

4. *Ibid.*, p. 33.

5. Bernardino de Mendoza quoted in Haynes, *The White Bear*, p. 55.

6. Charles Nicholl, *The Reckoning* (Picador edn, 1993), p. 116.

7. *Ibid.*, p. 105.

8. *Ibid.*, p. 105.

9. French, *op. cit.*, p. 36.

10. Alan Haynes, *Invisible Power, The Elizabethan Secret Service 1570–1603* (Alan Sutton, 1992), p. 18.

11. *Ibid.*, p. 19.

12. Christopher Butler, *Number Symbolism* (Routledge & Kegan Paul, 1970), p. 107.

13. *Ibid.*, p. 107.

14. Yates, *The Occult Philosophy*, p. 30.

15. Keats, 'La Belle Dame Sans Merci'.

16. Gospel According to St Matthew 10: 29.

17. Chambers, *op. cit.*, vol. II, p. 462

18. *Ibid.*, p. 455.

19. *Ibid.*, p. 456.

20. *Ibid.*, vol. IV, p. 295.

21. B.E. Jones, *Freemasons' Guide & Compendium* (Harrap, 1956), pp. 521–2.

Chapter 7

1. Andrew Gurr & John Orrell, 'Rebuilding Shakespeare's Globe' (Weidenfeld & Nicholson 1989), p. 102.

2. This was duly noted in *The Byrom Collection*, pp. 230–1.

3. Alan Q. Morton and Jane A. Wess, *Public and Private Science, The King George III Collection* (Oxford, Oxford University Press, 1993), p. 542.

4. Peter Northover, 'Analysis of Geometrically Engraved Brass Plates in the Boyle Collection, Science Museum' (1998), p. 1.

5. *Ibid.*, p. 2.

6. *Ibid.*, p. 2.

7. *Ibid.*, p. 3.

8. *Ibid.*, p. 4.

9. Private letter from Dr Peter Northover to Joy Hancox, 10 May 1998.

10. William Rees, *Industry Before the Industrial Revolution* (Cardiff, University of Wales Press, 1968), vol. II, p. 374.

11. *Ibid.*, p. 386.

12. *Ibid.*, p. 389.

13. M.B. Donald, *Elizabethan Monopolies, The History*

of the Company of the Mineral and Battery Works 1568–1604 (Oliver & Boyd, 1961), p. 88.

14. *Weekly Argus*, Monmouth, Thursday 25 September 1980.

15. Judith Russell, *Tintern's Story* (privately published), p. 16.

16. H.W. Paar & D.G. Tucker, *The Technology of Wire-making at Tintern, Gwent*, Paper, p. 16.

17. *Ibid.*, p. 16.

18. *Ibid.*, p. 16.

19. *Ibid.*, p. 16.

20. Rees, *op. cit.*, p. 394.

21. *Ibid.*, p. 396.

22. *Ibid.*, p. 395.

23. *Ibid.*, p. 584.

24. *Ibid.*, p. 589.

25. *Ibid.*, p. 604.

26. Donald, *op. cit.*, p. 111.

27. Rees, *op. cit.*, p. 384.

Chapter 8

1. Fenton, op. cit., pp. 73–4. The text can be found among the Lansdowne Mss in the British Library.

2. Rees, *op. cit.*, p. 386, note 78.

3. Fenton, *op. cit.*, p. 85.

4. *Ibid.*, p. 85.

5. *Ibid.*, p. 249.

6. Rees, *op. cit.*, p. 440.

7. Fenton, *op. cit.*, p. 78.

8. *Ibid.*, p. 247.

9. *Ibid.*, p. 246.

10. *Ibid.*, p. 5.

11. *Ibid.*, p. 23.

12. *Ibid.*, p. 26.

13. *The Life of Edward, Lord Cherbury*, ed. Sidney Lee, (London, 1886), p. 42.

14. Hannay, *op. cit.*, p. 124.

15. *Ibid.*, p. 129.

16. Rees, *op. cit.*, p. 390.

17. *Ibid.*, p. 390.

18. Chambers, *op. cit.*, vol. II, p. 225.

19. *Ibid.*, p. 226.

20. Hancox, *The Byrom Collection*, p. 46.

21. Jardine and Stewart, *op. cit.*, p. 130.

22. Fenton, *op. cit.*, p. 270.

23. Thomas Herbert, *Memoirs of The Last Two Years of The Life of King Charles* (London, 1813), p. 132.

Chapter 9

1. Morton and Wess, *op. cit.*

2. *Ibid.*, pp. 7–8.

3. Joy Hancox, *The Queen's Chameleon* (Jonathan Cape, 1994), *passim*.

4. Morton and Wess, *op. cit.*, p. 543.

5. Sitwell, *op. cit.*, pp. 192–3.

6. *Calendar of Scottish Papers 1563–1569*, vol. II, edited by Joseph Bain (Edinburgh, 1900), p. 140.

7. David Kahn, *The Code Breakers* (Weidenfeld & Nicholson, 1966), p. 92.

8. Shakespeare, *The Winter's Tale* IV iv.

9. Langland, *Piers The Plowman* quoted in Francis Klingender, *Animals in Art & Thought to the End of the Middle Ages* (Routledge & Kegan Paul, 1971), p. 371.

10. Jardine and Stewart, *op. cit.*, p. 502.

11. *Ibid.*, p. 503.

12. Alfred Dodd, *Francis Bacon's Personal Life Story* (Montana, USA, Kessinger Publishing Co., n.d.), vol. II, p. 542.

13. J.C. Cooper, *An Illustrated Encyclopedia of Traditional Symbols* (Thames & Hudson, 1979), *passim*.

14. Chambers, *op.cit.*, vol. IV, pp. 55–7.

Chapter 10

1. John Michell, *Who Wrote Shakespeare?* (Thames & Hudson, 1996), p. 147.

2. John W. Kopec, *The Sabines at Riverbank* (New York, Acoustical Society of America, 1997), p. 4.

3. Kopec, *op. cit.*, p. 178.

4. Michell, *op. cit.*, p. 144.

5. Bosanquet Deeds & Documents, 1536–1903 D.2034.L4, Gwent Record Office, County Hall, Cwmbran.

6. *Calendar of State Papers Domestic*, 7 May 1611.

7. *Acts of the Privy Council of England*, May 1613–Dec 1614, dated 22 November.

8. *The Complete Peerage*, vol. X, p. 413.

Bibliography

Place of publication is London unless otherwise stated.

Architekt & Ingenieur, Baumeister in Krieg & Frieden, Exhibition Catalogue (Germany, Duke August Library, Wolfenbuttel, 1984)

Aubrey, John, *Brief Lives*, ed. O.L. Dick (Penguin, 1987)

Axton, Marie, *The Queen's Two Bodies; Drama and the Elizabethan Succession* (The Royal Historical Society, 1977)

Bacon, Francis, *The Advancement of Learning* (Dent, Everyman Library, 1954)

——, *Essays* (Oxford, Oxford University Press, 1999)

Bagley, J.J., *The Earls of Derby 1485–1985* (Sidgwick & Jackson, 1985)

Bible, The

Black, J.B., *The Reign of Elizabeth 1558–1603* (Oxford, Oxford University Press, 1985)

Blatherwick, Simon, *London's Pre-Reformation Purpose-Built Theatres of the Sixteenth and Seventeenth Centuries* (English Heritage, 1998)

Bord, Janet and Colin, *Atlas of Magical Britain* (Sidgwick & Jackson, 1990)

Bowsher, Julian, *The Rose Theatre, an Archaeological Discovery* (Museum of London, 1998)

Bradbrook, M.C., *The Rise of the Common Player* (Chatto & Windus, 1964)

Bradney, Sir Joseph, *A History of Monmouthshire*, 4 vols (1904–33)

Burckhardt, Titus, *Alchemy*, trans. W. Stoddart (Stuart & Wilkins, 1967)

Butler, Christopher, *Number Symbolism* (Routledge & Kegan Paul, 1970)

Calendar of Scottish Papers, 1563–1569, ed. J. Bain (Edinburgh, 1900)

Calendar of State Papers Domestic, 1611

Chambers, E.K., *The Elizabethan Stage*, 4 vols (Oxford, Oxford University Press, 1951)

Churton, Tobias, *The Gnostics* (Weidenfeld & Nicholson, 1987)

Cirlot, J.E., *A Dictionary of Symbols* (Routledge & Kegan Paul, 1981)

Cooper, J.C., *An Illustrated Encyclopedia of Traditional Symbols* (Thames & Hudson, 1979)

The Complete Peerage (St Catherine's Press, 1945)

Coward, Barry, *The Stanleys* (Manchester, Chetham Society, 1983)

Crofton, H.T., *The Broughton Topography and Manor* (Manchester, Chetham Society, 1909)

Dawkins, Peter, *Arcadia* (Coventry, The Francis Bacon Research Trust, 1998)

——, *Bacon, Shakespeare & the Fra. Christian Rose Cross* (The Francis Bacon Research Trust, privately printed, 1991)

——, 'Dedication to the Light', *The Francis Bacon Research Trust Journal*, series 1, vol. 3, privately printed (1984)

——, *Francis Bacon, Herald of the New Age* (The Francis Bacon Research Trust, privately printed, no date)

Day, Barry, *This Wooden 'O'* (Oberon Books, 1996)

Delderfield, Eric R., (ed.), *Kings & Queens of England and Great Britain* (Newton Abbot, David & Charles, 1977)

Dictionary of National Biography (Oxford, 1917)

Dodd, Alfred, *Francis Bacon's Personal Life Story* (Montana, USA, Kessinger Pub. Co., n.d.)

Donald, M.B., *Elizabethan Monopolies: The History of the Company of Mineral and Battery Works, 1568–1604* (Oliver & Boyd, 1961)

Duncan-Jones, Katherine, *Sir Philip Sidney, Courtier, Poet* (Hamish Hamilton, 1991)

Edwards, Christopher, *The London Theatre Guide 1576–1642* (Bear Gardens Museum, 1979)

Evans, Joan, (ed.), *The Flowering of the Middle Ages* (Thames & Hudson, 1985)

Fenton, Edward, (ed.), *The Diaries of John Dee* (Charlebury, Day Books, 1998)

Foster, Richard, *Patterns of Thought* (Jonathan Cape, 1991)

Fox Davies, A.C., *The Wordsworth Complete Guide to Heraldry* (Hertfordshire, Wordsworth Editions Ltd, 1996)

French, Peter, *John Dee: The World of an Elizabethan Magus* (Routledge & Kegan Paul, 1984 edn)

Furcham H.W., *The Order of the Hospital of St John of Jerusalem* (1915)

Garin, Eugenio, *Astrology in the Renaissance* (Routledge & Kegan Paul, 1983)

Geoffrey of Monmouth, *The History of the Kings of Britain* (Penguin Books, 1966)

Gettings, Fred, *The Book of Tarot* (Triune Books, 1973)

Godwin, Joscelyn, *Robert Fludd* (Thames and Hudson, 1979)

Goodman, Frederick, *Magic Symbols* (Brian Trodd Publishing, 1989)

Gotch, J.A., *The Home of the Cecils* (T.C. & E.C. Jack, 1904)

Grillot de Givry, Emile, *Sorcery, Magic and Alchemy* (Zachary Kwintner Ltd, 1991)

Gurr, Andrew, and Orrell, John, *Rebuilding Shakespeare's Globe* (Weidenfeld & Nicholson, 1989)

Halevi, Z'ev ben Shimon, *Kabbalah* (Thames & Hudson, 1979)

Halliwell, J.O., (ed.), *John Dee's Diary* (Camden Society, 1842)

Hancox, Joy, *The Byrom Collection* (Jonathan Cape, 1992)

——, *The Queen's Chameleon* (Jonathan Cape, 1994)

Hannay, Margaret P., *Philip's Phoenix: Mary Sidney, Countess of Pembroke* (Oxford, Oxford University Press, 1990)

Hayes, Michael, *The Infinite Harmony* (Weidenfeld & Nicholson, 1994)

Haynes, Alan, *Invisible Power, The Elizabethan Secret Service, 1570–1603* (Stroud, Alan Sutton, 1992)

——, *The White Bear* (Peter Owen, 1987)

Heniger, S.K., *The Cosmographical Glass* (San Marino, California, USA, The Huntington Library, 1977)

Herbert, Sir Thomas, *Memoirs of the Last Two Years of King Charles* (1813)

Heywood, Thomas, *The Stanley Papers Part 1* (Manchester, Chetham Society, 1853)

Higgins, Frank C., *Ancient Freemasonry* (New York, Pyramid Book Co., 1923)

Hillenbrand, Robert, *Islamic Architecture* (Edinburgh, Edinburgh University Press, 1994)

Honan, Park, *Shakespeare, A Life* (Oxford, Oxford University Press, 1998)

Honigman, E.A.J., *Shakespeare's Lost Years* (Manchester, Manchester University Press, 1985)

Howard, Michael, *The Occult Conspiracy* (Vermont, Destiny Books, 1989)

Jardine, Lisa, and Stewart, Alan, *Hostage to Fortune, The Troubled Life of Francis Bacon* (Victor Gollancz, 1998)

Jones, Bernard E., *Freemasons' Guide and Compendium* (Harrap, 1955)

Jupp, Edward B., *An Historical Account of the Worshipful Company of Carpenters* (1887)

Kahn, David, *The Code Breakers* (Weidenfeld & Nicholson, 1966)

King, Sir Edwin, and Luke, Sir Harry, *The Knights of St John in the British Realm* (St John's Gate, 1967)

King, T.V., and Raines, F.R., *Lancashire Funeral Certificates* (Manchester, Chetham Society, 1869)

Klingender, Francis, *Animals in Art and Thought to the End of the Middle Ages* (Routledge & Kegan Paul, 1971)

Knight, Christopher, and Lomas, Robert, *The Second Messiah* (Century Books Ltd, 1997)

Kopec, John, *The Sabines at Riverbank* (New York, Acoustical Society of America, 1997)

Lee, Sir Sidney, (ed.), *The Life of Edward, Lord Herbert of Cherbury* (1886)

McCann, W.A., *Site of the Globe Theatre, A Geophysical Survey, Final Report* (MoLAS, 1998)

——, *Site of The Theatre, A Geophysical Survey, Report* (MoLAS, 1999)

McCrum, Robert, 'The Smell of the Crowd', *Observer Review*, June 1997

McIntosh, Christopher, *The Rosy Cross Unveiled* (Wellingborough, The Aquarian Press, 1980)

Mackie, P.C., McCann, W.A., and Brown, A., *The Site of the Globe Theatre, Interim Report* (MoLAS, 1996)

Mackintosh, Iain, *Architecture, Actor & Audience* (Routledge, 1993)

Maier, Michael, *Atalanta Fugiens, An Edition of the Emblems, Fugues and Epigrams* (Grand Rapids, Michigan, USA, Phanes Press, 1989)

Manchester Education Department, *John Dee's Manchester*, compiled by M.E. Dempsey, 1988

Mann, A.T., *Sacred Architecture* (Dorset, Element Books Ltd, 1993)

Michell, John, *The Dimensions of Paradise* (San Francisco, USA, Harper & Row, 1986)

——, *Who Wrote Shakespeare?* (Thames & Hudson, 1996)

Monmouth Weekly Argus, 15 September 1950

Morton, Alan Q., and Wess, Jane, *Public and Private Science, The King George III Collection* (Oxford, Oxford University Press & The Science Museum, 1993)

Munk, Rabbi Michael L., *The Wisdom in the Hebrew Alphabet* (New York, USA, Mesorah Publications Ltd, 1995)

Nicholson, Albert, *The Chetham Hospital and Library* (Sherrat & Hughes, 1910)

Nicholson, Peter, *A New Carpenter's Guide* (1858)

Northover, Peter, *Analysis of Geometrically Engraved Brass Plates in the Boyle Collection, Report* (Science Museum, 1998)

Overton Fuller, Jean, *Sir Francis Bacon* (Kent, George Mann, 1994)

Paar, H.W., and Tucker, D.G., *The Technology of Wire Making at Tintern, Gwent*, Paper

Parfitt, Will, *The Elements of the Qabalah* (Shaftesbury, Element Books, 1991)

Pennick, Nigel, *The Ancient Science of Geomancy* (Thames & Hudson, 1979)

——, *The Mysteries of King's College Chapel* (Wellingborough, The Aquarian Press, 1978)

Peters, John, 'Drama in Conflict', *The Sunday Times*, October 1995

Raines, F.R., *The Stanley Papers Part 2* (Manchester, Chetham Society, 1853)

——, *The Wardens of Manchester* (Manchester, Chetham Society, 1885)

Rees, William, *Industry Before the Industrial Revolution* (Cardiff, University of Wales Press, 1968)

Robinson, David, (ed.), *The Cistercian Abbeys of Britain* (B.T. Batsford Ltd, 1998)

Russell, Judith, *Tintern's Story* (privately printed, 1999)

Shakespeare, William, *Richard II*

——, *Richard III*

——, *The Winter's Tale*

Sitwell, Edith, *The Queens and The Hive* (Penguin Books, 1966)

Smith's Smaller Classical Dictionary (Dent, Everyman Library, 1937)

Sohmer, Steve, *Shakespeare's Mystery Play* (Manchester, Manchester University Press, 1999)

Steinberg, S.H., *Five Hundred Years of Printing* (Penguin Books, 1974)

Stow, John, *Survey of London* (Dent, Everyman Library, 1945)

Thomas, Keith, *Religion and the Decline of Magic* (Penguin Books, 1971)

Thomson, W.H., *History of Manchester to 1852* (Altrincham, John Sherrat & Son Ltd, 1967)

Trevelyan, G.M., *English Social History* (Longman, 1973)

Walker, D.P., *Spiritual & Demonic Magic* (Stroud, Sutton Publishing, 2000)

Wallace Murphy, Tim, *Rosslyn Abbey, An Illustrated Guide Book* (Rosslyn, The Friends of Rosslyn, 1993)

Westminster Abbey Official Guide, 1977 edn

Wickham, Glynne, *Early English Stages*, vols I and II (Routledge & Kegan Paul, 1963)

Wilson, Colin, *The Occult* (Herts, Granada Publishing Ltd, 1983)

Wilson, Derek, *Sweet Robin* (Allison & Busby, 1997)

Wilson, Ian, *Shakespeare, The Evidence* (Headline, 1994)

Yates, Frances, *The Art of Memory* (Routledge & Kegan Paul, 1984 edn)

——, *The Occult Philosophy* (Routledge & Kegan Paul, 1983 edn)

——, *The Rosicrucian Enlightenment* (Routledge & Kegan Paul, 1986 edn)

——, *Theatre of the World* (Routledge & Kegan Paul, 1969)

Index

Abbey, Tintern 173–4
Acoustical Materials Association 217
Acoustical Society of America 214
acoustics 61, 127, 188, 214–18
Acte for the Punishment of Vagabondes 5
Acts of the Privy Council 224
Advancement of Learning, The 24
Aeschylus 33
Al Aqsa Mosque 95
Alberti, Leon Battista 188
alchemy 37, 39, 41–2, 106–7, 131, 141, 162,
    168, 172, 190, 194–5, 202, 209
alchemy, philosophical 114
Allen, Giles 54
Alleyn, Edward 9–10, 128, 170
alphabets 88, 117
Alport Lodge 6
Althorp 10
amphitheatre, Elizabethan 131
amphitheatre, Greek 127
amphitheatre, Roman 36, 219–20
Anchor Terrace 61, 70–1, 74
Angiddy, river 148, 167
Anne of Denmark, Queen 108, 170, 226
Anthony, Francis 108
Arcadia 45, 106, 213
Aristophanes 26
Aristotle 33
Arundel, Earl of 7, 171, 184, 199–201
Ashmole, Elias 47, 176
astrology 14, 17–18, 131
astronomy 18–19, 106, 144
Aubrey, John 42, 102, 113, 200–1

Bacon family 223

Bacon, Anthony 23–4
Bacon, Francis
    his death 200–1
    with Dee 4
    George Herbert 164
    Gorhambury 113
    Knights of the Helmet 202–4
    legal ambitions 23
    masques 24, 203
    Mount St Alban's 218–20
    spies 172, 199
    wireworks 224–7
    witness for Alice Stanley 12
Bacon, Sir Nicholas 19, 23, 29, 150, 178, 199,
    212
Baconian Acoustical Levitation Machine 218
baptism 42
Barn Elms 43–4, 116
Barnes, Ellen 70
Bath 8
Battista della Porta, Giovanni 116
Bayly, Dr 32
Beaufort, Duke of 211
Beaumont, Frances 24
Benedictines 29, 99, 155
Benthall, Michael 68
Bernadino of Siena 17
Bernard of Clairvaux 28
Bezalel 89
Billingsley, Henry 33, 171, 219, 223–4, 227
Blatherwick, Simon 61, 69
Blessed Gerard, The 27
Bolingbroke, Henry 45, 97
Bosworth, Battle of 12–13
Bowsher, Julian 78–80

Boyle, Robert 138–9, 141, 152, 171, 177, 179, 210
brass plates 136–46, 178
Bristol 8, 147–8, 152–3, 227
British Library 58, 132, 157, 179
Bromley, Mr 162
Broughton, Manor of 12–13
Browne, Thomas 176
Bruno, Giordano 104–6, 112–13
Buchell, Aernout van 1
Buck, George 109, 164
Burbage, Cuthbert 54
Burbage, James 5, 17, 21, 23, 48, 54, 96, 139
Burbage, Richard 9–10, 33, 43, 103
Burde, John 151–2
Burde, William 152
Butler, Christopher 117–18
Byrom, John xi, 139, 199, 217
Byrom Collection, The xi, 60, 67, 74, 135, 179, 185, 204, 210, 213
Byrom drawings, *passim*

cabala 104, 180
Caerleon 36, 219
Caesar, Sir Julius 201
Calendar of Scottish Papers 182
Calendar of State Papers 224
Camden, William 14
Candish, Richard 41, 44
cardano grille 117
Carew, Thomas 164
Carey, George, second Lord Hunsdon 42–4, 48, 54–5
Carey, Henry, first Lord Hunsdon 11, 43, 52
Caroline, of Ansbach, Queen 177, 179–80
Carr, Robert, Earl of Somerset 24–5
Casaubon, Isaac 108
Casaubon, Meric 30
Catherine, Countess of Salisbury 28
Cecil, Robert, first Earl of Salisbury 19, 24, 49–51, 53, 212, 224
Cecil, Thomas, second Lord Burghley 49–50
Cecil, William, first Lord Burghley 4, 18–19, 23–8, 35, 37, 43, 49–50, 53, 105, 116–17, 148, 150, 157–60, 163, 208

Cecil, William, second Earl of Salisbury 28
Central Excavation Unit of English Heritage 78
Chadderton, William 5–11, 52–3
Chaloner, Thomas 15–16, 18
Chamberlain, John 24, 28
Chapter House 93, 96
Charles I, King 19, 40, 47, 56, 111–12, 163, 171, 174–7, 219
Charles II, King 56, 111, 171, 175–6, 219
Chaucer, Geoffrey 196
chemistry 37, 89, 106, 141
Chepstow 99, 101, 152, 159, 169, 173, 211–14, 216, 218, 224
Chepstow Castle 173, 212
Cheshire 6–7, 14
Chetham Society, The 14
Cistercians 99, 155, 211, 227
Civil War, the 16, 19, 111, 113, 175
Clark Laboratory, The 69, 71–2, 74–5
Clerkenwell 26–7
Clifford, Lady Margaret, Countess of Cumberland 44
Clink Prison, the 129
Cobham, Lady 42
Cobham, Lord 43, 50, 150
codes 43, 116–18, 172–3, 188
Cole, Humphrey 147
colour coding 2
Commonwealth, the 19, 56, 111, 113–14, 135, 164, 171, 176, 219
Company of Carpenters, the 63
Condell, Henry 103–4
Constable, Katherine 31
Corpus Christi 8
cosmography 18
Cotton, Robert 30, 175
Coventry 8, 52
Cratylus 91
Crickmore, Leon 210
Crosby, Theo 2, 57–9, 61, 63–4, 67
Cryer, Neville Barker 47, 185–6, 191–2, 194, 196, 198–9
cryptography 43, 227
Cunningham, William 18

Daily Express 211
Daily Telegraph 124
Daniel, Samuel 165–6
Davis, John 159–60
Day, Barry 68
De Architectura 33
de Bry, Johann Theodore 85, 111, 132, 171
de Bry, Theodore 36, 86, 115, 118, 122, 126, 132, 134–5, 226, 228
de Caus, Salomon 111, 113, 168, 171
de Hoghton 10
de Molay, Jacques 100
de Montfort, Simon 96–7, 100
De Silva 22
de Valence, family of 155
de Valence, Aymer, Earl of Pembroke 100–1
de Valence, Mary, Countess of Pembroke 153–5
de Valence, William 153
de Vere, Elizabeth 53
de Witt, Johannes 1
Dee, Arthur 31, 162–3, 176–7
Dee, Jane (Fromond) 52
Dee, John
   astrology 5, 18, 162–3
   Bear Garden 129, 131
   chemistry 37, 41
   codes 116, 118, 172–3, 188
   diaries 30
   Elizabeth I 2–5, & *passim*
   Euclid 67, 90, 106–7, 109, 219, 227
   godparents of children 42–7
   the Herberts 26, 35, 168
   hermetic texts 108
   imperial vision 36–7
   mining 45, 157–60
   Monas Hieroglyphica/Monad 151, 162, 204
   Mortlake 31–2
   Prague 39–40, 104–6
   concept of theatre 34, 90–3, 118, 122, 124, 126–7
   removal of theatre 54–5
   Warden Manchester 6, 51–5
   white magic 113, 132
Dee, Francys 44

Dee, Madimi Newton 42–3, 50
Dee, Margaret 44, 46, 49, 52
Dee, Michael 45, 46–7
Dee, Rowland 36
Demainbury, Stephen 178
Department of Greater London Archaeology, Museum of London 60
Derby, Earls of (*see* Stanley)
Devereux, Robert, Earl of Essex 24, 45, 166, 170, 172
Dissolution of the Monasteries, the 33, 101, 148, 169, 175, 220, 226
Dittrechstain, Lord and Lady 46
Dome of the Rock, the 95–6
Donald, M.B. 212
Donne, John 164
Dover 8
du Puy, Raymond 27–8
Duckett, Anthony 158
Duckett, Jeffrey 158
Duckett, Lionel 157–60
Duckett, Richard 159
Dudley, Ambrose, Earl of Warwick 50, 160, 199, 226
Dudley, Robert, Earl of Leicester 17, 18, 50, 54, 106, 150, 199
   and Amy Robsart 209
   and Dee 2–3, 5, 30–2, 35, 37, 39, 42, 105, 159
   and Elizabeth I 5, 20–2, 97–8, 116, 165, 182, 184, 192, 195, 203, 208
   and Theatre 5, 21, 23, 26, 96, 156, 171, 203
   and William Chadderton 5–8
Dudley, Robert II 164
Duke of York's Men 170
Dyer, Edward 30–1, 37, 45, 106–7

Earl of Essex's Men 8
Edmund, 'Crouchback' 97
Edward the Confessor, King 100
Edward IV, King 101
Edward V, King 6, 26, 101, 117
Edward VI, King 6, 26, 117
Egerton, Mary 174
Egerton, Thomas 13

Elector Palatine, Frederick 24, 109, 111, 113, 164, 170
Elizabeth of Bohemia (Electress Palatine) 24, 108–12, 115, 168, 170
Elizabeth I
  her character 20
  and William Cecil 4, 18, 25, 116
  and John Dee 3, 15, 29, 31–2, 37, 39, 40–4, 46–9, 50–1, 55
  and Robert Dudley 5, 97–8, 182–4, 192, 195, 203, 208, 229
  and Earl of Essex 45
  and Lord Edward Herbert of Cherbury 164
  and William Herbert, first Earl of Pembroke 103, 226
  at Kenilworth 20–3
  love of theatre 29, 36, 126
  Priory of St John 28
  religious policy in Lancashire 7
  and Ferdinando Stanley 7, 9–11, 13
  and Henry Stanley 7
  and William Stanley 53
  and Sir Francis Walsingham 116
Elizabeth II, Queen 64
Encyclopaedia Britannica 218
English Heritage 70, 79
Essex, Countess of 44
Eton College 44, 220
Euclid 3, 33, 67, 171, 219, 223, 227
Euripides 33
Ezra 89

Fabyan, Colonel George 214–18
Fairfax, Lord of Cameron 175
Faustus 113
Fedor, Emperor of Russia 40
Ferrers, George 21
Festival of Firsts 64
Ficino, Marsilio 33
First Folio Edition 28
Fitton, Mary 103
FitzGilbert, Gilbert, first Earl of Pembroke, 'Strongbow' 99
FitzGilbert, Richard, second Earl of Pembroke 99

Florio, John 105
Fludd, Robert 108
Frankfurt 40, 107, 111, 115, 132
Frederick, Elector Palatine 24, 109, 111, 113, 164, 170
Freemasonry 185, 226–7
Friedmann, William 216–17
Frobisher, Martin 107, 168
Fromond, Jane (Dee) 31–2

Gager, William 165
Gallup, Elizabeth 216–17
Gardner, Robert 162
Garnier, Robert 165
Gascoigne, George 21–3
Gaunt, John of 97
Geoffrey of Monmouth 36
George III, King 178
Gesta Grayorum 24
Gilbert, Adrian (Awdrian) 35, 41–2, 159–60, 168
Gillom, Fulke 10
Giorgio, Francesco 117–18
Gleason, John 69, 135
Gorge, Thomas 50
Gorhambury 19, 29, 36, 113, 178, 201, 220
Grays Inn 22, 24–5
Gresham's College 105, 227
Greville, Fulke 45, 105–6
Grimston, Harbottle 113, 201
Ground Penetrating Radar (GPR) 70–2, 75
Gurr, Andrew 64, 67
Guthrie, Tyrone 68
Gwinne, Matthew 105

Hackney 69
Haggai, Book of 28
Hall, Joseph 28–9
Halsall, Jane 12
Hanbury, Richard 152, 159, 224
Hanson, Lord 60–1
Hariot, Thomas 115
Hatfield House 19
Haynes, Alan 117
Heavens, the 17, 93, 142, 188

Hechstetter, Daniel 157–8
Heidelberg 111, 113, 164
Heminges, John 103–4
Henry I, King 98
Henry II, King 99–100
Henry III, King 12, 93, 97, 99–100, 153–5
Henry IV, King 45, 97
Henry VII, King 13, 36
Henry VIII, King 6, 11, 13, 36, 44, 101, 153,
    155, 165, 171, 223
Herbert, Earls of Pembroke, first creation
    William, first Earl 101, 151, 156, 162–3,
        221, 223
    William, second Earl 101
Herbert, Earls of Pembroke, second creation
    William, first Earl 5, 101, 147–8, 150, 165,
        167–8
    Henry, second Earl 35, 99, 102, 104, 165–6
    William, third Earl 102–4, 106, 109,
        167–8, 175–6, 200, 226–7
    Philip, fourth Earl 102, 104, 106, 166, 168,
        175, 226
Herbert, Edward, Lord of Cherbury 163–4, 171
Herbert, George 221
Herbert, George (Poet) 51, 164
Herbert, Henry of Chepstow 159
Herbert, Sir Henry 109, 164
Herbert, John 49, 51
Herbert, Mary 41, 106, 159, 161, 163, 165
    (see Sidney)
Herbert, Mary of St Julian's 162, 176
Herbert, Richard 174
Herbert, Thomas 35
Herbert, Thomas, of Tintern 174–7, 200, 223, 227
Herbert, William 162, 172
Herbert, Sir William, of St Julian's 151–2,
    156, 162–3, 172–3, 219, 223–4, 227
Hermes 192, 194–5, 202, 209
Hermes Trismegistus 90–1, 96
Hesketh, Richard 11, 53
Hesketh, Robert 10,
Hesketh, Thomas 8, 10
Heywood, Jasper 165
Hickman, Bartholomew 44

Hillenbrand, Robert 93, 96
Hinckens, John 149
Hipparchus 92
Hobbes, Thomas 200
Hollar, Wenceslaus 62, 133
Hollybrook Ltd 71
Honan, Park 26, 103
Hond Operative Masons 29
Hondius, Jodocus 133
Hope, Polly 64
Horace 33
Howard, Frances 24
Howcroft, Peter 81, 85
Humphrey, William 147
Hunnis, William 165
Hunsdon, Lord (see Carey)

Illustrated London News 211
Inner Temple 23–4, 100, 203
Inquisition, The 105
Invisible College 111, 141, 227
Ipswich 8
Islamic symbolism 93

James I, King 19, 23–4, 28, 44, 47, 54,
    101–3, 107–9, 111–13, 164, 168–71,
    176, 199, 209, 226
Jamnitzer, Wenzel 141, 178, 227
Jew of Malta, The 10
Jewell, Simon 165
Johnson, Kevin 144
Jones, B.E. 131
Jones, Inigo 103, 109, 111
Jones, Thomas 49
Jonson, Ben 19, 102–3, 109, 111, 164, 166
Jordan of Bricett 27

Katherens, Gilbert 17
Kayser, Barnes 149
Keats, John 127
Keeper of the Great Seal 19, 44, 49, 199
Kelly, Edward 39–43, 47, 107
Kemp, William 43
Kenilworth 20–2, 26, 165

Kenyon, George 54
Khunradt, Heinrich 40
King, Rosalind 81
King's College Chapel 96
King's Men, The 103, 108–9, 111
Knights Hospitaller 27
Knights of the Helmet 203, 228
Knights of the Temple of Solomon 27
Knowsley 6, 8, 10, 12
Kopec, John W. 214, 217–18

L'Aumone 154
Lady Bewty 23
Lady Elizabeth's Men 24, 109, 170
Lancashire 6–7, 9, 10–2, 14, 51
Lancaster, Earl of 97, 100
Laneman, Henry 33
Langland 196
Lant, Thomas 226
Laski, Albert 39–40, 45, 105–6, 131, 158
Lathom 6–8, 10, 14–18, 52, 93, 113
latten 147, 149, 152, 168
Laurence, Lord Hastinges 101
Leibniz 179
Leicester, Earl of (*see* Dudley, Robert)
Leicester, earldom of 96–7
liberty 48
Lord Admiral's Men 9, 43
Lord Chamberlain 11, 43, 55, 104, 108–9, 169
Lord Chamberlain's Men 11, 33, 43, 52, 108
Lord Dudley's Players 5
Lord Treasurer 18, 25, 29, 37, 49–50

McCann, William, A. 69–71, 74–6, 80–1, 85
McClean, Adam 179
McCudden, Simon 60
McCurdy, Peter 64
Magical Calendar, The 132
Maier, Michael 40, 107–8
Manchester 5–6, 8, 10, 12–14, 47, 49, 51–2,
    54, 81, 163, 213, 215
Manutius, Aldus 115
Marlowe, Christopher 1, 10
Marshall, Gilbert, Earl of Pembroke 100

Marshall, William, Earl of Pembroke 99–100, 153
Martin, Richard 107, 124, 152, 159
Mary, Queen of Scots 7, 97, 112, 172, 182
Mary I 6–7, 20, 32
Mary Tudor (sister of Henry VIII) 14, 44
Masque of Flowers 24
masques 8, 21–2, 24, 100, 103
Massinger, Arthur 165
Massinger, Philip 102, 165, 168
Master of Requests 49, 51
Master of the Revels 26–8, 108–9
Mastership of the Game 128
Maximilian, Holy Roman Emperor 31
Mercury 17, 38, 194, 202–4, 209
Merian, Matthias 133–5, 171–2
Michell, John 91, 211, 218
Middle Temple 23
Middleton, Thomas 166
Mineral and Battery Works 145, 147, 150,
    152, 159, 212
mines 41–2, 145, 147, 150, 157–60, 162
Mirandola, Pico della 33
Moffet, Thomas 37
Mohammed 95
Moiseiwitsch, Tanya 68
Monad 2–4, 43, 162, 172–3, 194, 203–4
Monas Hieroglyphica 3–4, 31, 38, 90, 107, 117,
    151
Mortlake 5, 31–2, 35, 37, 41–3, 47, 49–50,
    102, 105–6, 129, 151, 156, 160, 162,
    172, 173, 176
Morton, Alan 178
Moses 90–2
Mount St Alban's 212, 218–19, 224
Munk, Michael L. 88–9
Murcell, George 67–9, 75, 77
Museum of London 60, 70, 78–9
Mysteriorum Libri V 41

Nashe, Thomas 166
Neville, John 68, 185
New Temple, London 99–101
Newton, Isaac 171, 179
Newton, Madimi 42–3, 50

Nichols, John 19
Norden, John 62, 133
Norfolk, Duke of 150, 182, 184
Northover, Peter 144–6, 156, 161
Norton, Thomas 227
Nottingham 8
number symbolism 87, 117, 122, 180
Nuremburg 61, 141
Nurtons, The 223

open-air theatre 188
Oppenheim 111, 115
Order of St John 26
Orrell, John 64, 134
Overbury, Thomas 25
Ovid 33
Owen, Orville 211–14, 216–19, 224

Paddy, Sir William 108
Palladio 126
Pallaphilos 203
Pallas Athene 203
parametric 81, 119, 131, 137–8, 144
Paris Garden 34–5, 47, 129
Parker, Henry 15–18
Parr, Katherine 101, 165
Peacham, Henry 104
Peacock, Kenneth 81
Pembroke's Men 102
Pembroke, see
   de Valence
   FitzGilbert
   Herbert
   Marshall
pentalpha 131
Pepler, Mr 160
Phelippes, Thomas 4, 116, 172–3, 199
Philip, Prince 64
Philip II, of Spain 6–7, 117
Philip the Fair 100
Phillips, Augustine 102, 172
Physiologus 196
Plato 33, 91, 118
Platter, Thomas, of Basle 129

Plummer, Christopher 68
Prague 40, 45–7, 104, 106, 113, 160
Precession of the Equinoxes 92
Prestwich 163
Prince Henry's Men 108
Prince's Men 170
Priory of Goldcliff 220–1
Prospero 109, 113
Puckering, John 24, 44, 49
Puritans 2, 8, 56, 133, 171
Pythagoras 88, 91

Quatuor Coronati 185
Queen Anne's Players 170, 226
Queen's College, Cambridge 5
Queen's Players 8

Raleigh, Walter 112, 172
Randolph, Ambassador 182
Rawley, William 200
recusants 6–8, 11
Rees, William 124, 147, 150, 159, 167,
   212
Richard II, King 45, 97
Richard III, King 12–13, 101
Robsart, Amy 209
Romff, Lord 46
Roosevelt, Theodore 216
Rosicrucians 217
Rosslyn Chapel 96
Round Church 95
Royal Society 105, 111, 137, 139, 141, 171,
   180, 227
Rudolf II 31, 40, 45–6, 106–7, 113
Rufford Hall 10
Rylance, Mark 59–60, 80

Sabine, Paul Earls 215–16
Sabine, Wallace Clement 215, 218
St Alban's 29, 201, 220
St Alban's Chapel 219, 221
St Benedict 155
St George's Theatre 67–9, 127
St Julian's 162, 163, 219, 221, 224, 227

St Mary, Redcliffe 227
Salisbury, Earl of (see Cecil)
San Francesco della Vigna, Church of, Venice
    117
Sancto Clemente, Gulielmo de 46
Sandrart, Joachim von 171
Schutz, Christopher 147–51
Schweighardt, Theophilus 179–80, 184–5,
    188, 204, 206, 208–9, 224, 226–7
Science Museum 136–8, 143–4, 177–8, 180,
    204, 209, 211, 213, 227
Scrope, Lord 17
scruff 153
secret service 116
Shakeshafte 10
Shakespeare
    authorship debate 210–11, 217–18
    art *v* nature (*Winter's Tale*) 190–1
    attitude to animals 128
    death 103
    father, John 170
    First Folio 35, 103–4; Charles I's copy 177
    in Lancashire 10
    linked with Pembroke's Men 102
    treatment of Dee (*Tempest*) 109
    treatment of John of Gaunt (*R. II*) 97
    treatment of Stanleys (*R. III*) 13–14
Shakespeare, works of
    Antony and Cleopatra 27, 166
    As You Like It 102
    Comedy of Errors, The 203
    Hamlet 128
    Henry IV 27
    Henry V 34, 64–5, 182
    Henry VI 10, 13–14,
    Julius Caesar 34, 64, 109
    Merchant of Venice, The 17
    Much Ado about Nothing 109
    Othello 109
    Pericles 103
    Richard II 45, 97
    Richard III 13–14
    Tempest, The 109
    Titus Andronicus 10, 102, 128

Twelfth Night 24, 28
Winter's Tale, The 64–5, 190, 191
Shapiro, I.A. 133
Sherwood, Frederic 214, 217–18
Shoreditch 17, 33, 54, 69, 75
Sidney, Henry 99, 102, 150, 160
Sidney, Mary 35, 102, 106, 165 (see Herbert)
Sidney, Philip 2, 30, 37, 44–5, 105–7, 115,
    160, 165–6, 213, 226
Sidney, Robert, Lord Lisle 224, 226
Skydmore, Lady Mary 50
Sloane, Hans 179
Smythe, Thomas 151
Smythe, William 147, 150
Solomon, King 89
Solomon's Temple 19, 29, 95, 118
Somerset, Edward, fourth Earl of Worcester
    170–2
Somerset, Henry, second Earl of Worcester
    169
Somerset, William, third Earl of Worcester
    148, 170
Sophocles 33
Southwark 1, 54, 61, 99, 129, 228
Southwark Bridge 61
Spearshaker Lecture 60
Speckle, Daniel 85
Spencer, John and Alice 10
Stanley, Edward, Lord Monteagle 13
Stanley, Ferdinando, Lord Strange, fifth Earl of
    Derby 8–13
Stanley, George 14
Stanley, Henry, Lord Strange, fourth Earl of
    Derby 6–8, 11–15
Stanley, Lady Margaret (Clifford) 6–7, 12–15
Stanley, Thomas, first Earl of Derby 13–14
Stanley, Thomas, second Earl of Derby 8
Stanley, William 13
Stephen, King 99
Stowe 129
Strange, Lord and Lady 6–10, 13, 102, 128
Strasbourg 85, 115
Street, Peter 54, 63–4
structural matrix 85

Suffolk, Earl of 24
Summerson, John 58

Tabernacle 89
Taylor, Ian 212–14, 217, 218
Templars 27–9, 95–6, 99–101
Temple Church 95, 99, 101
Thames 1, 33–4, 47, 54, 61, 63, 65, 85, 99,
    109, 129, 133
Theatre of the World 69
theatres
    Bear Garden 35–6, 47, 128–9, 131, 133–4
    Curtain 1, 33–6, 47, 75, 108
    Fortune 1, 2, 54, 63–4, 108, 111, 211
    Globe (First and Second) 1–2, 4, 11, 19, 33,
        43, 45, 48, 54–8, 60–3, 67, 69–71, 74,
        77, 80–1, 85–7, 92, 96, 108, 111,
        118–19, 122–6, 129, 133–5, 172
    Globe, reconstructed 2, 56–69, 71, 80, 87,
        127, 133, 214, 217
    Hope 1, 17, 35, 111, 172
    Newington Butts 43
    Rose 1, 9, 10, 13, 40, 47–8, 54, 61–2,
        77–80, 87, 90, 95, 133, 170, 179, 200,
        204, 206
    Swan 1, 47–8, 102, 133–4
    Theatre 1, 5, 11, 14, 17, 20, 26, 33–4, 43,
        47–8, 54, 55, 63, 67–9, 75, 76, 77, 80,
        90, 92, 115, 139
    Whitefriars 109
Theobalds 18–19
Thibault, Gerard 171
Thoth 90
Throckmorton, Nicholas 182
Tilney, Edmund 27, 109
Tintern 146, 149–51, 156, 161–2, 167,
    169–70, 172–8, 199, 211–13, 218, 220,
    223–4, 226–8
Tintern Abbey 99–101, 145–6, 148, 151, 153,
    155, 159, 169, 212, 221
Tintern Parva 153, 173–5, 223–4, 227
tiring house 1, 19, 63–4, 126
Titus Vespasian 10
Tree of Life 39, 198

Trellech 167–8
Trinity College, Cambridge 26
Trithemius, Abbot, of Sponheim 116, 132
Triumphes and Mirthes 64–5
Truefitt, George 68–9

Verulam, city of 36, 220
Verulam, Baron of (*see* Bacon, Francis) 220
Virgil 33, 107
Visscher, Jan Claes 86, 133–5
Vitruvius 33, 67, 90, 92, 115, 118, 188

Walsingham, Lady Frances 42–5, 160
Walsingham, Sir Francis 4, 32, 35, 43–4, 116,
    158–60, 163, 172–3, 199
Wanamaker, Sam 56–7, 61, 64, 68–9
Wanamaker, Zoë 64
Warden of the Church and College of
    Manchester 5
Warwick, Countess of 49–50, 52, 54
Wedel, Lupold von 129
Welsh Office, The 148
Wess, Jane 144, 178
Westminster Abbey 93, 96, 100, 153–5
Wexford 153
White, John 115
White Mountain, Battle of the 113
Whytehead 223
Wickham, Glynne 109
Williams, Abbot 154
Williams, John 220
Williams, T. 145
Williams, William 147
witches 112, 113, 131
Witherborne, Dr 200
Worcester, Earls of (*see* Somerset)
Wurtemburg, Duke of 18
Wyche, Richard 155, 175, 223

Yates, Francis 17, 24, 67–9, 106, 123, 127

Zachaire, Denis 114
Zoroaster 91, 186
Zutphen, Battle of 45, 226